HEADING HOME

ON STARTING A NEW LIFE *in a* COUNTRY PLACE

Lawrence Scanlan

Doubleday Canada Limited

Canadian Cataloguing in Publication Data

Scanlan, Lawrence
    Heading home

Hardcover ISBN 0-385-25536-5; paperback 0-385-25674-4

1. Camden East (Ont.) — Social life and customs.
2. Country life — Ontario — Camden East. I. Title.

S522.C3S33 1996   971.3'59   C96-930584-2

Cover design by Tania Craan
Text design by Heidy Lawrance Associates
Printed and bound in the USA

Published in Canada by
Doubleday Canada Limited
105 Bond Street
Toronto, Ontario
M5B 1Y3

CONTENTS

For Ulrike

ACKNOWLEDGEMENTS

Writing a book is such a solitary adventure. On the other hand, acknowledgement pages are never short. Many people influenced this project and I want to thank as many of them here as I can.

The book owes much to the authors listed in the bibliography and to those individuals quoted in the book or who took the time to speak with me. Thank you all.

Some of the ideas here appeared in different form in *Harrowsmith*. My colleagues at that magazine between 1990 and 1993 made my work better and gave me many laughs to boot. I miss them still.

Thanks to everyone at Doubleday, and especially John Pearce, Don Sedgwick and Maggie Reeves. I was buoyed by their support and genuine interest in every phase of the book's development. Shaun Oakey, the book's copy editor, was diligent, fussy and insightful. I was glad of his marginalia, in tiny perfect script on yellow Post-it notes.

Literary agent Jan Whitford has become a good friend and a trusted advisor; the structure of the book owes much to her imagination.

Many friends read the manuscript and made valuable suggestions. Any mistakes in the book, therefore, must be laid at their feet. Just kidding. Thanks, therefore, to Michael Webster (once an editor, always an editor), and to Jane and Peter Good (our neighbours to the north). Thanks to David Carpenter for the great gift of his friendship. To M.T. Kelly for his kindness and encouragement. To Shelley Tanaka for her honesty and wit.

I want especially to thank Cynthia Holz, who read the manuscript more carefully and critically than perhaps I wanted her to, but I am grateful that she did. Alexander Scala read the text with a sharp eye and, as usual, gave me much to think about.

Allison and Patrick Good, Bev and Sue Smallman, Wes and Pat Garrod and their sons Wes Jr. and Chad, Susan Rogers, Anne Rutherford, Wayne Grady, Jennifer Bennett, Andrew Nikiforuk, David Archibald, Michael Todd, Mike Berry, Heather Clemenson, Mary Lou Fraser, Shelagh Rogers, Sharon Butala, Stuart McLean, Sandra Birdsell, Norman Bell, Donnie McLean and Jamie Swift all helped in myriad ways. As did the music of Miles Davis, Chet Baker, Sonny Rollins and Pharoah Sanders.

Certain debts close to home can never be repaid. Ulrike Bender has been throughout this project — and all others — sounding board, collaborator and in-house editor. She challenges and praises, adds and subtracts, and sustains me every step. Our nine-year-old son Kurt helped inspire the book and I called on him often for his thoughts. Bern and Clarissa Scanlan, Jacob and Wilma Bender have helped me in countless ways and I am very much in their debt.

May the people of Camden East, and especially our neighbours on Mill Street, see the book as a tribute to them and to all who live in little places.

PROLOGUE

This is a book about a journey. The journey from the city to the country, and then by degrees, towards understanding how to live in the country. (By country I mean villages and small towns and acreages in between.) I liken it to learning another language: fluency seems just over the next rise, or the one after that. In the meantime, you never stop learning new phrases, or torturing syntax.

City and country, I now know, are not separate nations but separate planets. Yet the two planets, it seems to me, are edging closer to one another.

I have lived on both planets, and admire both. Though I prefer the country, I appreciate cities now more than I ever did when I lived in them: family and friends, culture and sports, business and pleasure constantly pull me to the metropolis and I go happily, knowing what's there. The view the other way, though, is skewed. City friends with no direct experience of country life either imagine it to be edenic and yearn for it in a romantic, hopeless way, or are a little appalled and wonder why I have chosen banishment to a backwater. I mean in this chronicle to cure both illusions.

The book is only in part about me and my family learning to speak the language of the country. Each of the twelve chapters — one for each month of the year — weaves the particular (life in our village in southeastern Ontario and its cast of characters) and the general (country life and all that that entails for anyone who would quit the city), and each ends with entries

from my diary specific to that month in 1995. Like all journeys, this one features equal parts smooth sailing and bumpy
rides, and puzzling over maps as we try to find our way.

At the heart of the book is the notion that for many of us,
place now matters a great deal. The book poses the question,
Why not a small place, a country place? Canadians have long
huddled in cities along the southern border, as if for warmth.
We are a land blessed with land, so why do we insist on crowd-
ing the urban edge?

I take some comfort in knowing that this seems to be changing. There is a move on, and though not without its worrying
aspects, it is taking more and more of us past city limits. If you
have lived all your life in big places, then the small and the
tiny will seem strange and daunting. You will need a guide,
encouragement perhaps. I hope this book, by turns personal
and practical, and as clear-eyed as I could make it, does the trick.

Camden East, Ontario

January

A RIVER RUNS THROUGH IT

A rare thaw is transforming the snow dumped on us the week-end before into something I rarely see this time of year. From my vantage — a 130-year-old house in the village of Camden East, Ontario — I look out on water before me, water behind me.

The rhythms of winter here cause a small pond to form at the base of the hill that ascends from our south-facing house to the east–west road, the Yarker Road. The village sits in a modest valley, with the river (and our house) occupying the valley floor. The hill, a treeless sloping acre behind the village's general store, is vacant, and so it serves as a kind of tilted commons. There on the grass are held our flea markets and fund-raisers under circus-sized tents, our community fairs and fireworks displays.

In summer, the hill is an almost private playground. When I hit flyballs to my nine-year-old son, Kurt, I bat from the bottom of the hill, by a mostly buried flat rock that serves as home plate. In winter, the hill is used for tobogganing, although those wooden contraptions have given way to GTs — a plastic saddle with steering wheel over ski runners.

Right now, the pond widens by the hour as the snow turns to slush and the slush to water before trickling down the hill. A neighbour across the street to the southeast, Lyle Lawlor, now in his sixties, was born more or less on the spot where he now lives. His property line takes in almost half the hill, and his favoured position in summer is out on his back deck, chin on the wrist on the railing, watching the hill for signs of activity. When Kurt and I play ball, Lyle is often that lone fan in the stands.

A five-foot, seven-inch wisecracker in a ventilated baseball cap worn year-round at a jaunty angle, Lyle says his calling card should read "Jack of all trades, master of none." By trade a welder and pipefitter, he is on the side an electrician, plumber, carpenter, small engine repairman and, in winter, he ploughs snow for a fee; neighbours' sidewalks, like ours, are free. Mostly, though, he's a character. An original. A guy who knows the village and the roads all around and a funny story about most who reside there, especially the born-and-breds — the Hinches, the Skinners, the Galbraiths, the Suttons. The village is home to several other Lawlors, and if you draw a line between the houses of the Lawlors and the McCormicks and the Williamses — other old Camden East families — the lines cross to form a little galaxy.

The crazy January rain is coming down so hard today that I feel compelled to drive up to the Yarker Road and wait for Kurt's school bus in front of Lyle's house — "Lyle's Small Engine Repair" says the handmade sign by his garage. The bus stop is only 150 yards from our house, but right now that would be a long swim home for a little person.

I drive up and park behind the spot where the bus, which is never late, will disgorge its passengers five minutes from now. On the sidewalk is a teenage girl from the day care waiting in the wet for her kindergarten charges. She must be new; I don't recognize her. Perhaps I should invite her into my car and out of the downpour? No. She and I have both read too many newspaper stories about girls and men.

From my left comes an angel in a baseball cap. Lyle, who sees all in the village, has emerged from his house with an umbrella, which he hands to the girl. I cannot hear their conversation, but by their body language I can imagine it.

"Young lady, you're lookin' like a drowned rat. You take this." Man holds umbrella out to her.

Girl shrugs shoulders. "Oh, it's okay. The bus'll be here in a minute."

Man holds it out to her again. "You're wet. And the kids'll get wet. Now take it. And bring it back tomorrow or some other time."

Little smile. "Thank you."

Man leaves. As gleeful as Gene Kelly. Singing in the Rain.

I roll down my window and tease him. Tell him what a good Boy Scout he is. Truth is, I am touched by this moment in the life of my village. There are enough such moments to make it a fine place to live. *My* village.

Lyle tells me that the skating pond has never failed to form at the base of the hill. The natural rink is tiny, though still a chore to shovel. Kurt learned to skate there, and few children in the village have not skated there, or played shinny there, or at least GT'd across the pond's surface at the end of a run down the hill.

Kurt is drawn to the pond. In winter he laces up skates and plays hockey there by the hour. In spring he dons rubber boots and leads boats on long string across the shallows. Keen and confident, Kurt is slim and fair, with hazel eyes and a light dusting of freckles across the bridge of his nose. He was born in 1986, ushered into the world most auspiciously by a midwife named King and a doctor named Swift. The field has been his playground since the beginning. Most of the time it's empty, but a sheet of ice in winter or a miniature lake in spring always draws children to the base of the hill.

I said there was water behind me too. I refer to the Napanee River — and you would offend me were you to call it, as some visitors do, a creek. Now forty feet wide and moving at a clip past the high bank on which our house sits, the river encounters thick ice just downstream of us. The bizarre thaw has upstream reopened the river, which till now has been more ice than water. I warily walk the steps down the steep bank. If I slipped in, the rolling waves would snare me and the icy shore would block my escape; the cold of the water, I well know, feels like hundreds of sharp needles pressed deep into bone. Creek, indeed.

The Napanee starts in the northeast at the Cameron Swamp, also known as the Verona Bog, which is fed by various northern streams and lakes, some as deep as eighty feet. Between the bog and the town of Napanee downstream, the river drops two hundred feet, and the falls at the villages of Yarker, Newburgh and Camden East, where the water cuts through limestone cliffs, are spectacular in places: rapids along the way draw kayakers and whitewater canoeists each spring. In the nineteenth century, before water levels could be regulated, the river was wild: the drop at Yarker was 26 feet, and during freshet, spring breakup, you could hear the falls for five miles.

The author Michael Ondaatje mentions the Napanee River in his novel *In the Skin of a Lion*. He describes how logs were sent downriver from the Depot Lakes early this century, past Yarker, past our house (though it gets no mention), and on to the town of Napanee before being towed to sawmills along Lake Ontario. Ondaatje names the Rathbun Timber Company, and Hugo B. Rathbun was indeed the timber baron in this area.

The Camden East Township history describes the singularly fine stands of pine and oak and hemlock that grew here, how any logs harvested had to be no less than twenty inches across at the top. Settlers were astonished to see trees that rose seventy feet before branching, and a foot-thick carpet of moss and pine needles on the virgin forest floor.

Ondaatje describes how men called river drivers kept the log booms moving, using twelve-foot pike poles and dynamite to break up jams. No one knows how many men lost their lives working on the river, or how many women and children have drowned in it, but the number is high.

I have skated on the Napanee River, downstream where it always freezes solid, and so one scene in particular from *In the Skin of a Lion* feels close to home. The loggers are skating at night, playing a game. Each holds a sheaf of cattails whose tops are on fire. The eleven-year-old boy looking on is transfixed. "Skating the river at night," Ondaatje writes, "each of them moving like a wedge into the blackness magically revealing the grey bushes of the shore, *his* shore, *his* river. A tree branch reached out, its hand frozen in the ice, and one of them skated under it, crouching — cattails held behind him like a flaming rooster tail."

The italics are the author's, but I understand that boy's possessiveness. The river is a great gift. It has soothed me more times than I can remember. I have swum, fished, canoed there, and watched it with unfailing interest ever since coming to live in this house fifteen Januarys ago.

My journey from city to country begins in January 1981, when I was thirty-two years old. After living for two and a half years in the Selkirk Mountains of British Columbia, where I had been the editor of a small daily newspaper (the *Nelson Daily News*, aka *The Snooze*), I landed a job with *The Whig-Standard* in Kingston, Ontario. Though locals sometimes sneered at it and called it *The Sub-Standard*, it was then an independently owned, often fine mid-sized daily and was about to enter a golden era that coincided with (was no doubt occasioned by) my arrival.

The paper was not the problem. Sleep was the problem.

Twelve years later, I would describe my dilemma in an editorial in *Harrowsmith* magazine, another career stop.

"My job," I wrote, "compelled me to work twice as many nights as days. No pillows or earplugs or drawn blinds would defeat the city's noise, and sleep by day came in fits and starts, or not at all. I was the night editor of a daily newspaper in a burgh notable for its old stone buildings and many jails. And

I remember with clarity scanning the news wire during one of those interminable nights and seeing the report of an experiment in which houseflies were made to adopt essentially *my* hours. Shift-work bugs, the scientist discovered, died young."

Kingston should have been ideal, and in many ways it was. Home was a graceful nineteenth-century limestone house on Rideau Street carved into four ample apartments. The owner, a purist after my own heart, had sanded and polished the wide-pine floors, installed period windows, approached the restoration with an eye to history.

The building had the misfortune to be attached to a Canadian Tire store, but even that esthetic heresy had its appeal. As a friend assured me, "You are never in doubt about the seasons with a Canadian Tire store so close. Just look in the window. Plastic snow shovels means winter. Plastic lawn chairs means summer." *The Whig* was a five-minute walk away.

And living in Kingston meant a kind of homecoming: my grandparents, Leonard and Gertrude Flynn, lived on Markland Street, two minutes away. I had spent idyllic summers as a child at their farm near Tamworth, about twenty-seven miles northwest of Kingston. I liked the city's manageable size, its old-stone character. Robertson Davies had once proclaimed Kingston a magical place because it stood by two epic bodies of water, the St. Lawrence River and Lake Ontario. It seemed a humane middle ground between smalltown Nelson and uptown Toronto.

But the city would not let me sleep.

My job had me working a month of days followed by two months of nights. What made the rotation unbearable was that I am a light sleeper and the city has a heavy tread. The pounding stereo of our neighbour, the grinding gears of transport trucks, the idling motors of cars perched on the sidewalk as the owners popped in to Canadian Tire: all that daytime noise poured into our lovely bedroom overlooking the street. My choice was no choice at all. Open windows let in din; closed windows kept in summer heat. Neither fostered sleep.

I coiled each day on a mattress in a spare room little bigger than a broom closet with pillows wrapped round my ears. Perversely, I began to *listen* for noise, to sniff for diesel fumes. In mind and body I heated up, like the orange Honda station wagon I then drove with its forever ailing water pump. Every chance I got I retreated to the family cottage at Buckhorn Lake two hours away. I burned with a hot hate for the place I then called home.

When I spotted that article about flies' lives cut short by shift work, a light went off in my sleep-deprived brain. My partner, Ulrike, and I began reading the real estate pages of *The Whig*. If an apartment in the city meant noise, then its clear opposite, a house in the country, had to mean quiet.

Ulrike was born in Germany, came here as a baby. What first drew me to her were her deep brown eyes, her robust laughter, and some exotic European quality we both laugh about now. When I met her, twenty-two years ago, she was a student of languages who spoke fluent German and French, and it seemed she would become a translator. Exotic, indeed.

There was a precision about her, which impulsive sorts like me find appealing. The attraction was of opposites. She played the piano; musical training, sadly, is missing from my education. She was good with numbers; I much prefer words. One time early in our courtship I watched her dash off a sketch and was amazed by the speed and accuracy of the rendition; to me, it was like watching an alchemist turn lead into gold.

Ulrike retains what I take to be a Teutonic sensibility. She prefers order to chaos and discovered, too late, that the Irish are chaos incarnate. My city-induced chaos had become her chaos, and so our desire to escape was mutually felt.

After agreeing that we could tolerate a commute of twenty miles or so, Ulrike drew a radius around the city and we began searching. We drove out to the countryside on weekends, and it was a measure of my desperation to flee the city that I fell in love with just about every country property we looked at.

My first love was a sprawling limestone farmhouse near the village of Moscow and not far from Odessa and Verona — proof of the cosmopolitan leanings of pioneers in these parts. The property included a barn and a hundred acres. Perhaps I could build a cabin in the centre of it, and there, at last, go to sleep?

The tenants, fearing eviction, did their utmost to dissuade us from buying. My memory serves up these details: a vaguely Appalachian family comprising a silent woman and many small ones, all spoken for by a hatted, puggish man with bad teeth and thatched red beard. I remember him pointing into the cupboard below the sink where something — rats big as cats, he whispered lest the realtor hear — had been gnawing at the pink insulation; tales of pipes that froze in winter; floors, each with its own crazy tilt; door jambs a mile off plumb; and all around the periphery of the house straw piled two feet thick. To ward off the cold, confided redbeard, who shivered his shoulders to imply they froze nonetheless. We left the stone house to him and his clan.

From a real estate catalogue we had clipped a picture of the house, and it lies yet in the oak filing cabinet in my office. The file is labelled "House." Another photograph depicts a cedar-siding chalet with ten acres of woodland near the village of Yarker. The woods offered the prospect of walks and firewood for life, and because the house was set well back from the road, it would be private, it would be quiet, it would be heaven. We made an offer. Offer rejected. I was crushed, as a fly — for I had flies on the brain — is crushed by a flyswatter.

But by degrees we were getting closer to home. Yarker is a mere five miles from Camden East, and we looked at two houses there in December 1981. The first was a new one-storey on the southern edge of the village, right on the edge of Ulrike's drawn radius. The owner was Bernie Duhamel, and he would offer us our first lesson in country living. The lesson was about fire, and whenever I get lax about cleaning woodstove chimneys or replacing batteries in smoke detectors, I think of Bernie. Chimneys get swept, detectors are made to blink again.

Bernie is a small but sturdy block of a man who walks as if he just got off a horse. He has a goofy quality, loves to be teased, and I have always been drawn to people like him. The house that Bernie built — for he was a carpenter, among other things — was a monument to fire prevention. The doors were of heavy metal. The H-shape, with the front door at the short stretch between the two longer sections, allowed quick exit. Every room had a smoke detector. The single storey meant no danger of being trapped upstairs.

You never forget a house fire, but Bernie's story concerned a fire at night in the country in an old clapboard house — it stood where this new one had been raised — and it made a deep and lasting impression. It was a bitter-cold February night. Bernie had bought a radiant heater and left it on to stop pipes from freezing in a back room. Something woke him in the small hours, maybe the sound of windows popping in the intense heat. It dawned on him that the house was roaring as the fire demanded more and more oxygen to fuel the flames. He could see foul black smoke pouring up through the cracks between the old pine floorboards. The heat below acted like a giant bellows, and it seemed the whole house would burst.

His panic mounted, for Bernie could find no sign of his wife, Jenny, or their two young daughters. His shouts went unanswered. Crawling on his hands and knees to avoid the smoke, he finally found Jenny in an upstairs closet, where she had huddled with the two girls and prepared to die. Bernie rallied them all to a bedroom window, smashed it with his fist and hurled out his daughters one by one onto the barren ground below. There had been little snow that year. Then he pushed out his wife, who, still numb from panic, would not jump of her own accord. Finally, Bernie leapt.

Strangely, miraculously, none suffered serious injuries. It was as if they had drifted down on the cold itself. But fire would haunt them, and the new house would be designed with fire in mind. They knew, and Ulrike and I then knew, that a nineteenth-century frame house can be consumed with unnerving speed.

The aftermath of the fire told us a lot about the village. When Bernie set out to build a new house, village carpenters, plumbers, electricians, drywallers came round to help. "I had to shoo them away at the end of every day," Bernie said, laughing. Years later, he built a tennis court and invited the village to use it. His way of saying thanks.

A week later, we looked at another house in the village. The owners were out but had left the front door unlocked, as was, we learned later, their custom, and in walked the three of us: a novice agent yet to sell her first house, Ulrike and me, yet to buy our first.

We were drawn to the kitchen at the north end, a huge affair one step down from the rest of the house where an upright woodstove in the corner threw off an inviting heat. Someone, cleverly, had been baking earlier, and an enticing aroma wafted everywhere, redoubling the homey feeling.

A long pine harvest table, solidly built and seemingly for this room, occupied a spot near sliding glass doors eight feet wide and almost as high, so that over morning coffee you could look out to the Napanee River, which coursed by not thirty feet away. The ample old-pine cupboards, like the harvest table, had been rescued from boards in the summer kitchen — an addition to farmhouses that isolated heat generated by cooking during hot weather — and refashioned by a cabinetmaker. This explained the cupboards' worm holes, which I took as marks of character. The harvest table bore a four-inch black scar on one side, perhaps from a near-fire, so these boards too had tales to tell. Eight highbacked wooden chairs were pushed in round the table, and we ran our fingers over the spindles as we passed them.

An island of smaller old-pine cupboards affixed to the ceiling ran half the width of the kitchen and directly over the sink, so that even washing dishes one could look out to the river (and, as I learned later, bop one's head on the pine). The entire kitchen ceiling and that of the master bedroom upstairs, along with hip-high wainscoting in the living room, were made of five-and-a-half-inch tongue-in-groove pine. Renovations had been executed with care.

I liked the honeyed wide-pine floors that ran throughout the house. I liked its nine-foot ceilings, odd angles, the rounded lines of the bannister leading upstairs, the cherry-glass in the formal front entrance historically used only on Sundays. The place had a *feel* to it. Pre-Confederation, on a three-quarter-acre riverfront lot near the centre of the village. Flanked on three sides by century maples and on the river side by elm and ash.

We made an offer that night.

We had questions for the owners, though. Lots of them. I still have the list of twenty-seven in our House file. Number one reads: "What is clapboard?" Number nine: "Did you find it a quiet spot?"

Evidently they did, as have we, for the most part. There was that summer the gospel singers with loudspeakers occupied the hill, but that's another story.

Our offer of $48,800 was accepted (harvest table, chairs and woodstove were extra), and I mention the price because cheaper housing is just one answer among many to this book's key question: why people move from the city to the country.

In the 1960s and 1970s in North America there occurred a back-to-the-land movement, a "rural renaissance." Typical were the hippies whom Ulrike and I saw living in the Slocan Valley north of Nelson. They were dodgers all, Americans who had come up years before to evade the draft and the Vietnam War, or Canadians who had dropped out. They found a bit of lowland, raised a few goats and sheep, grew vegetables and marijuana. The men wore long hair, the women long skirts, they had babies named Meadow and Starlight.

Those exiting the city in the seventies, though, were not all hippies in headbands. Census data, in the U.S. especially, showed a marked blip as mainstreamers too, responding to the

Arab oil embargo, sought energy independence through wood-heated places in the country. But the exodus did not last.

The evidence for another major urban exodus in the 1990s is contested by some. We do live in constant motion, to and from cities, which, everyone knows, seem always to be growing, small towns forever to be dying. Yet when I piece together the mosaic of data, anecdotal evidence, demographic studies and prognostications, a picture emerges of city people in great numbers shifting to the country and smaller places, where they are convinced the grass is greener.

"For the first time in history," writes Stanley R. Barrett, a professor in the department of sociology and anthropology at the University of Guelph, "more people have been moving from urban to rural areas than the reverse." He wrote a book in 1994 called *Paradise: Class, Commuters, and Ethnicity in Rural Ontario,* a lively study of a real town he coyly calls Paradise. For some disgruntled locals, apparently, the migration constitutes Paradise Lost; some delighted newcomers, though, sing the praises of Paradise Found. Of this much, Barrett is certain: the move is on. Some academics call it the population turnaround.

Urban refugees, Barrett discovered, seek a better quality of life, an affordable home and enough space for kids and dogs to run in, horses to graze on, and with room to spare for flowers and vegetables and trees. The desire for more space, I am convinced, lies behind a great many moves from the city.

David Foot is a professor of economics at the University of Toronto with a particular interest in the postwar baby-boom generation, that one-third of the Canadian population, nine million strong, born between 1947 and 1966. "When I look at the census data," says Foot, "and especially location by age, I see incontrovertible evidence: as you get older, you want out of the city. Baby-boomers need escape from the bustle of city life, as ageing people do. They want peace and quiet. They want room."

Foot is a prognosticator, as is Faith Popcorn, a former Wall Street advertising executive whose company computer-analyzes manufacturers' data to make predictions about the future. You may put no faith in someone named Popcorn, but her book, *The Popcorn Report,* had a stranglehold on bestseller lists for almost two years after it was published in 1991.

"City people," she told me, "are getting burned out by work. To them, the city means boundless stress, trying to live ninety-nine lives. More and more people are going to try and live a better, more ethical life by moving to the country. And they're willing to make 20 to 40 per cent less income to do it." Popcorn writes: "What they really long for is to change their jobs, move to the country, and live on fifteen thousand dollars a year." She calls it cashing out to the country or eco-settling.

"For the first time in the history of mankind," Popcorn writes, "the wilderness is safer than civilization. There are no crack vials in the wilderness, no subway murders, no asbestos, no Scuds." Her data — which she had no interest in revealing to her readers or to me — told her that city folk who dream of moving to the country are now acting on that dream.

The notion of urban angst and rural bliss is simplistic and not at all new. It's been stoked by literature, often nostalgically, for centuries. The twentieth century has witnessed a breathtaking migration of people from farms and small places to cities, but somehow we never stopped looking back longingly at what was.

In 1972, a U.S. presidential commission published one of the first analyses of residential preference. The great majority of Americans, it revealed, prefer small towns or open country communities to large metropolitan areas. Seventeen years later, a Gallup poll got the same result: only 19 per cent said they want to live in a city.

American demographer Calvin L. Beale has been plotting urban and rural migration patterns for a long time. He is convinced that "counterurbanization" marks a fundamental population shift in the United States. He observes, for example, that three in four nonmetropolitan counties gained population between 1990 and 1994, "a stunning reversal following a decade of rural decline" and one rooted "in longterm economic changes that favor nonmetro areas, along with the strong conviction of many Americans that smalltown life is better than big-city life."

Another academic, Jack Lessinger, now retired from the University of Washington, has similarly charted the movement of disaffected urbanites into outlying towns and villages, what he calls penturbia. By 2020, he boldly predicts, half the American population will live outside cities, and the urban real estate market will crash.

In the *Journal of the American Planning Association,* three planners observed in 1994 that "the exurbs" — rural places in the urban shadow and now home to 60 million Americans — make up the fastest-growing component of the continental landscape. Urban people, the planners say, see rural areas as kinder, gentler places with a deeper sense of community. Urbanites are fleeing high city taxes and buying cheaper houses in the country. Technology offers them flexible schedules and home offices. They want to retire in small towns. They want space, green space, and, of course, they want privacy.

Canadians share similar sentiments. In their book *The Big Picture: What Canadians Think About Almost Everything,* published in 1990, Canadian pollsters Allan Gregg and Michael Posner reported that almost 70 per cent of Canadian urbanites, if given a choice, would live in the country. Gregg and Posner wrote that in the 1980s "those who stayed in larger cities began to seriously question the quality of their lives and their legacy to their children."

Quality of life.

Remember my *Harrowsmith* editorial about shift-work flies that died young? I had written it as a companion to a feature article describing how people were leaving city for country but using technology to stay connected. As for why they left the city, here is what I wrote: "I was recently reminded of my own move to the country as I sat in the backyard of a Toronto friend one cool fall night and listened to the ennui that poured from my city cronies, all of them wound tight as coils and seeking blessed relief in strong drink and a hot tub. As they saw it, swarming — the current name for collective urban thuggery — menaced their children. Stress and gridlock spared no one. Mortgages devoured their money, and where the time went, no one knew."

Consider these episodes reported in Toronto in 1995. In January, a high school in Scarborough — where I lived as a youth — requested daily police presence because of violence involving knives and guns. In April, a union official was labelling assaults on transit drivers "an epidemic" and calling for Plexiglas shields at drivers' backs. In May, candidates in the provincial election complained that even during the day, many people would not open their doors to a stranger. October saw a ticket-taker murdered at the Victoria Park subway station, the one closest to the house where I grew up. He was the first Toronto transit employee to die violently on the job.

A Statistics Canada survey released in 1994 told us what we already knew: the countryside is a lot safer than the city. City residents were 67 per cent more likely to be robbed and 44 per cent more likely to be assaulted than their rural counterparts. Theft was 58 per cent higher in the city, vandalism 68 per cent more prevalent. No suprise, then, that city residents were much less likely than rural people to take a bus or walk in their neighbourhoods after dark, and twice as likely to have installed new locks or burglar alarms, taken a self-defence course or changed their telephone number.

It seems to have escaped notice that crime in cities all over North America declined significantly in 1995; the *perception* persists that cities are dangerous, and becoming more so. Talk, for example, to Michael Berry, a relocation expert with PHH Relocation Services in Toronto, a firm that moves fifty thousand families a year around the world, and he will tell you that Canadians now view Toronto as someone from Iowa views New York: as mugger city. "In the past ten years," he says, "people here have definitely changed about how comfortable and secure they are. If there's a better way to live, they'll consider it. There's far greater acceptance of rural areas now." Berry is amused by all this, for he grew up in American cities, and by that yardstick Toronto is still — by a mile — Toronto the Good.

But it is the price of housing in Toronto the Good and other cities that has many urban dwellers saying good riddance. Berry's firm did a comparative analysis of houses of equal quality in Toronto, Calgary and Vancouver — downtown, in the suburbs a thirty-minute drive from city centre and in the countryside one to two hours away. They picked as a benchmark a two-storey ten-year-old Toronto house in East York on a 50-by-100-foot lot. The house was 2,000 square feet, with three bedrooms, two full bathrooms, a finished basement, a living room, dining room and attached garage. It cost $335,000 in 1995; its suburban counterpart cost $225,000, and its exurban equivalent $210,000. In Calgary, the figures declined from $235,000 to $175,000 to $150,000 as you moved from city centre to suburb to countryside. In Vancouver, the figures were $485,000, $300,000 and $230,000.

A study in Alberta in 1991 comparing rural and urban costs of living showed that the typical urban family spent $884 a month for shelter, including maintenance and repairs; the rural family spent $230. Only 6 per cent of rural families surveyed paid any rent or mortgage, suggesting that the overwhelming majority of rural people own their own homes free and clear.

Those numbers, which tell me you can live for less in little places, may shed some light on other numbers that I also found intriguing. Another Statistics Canada study, this one published in 1994, came to this conclusion: generally Canadians born in Canada are leaving the big cities — especially Toronto, Montreal and Vancouver — in droves, and immigrants are arriving to take their places. Where is the former bunch going?

It seems they're going to smaller places. A 65-page federal document called *Rural Canada: A Profile,* published in 1995, looks at population changes between 1981 and 1991 and concludes that the greatest growth is occurring in small cities and surrounding countryside (so-called intermediate areas) and in rural areas around big cities (metro-adjacent areas).

Ponder these numbers. Canada's urban population as a whole increased over that decade by 14 per cent, its rural and remote population by only 6 per cent. But in Ontario, intermediate areas grew by a whopping 21 per cent. Metro-adjacent areas grew by 16 per cent in Ontario, by 19 per cent in B.C.

Similarly, rural areas within fifty miles of western cities are witnessing dramatic growth. Winnipeg, for example, has ceased to grow, but its perimeter communities have expanded by 100 to 200 per cent in the past thirty years. Saskatoon, Regina and Edmonton are similarly casting a wide urban shadow.

To some extent, wealth is also leaving the city. *Rural Canada* figures suggest that per capita income between 1980 and 1990 grew by only 10 per cent in cities but by 19 per cent in intermediate regions. The gap was even higher in Ontario.

These data all point to movement, and it would be a mistake to see it as unique to North America. In his book *Conflict and Change in the Countryside,* published in 1990, British geographer Guy M. Robinson observes that the population of Europe's inner cities — he lists Frankfurt, Stockholm, Amsterdam, Copenhagen, Vienna, Birmingham and Paris — has been declining markedly since the 1970s. "In France," he writes, "counter-urbanization has represented the first net out-migration from Paris and its region since records of migration were first kept." The bigger the city, he finds, the greater the move out to small towns and countryside.

Maybe all these people on the move are like me: we like what the city has to offer, we just don't want to live there. As the pace of city life picks up, its alternative, living in the country, looks better. Many of those who have full-time jobs are frantically working harder and longer hours every year: 22 per cent of Canadians toil for fifty and more hours every week. An estimated 700,000 people work at one full-time job and moonlight at another. Americans on average work 158 hours a year more and take 15 per cent less time off than they did twenty years ago. Fashion gave us the dubious leisure suit, but what happened to all that leisure time that was supposed to be the byproduct of technology?

American industry loses up to $75 billion each year because of absenteeism, company-paid medical expenses and lost productivity — much of this blamed on stress. The list of best-selling drugs in North America includes an ulcer medication, hypertension and headache pills and a tranquillizer.

There is no escape from stress. In the country, the lament is much the same as it is in the city. Those of us with jobs worry about keeping them. Time and money seem always in short supply. As city people do, we dig holes for ourselves. Maybe, we fret, we shouldn't have bought all that land, leased that new half-ton, built that pond.

But rents and mortgages and property taxes don't punish our bank books the way they do in the city. And though rural attractions are apparently few, they are, many of them, free. A walk in the forest, a paddle on a river. Commuting, because often done along concession roads and not freeways, frazzles us far less. There is less of just about everything in the country save space — and stress.

The city winds me up, and there are times when I *want* to feel driven. The country is more inclined to calm me, and I need tranquillity too.

January 16. The Napanee River has gone mad. Two days ago it was silent, completely iced over downstream, and upstream reduced to a narrow gap in the ice. Today, after forty-eight hours of head-shaking weather — 15-degree Celsius temperatures that broke all kinds of records, and a driving all-day, all-night rain — the ice on the river and the snow on the land are both gone. Even the pond at the base of the hill is no more. I reckon the frost in the ground below it thawed as well and the water simply found its way down to the next level. Found its way, that is, to the river.

The river is now racing to Lake Ontario. Last night I sat in the dark at the harvest table and watched it rush past, a column of light from the Bakers' driveway lay across the river like moonlight — a stick to measure the river's speed. The river is a roiling, tumbling act now, fifty feet wide and still rising, springlike and loud. A frothy river with whitecaps, a river to drive logs on. A river, mind, not a creek.

February

COMING TO CLARK'S MILLS

The village of Camden East (pop. 250) is what some might mockingly call so small that to blink while passing through is to miss it. Ulrike and I came to realize that the village was more than simply the *absence* of size and bustle; it was the presence of something — a feeling, a sensibility, a sense, finally, of place.

I will draw you a little map to get you to the village, and to help you find your way once there.

Drive north six miles on the Camden East Road from the 401 — the Trans-Canada Highway — midway between Kingston and Belleville. Toronto and Montreal lie equidistant to the west and east. The road, also known as County Road 4, is a rolling, curving two lanes that cuts past farmers' fields and pastures carved out of forests and lined with hedgerows. It descends, finally, into the village.

At the southern edge of the village you will pass on your right a garage called Camden Motor & Sports, where you may spot one of our twelve-year-old vehicles (we have three, including one on hold in the bullpen of my driveway) being attended to by a wiry little mechanic in blue overalls named Bob Hartin.

Bob revs on the high side, but I like the way he moans about the price of new parts and creatively plucks used ones from the heaps beside his garage. I like the way he complains about working too hard and earning too little, then laughs about it with a shrug and a "What can you dew?" I like his stories, about people I know and others I'm glad I don't, and how he punctuates his tales in the middle with a "Mind you ..." and then turns the other way, like a river reversing.

Bob collects moths, some as big as birds. On summer nights the moths are drawn by the dozen to the bright light above his sign; some end up inside glass-covered boxes on the walls of what you might call Bob's office.

Drive on to the four corners where a blinking red stoplight suspended in the middle of a tangle of wires at the intersection halts traffic in all directions. Most drivers oblige. Now and again one leaves a little rubber to announce his departure.

Traffic at the four corners is light, but heavier than when we first came here. I often see gleaming silver tanker trucks, with "Cold Beautiful Milk" written in blue on the side, taking milk from farm to factory; big square Sealtest trucks bring back the milk — in a perfect world the very same milk — in pasteurized form. Those fat blue tanker trucks with the black rubber hose wound at the back? Smith's Pumping Service trucks, which mercifully haul away the stuff in our septic tanks. Wagar's Water Wagon trucks will deliver when cisterns and wells won't. The Chalk Well Drilling rig, an unwieldy red truck with water diviner George Chalk at the wheel, signals that somewhere an old well has run dry, somewhere a new one is in the offing.

Past the four corners they all go. Horse vans. Cattle trucks. The odd transport. A logging truck or two. Tractors pulling hay wagons. Diggers on flatbeds. Pickups. Cars, of course. For about an hour in the morning and late afternoon, the four corners are busy — sometimes three vehicles stop all at once. But by day, and certainly by night, it's pretty quiet.

Note the colours at the four corners. On the southeast corner is a red-brick two-storey building with ornate yellow cornices and a roof that slopes back from the facade. Makes me think of buildings in old westerns. At the turn of the century it was the Farmers Bank building, a cooperative that went calamitously broke in 1910. Later it became the first home of *Harrowsmith* magazine, then a crafts store, then Camden East Community School.

At the moment it is the shared home of the Camden East Community Day Care (where Sarah Whaley-Vallis and her staff look after a dozen or so preschoolers), Canada Post (where Marg Kelly the postmistress both receives and disseminates the little dramas and details that constitute village news) and the Lennox & Addington County Public Library, Camden East Branch. Open Wednesday evenings and Saturday mornings (librarian Mary Lou Fraser caters to a small but devoted readership).

On the northwest corner is an imposing grey and black counter to the red and yellow of the old bank building. The magnificent grey limestone suggests permanence, and the black shingle roof looks new, but at the moment the proud building is empty. "New price, $195,000" the For Sale sign reads.

For more than a century, the limestone structure had housed a general store, its stone outbuilding serving also as a granary. A photograph taken at the four corners around 1910 shows a hatted man in a wagon pulled by two greys coming south. A classier black buggy, its single horse facing north, is parked outside a porched version of the general store, then called Steadman's. The dirt road cuts north over the bridge across the Napanee River and through a thick canopy of trees.

Today, a green sign erroneously proclaims the limestone edifice as the home of the *Harrowsmith* Magazine and Bookstore. The magazine's mailroom was until fairly recently located here, as was the bookstore, but its editorial home was the sprawling Williams mansion across the river. The only sign of life around the limestone building these days are the three or four donkeys that local entrepreneur Larry McCormick has for years kept in the fenced riverfront field west of the building.

The donkeys, a tourist attraction of sorts, have long dined on the carrots and, occasionally, the fingers of both locals and visitors.

In this northwest part of the village north of the river lie two short streets: Dow Street, with one house, and Queen Victoria Road, with three houses, including the Williams mansion, where a portrait of the old queen for years sternly overlooked the stairwell.

The southwest corner of the village's only intersection is paved and serves as a parking lot, often full. It is in this most heavily populated southwest quadrant of the village that you will find relatively longer streets — Shorey and Johnson. The southeast quadrant features no side streets at all.

Finally, in the northeast quadrant lies Mill Street, with three houses, including ours, and, on the north side of the river, the river road (or Riverview Drive, its newer name), which follows the river upstream towards a tiny new subdivision of mammoth houses on mammoth lots carved in the mid-1980s out of a farmer's field. Here the street names are inspired not by simple reference points — long-dead people and still-remembered places — but by something else. Here are Heritage Drive, Pine Ridge Court and Springbrook Drive.

Elsewhere in the village, most houses hug either the river or the main roads going — as pointed green signposts at the four corners indicate — north to Centreville and Tamworth, south to the 401 and the Camden Braes Golf Course, east to Yarker, west to Newburgh and Napanee.

On the northeast corner stands the relative newcomer on the block — McCormick's Country Store. It was built in 1967 on the site of an old hotel, the Dominion House. Larry McCormick remembers tearing down the remains of the old place and finding in the subfloor beneath the bar little turn-of-the-century nickels, for that was the price of a beer in those days.

The village once boasted (not all at once, mind you) five hotels (along with the Dominion House there were the Addington House, the Warner Hotel, the Duncan Hotel and the Ramsay House), three churches, an Orange Hall, a flour mill, a carriage shop, a cheese factory, a woollen mill, a distillery, a brewery and its counter, a division of the Sons of Temperance.

The village dates from 1818 and started as a mill town, drawing mostly Loyalist and Irish settlers, among the latter two brothers, William and Hugh Saul, who are buried beside each other in St. Luke's Anglican Church cemetery. I can see its headstones on the rise if I look north from our kitchen. The Sauls were stonemasons, superb craftsmen who built several dozen churches and twenty-nine rather grand houses in the township, including the stone building at the four corners.

Several luminaries from Canadian history had a hand here. John Graves Simcoe, first lieutenant-governor of Upper Canada and founder of York (later Toronto), owned a thousand acres around Yarker, and the land stayed in his family until 1840. Sir John A. Macdonald once owned a frame-and-log house nestled into a hillside on the road between Camden East and Yarker, though he never actually resided there. As a young lawyer, he lived and worked in Napanee for several years.

In 1821, a man named Samuel Clark, who strikes me as a wary, worrisome sort by his photograph, bought the mill here, then built a woollen mill and a sawmill. This amassed him a small fortune. Soon enough the village, knowing which side its bread was buttered on, came to be called Clark's Mills. But fire or flood would destroy every mill that Squire Clark built, and in 1866, the village — still flexible in matters of bread and butter — changed its name. It then occupied centre stage in the Township of Camden East, named after the Earl of Camden, a former Lord Chancellor of England. Camden East it was, and remains. There is also a Camden West, I am told, in southwestern Ontario.

Larry McCormick once wrote a historical account of the village and offers this bit of trivia: in the early 1880s, Camden East was home to the best baseball team in the district. They were known as the Useless Nine. In the early 1900s, the grandfather of hockey great Bobby Hull lived in Camden East. Maybe John Hull skated on the Napanee River?

Ah, but I'm ahead of my story. Let us return to the four corners of Camden East, and the southeast corner in particular.

McCormick's Country Store is a low-slung affair whose round-log architecture is ad hoc all the way. Its most northerly addition, once a winter storage place for apples and now home to rental videos, looks gangly and towers over the rest. At the back of the general store/café/deli/gas bar/video outlet/nursery (plants, not babies) is a series of sloped lean-to additions, each one tacked onto the one before and by architectural necessity lower than the one before. The last is a kind of storage corral, but clearly the accumulation of stuff has outpaced the additions, for more stuff — an old Esso sign, wooden crates, a tiered vegetable stand — leans lazily against the corral under a thin blanket of snow.

One neighbour, Lyle I think it was, once joked that Larry would only stop building additions when the roof line finally touched the ground. Still, a coat of paint the deep red that maples turn in autumn lends a unifying effect to the sprawling little empire that Larry built. Even the chip truck on the lot — a snub-nosed retired school bus that now sells fries, poutine and hot dogs — is all-white with a broad bottom stripe of that autumnal red.

Depending on the season, a few guys in seed company baseball caps lean on planters outside the store, or sit on low stools at the counter, or stand in a small circle just inside the door by the vegetables, peering over coffee in styrofoam cups at customers coming in. They say "Hey" and tease those they know, talk of weather and crops and baseball and I don't know what else for hours at a time. Every Sunday morning a bunch of farmers, including the township reeve, meets for coffee in the store at seven-thirty, and then some of them may go to a drive-shed down the road for beers. In the rolling hills of Lennox & Addington County, Camden East is a capital city of sorts, and McCormick's Country Store is as downtown as it gets.

We came in February 1981. Of the move I remember little, perhaps because our possessions were so few. We were light and mobile then.

The day of the move was bitterly cold, but bright. A neighbour, George Gauld, who lives two doors away on our street, Mill Street — the huge foundation stones of the old mill can still be seen upriver, at the falls near his house — sauntered by out of curiosity. And we were glad of his curiosity. Because though our just-purchased house seemed huge, our queen bed would not pass up the stairs, and all my ideas for solving the conundrum involved a chain saw.

George had a better idea. Then in his thirties, he owned a thick head of black hair and still used the word *sir* a lot, perhaps from his time in the military. He is a technician who maintains the CBC Radio tower in Kingston and who knows a little, no, a lot, about the important things in life. Plumbing. Carpentry. Electricity. Home Maintenance. George approaches mechanical problems with just the right blend of detachment and engagement. He takes to challenges such as beds-too-big-for-stairs like a crossword addict takes to the Sunday paper.

George's solution was to haul the bed up through a second-floor bedroom window. He calmly and efficiently removed the big storm window from outside, the sashes from inside. We tied a rope around the bed as you would wrap a Christmas parcel and then he started hauling. My job was to climb the TV-antenna tower that ran up past the window and to both guide the bed and push from below while making a lot of grunting noises. George must be immensely strong, for he essentially hauled that bed in by himself.

Moving from an apartment in the city to a 2,200-square-foot two-storey house was like moving from cottage to castle. We had no clue what to do with all this space, but this much we did know: now burdened with a mortgage that made my hand shake as I wrote the cheque, we were not going to heat every cavernous room. We simply shut doors to the parlour and to two unused bedrooms upstairs, even stuffing blankets along the bottom to keep out the arctic drafts that swirled along the floors.

"You're in the old Edgar place?" villagers would ask. "It's nice — in summer." Thus began the war to stay warm in winter in an old country house, and we would fight it over a period of years with salvoes of insulation and weatherstripping and modern windows. We worried that big heating bills would topple us if we left the thermostat at the 22-degree Celsius comfort benchmark. We set it therefore at 18 degrees by day, 15 by night, and heated with wood as much as possible.

Only a little heat, I'm afraid, found its way to the second floor, owing both to the L-shaped configuration of the house and to the lone heating vent upstairs — in the hallway. We convinced ourselves that sleeping in a cool bedroom is healthful, donned pyjamas (in my case sweatpants and T-shirt) with Olympic speed and acquired both the best duvets we could find and high-tech slippers the size of mukluks. I learned to love reading in the kitchen at night, the stove offering quiet company and a special warmth that seems to come only from wood.

Meanwhile, we were settling in. Every day after work in Kingston — my new job as book editor at the newspaper mercifully ended the night shifts — Ulrike and I would stop at the corner and drop into Hartman's General Store, which then also housed the post office. (A few years later the store would be sold and become the *Harrowsmith* bookstore.)

The store had been called Hartman's since the depression, and some price-stickers, dusty ones anyway, could only have dated from the thirties. The proprietors were Ferd and Hope Hartman. You know you are in the country when your neighbours have names such as Fern, June, Levern, Fenwick, Garth, Basil, Elwyn, Elmer, Elberne, Godfrey, Earl, Aevon, Percy and Hubert — names plucked from my village-and-area telephone listing, and names I like, maybe because they seem from another time.

The store had everything you would need to bake a pie, catch a fish, dig a garden, shade your head from the sun, clean your tub, hang a door ... and whatever you needed but could not find Ferd would likely locate in a back room, of which there must have been a dozen. (In one village general store I know of, you can even get a beer if you ask the bootlegger nicely.)

Ferd would stand to the right of the cash register, resting with his knuckles on the oak counter and waiting with what I took to be amused anticipation. I never saw him get excited; but then I never saw him glum either. He had the body of Baby Huey, a head like an egg and eyes like Mr. Magoo's. He was tall and stooped, and as even-tempered as a kindly old dog. When the store was sold, the soft, wide-pine floors were all sanded before the bookstore moved in, but there remained a depression in the floor where Ferd had stood for decades.

That first spring in Camden East, when I had to build an enclosure for chickens bought on a whim at a farm auction, I got advice from Ferd on necessary hardware, his thoughts on chickens, and I thought I caught his grin. Living in the country was all a great adventure for me. I may have been thirty-two years old, but in spirit I was the boy gathering wood for my tree house, and Ferd was the grandfather chuckling as he remembered his own first tree house, his own first chickens.

We were actors in a play. Most days it was *Much Ado About Nothing*. Other days it was *The Comedy of Errors*. I loved my role, loved my wide-eyed character. Had chickens somehow offended local etiquette or bylaws, Ferd would have said so. I took his help as a blessing of sorts, and I came to know that Ferd would pass on my little bit of news, like a columnist in a tiny weekly writing up social notices.

"So I guess that young couple that bought the Edgar house from the Finucans are goin' to raise chickens. He was in here t'other day ..."

He was in here t'other day asking a lot of questions, Ferd might have said. We had never owned a house, never lived in the country, never lived in a village. Our first few years here felt like one long first day on the job. You hope to find one or two kind souls to answer all your questions. I soon had the impression that we were surrounded by kind souls, and a good thing too, for we had an endless supply of questions.

Q. What do you do with your garbage?

A. Take it to the dump on Saturdays or pay a guy with an old pickup to do it for you.

Q. Couriers won't deliver to a box number in a post office. What do we tell them?

A. Have them deliver it to McCormick's, and Annabelle Skinner or Lou Coyle will call you to come and get it.

Q. How do you order in pizza or Chinese food?

A. You don't. (Eventually Newburgh got take-out pizza, Rosie's, but Chinese food still requires a trip to Kingston.)

Q. Who can install the ceiling fixture Aunt Loretta gave us? Who can fix that faucet? Who can tune up the lawn mower?

A. Lyle, Lyle and Lyle.

My grandparents, especially, took great joy in hearing details of our sometimes bungled country apprenticeship.

Early that first summer we planted in the garden two entire rows of zucchinis, which we naively fertilized with manure, unaware that zucchinis require no such encouragement. I marvelled at the *Day of the Triffids* foliage that grew in semi-tropical tangle and the watermelon-sized fruit that lurked in the shadows. Our first winter a pipe burst in the basement and I had no clue how to stem the flow, knowing only enough to call over our aged neighbour to the east, Allan Carroll, who came and calmly turned the pressure valve and likely grinned all the way home. Another time I installed eavestroughing on the front porch. "I see Larry put up a raingutter," a neighbour up the way remarked to Ulrike. "It's got a bit of a lean onto it." Indeed it did, for the porch tipped slightly one way and I wanted the water to flow another, so when I screwed in the gutter I put a bit of a lean onto it. Then I called in the pros. The apprenticeship continues.

Having lived in the house no more than three weeks, we drove one Saturday to Napanee for groceries. It had snowed heavily and was snowing again. The prevailing westerly wind, I knew, would fill in our driveway and I would be an hour shovelling it.

But when we got back, the driveway was clear, the banks piled high with snow and edged with that clean vertical slice that snowblowers make. The guardian angel turned out to be Allan Carroll. He lived in one of the grand old houses of Camden East, what everyone today calls the Squire's House, after Squire Clark. (For himself, Samuel Clark had built a sturdy house of four-by-four framing and, for his sons to live in, a house next door to the west. Our house now.)

I felt a kinship with the Carrolls, for their kin and mine had also been connected. Allan and his wife, Coral, once farmed near Tamworth, and their cousins were immediate neighbours to my grandparents Leonard and Gertrude Flynn. When, one winter morning in 1932, the cookstove blew up and almost killed my grandmother (150 stitches were required to close the wound and all her life she bore a cleft-like scar on her right cheekbone), the neighbours, the Carrolls that is, came first. They thought the house had caught fire. That the Flynns and the Carrolls admired each other was considered something in those days, because the Flynns went to a Catholic church and the Carrolls to a Protestant one.

Allan and Coral sold the big property in 1985, when it got to be too much, and moved from Camden East to Napanee. When Allan died in 1991, they buried him in the graveyard of St. Luke's. Coral joined him in 1994. From that vantage, they have, in a manner of speaking, a view of the village and the house they called home for forty-five years.

When I think of them as a couple, I think of their constitutional: driving into Napanee in the Oldsmobile every Sunday at precisely 4 p.m. for a meal at the Superior. They sat in the same place, had the same meal, just nodded to the waitress and it came. His was liver and onions. Hers was steak.

Coral liked to paint, and we still have one of her watercolours that takes in a view of our house from hers, with Larry's old Texaco sign peeking out over the roofline. A gracious lady with a chirpy voice, she slapped her knees when she laughed, which was often. Coral's home-made carrot wine, to which we were treated one Christmas, tasted treacle sweet.

I remember Allan's huge hands, gnarled as oak, his shoulders squared-off like granite slabs, and the stories neighbours told of his once Bunyanesque strength. I can see him still, sitting stiff-backed in the kitchen at dawn (for farmers always rise at dawn), in the dark (to save electricity), waiting for the sun to rise so he could get on with his day. In spring, summer and fall, that day always included some gardening, and in winter there were always neighbours' driveways to snowblow.

He was there if we needed him. And we would. All of our neighbours on Mill Street would be pressed into service while we learned, learned about woodstoves and wells and water pumps and septic tanks, the elementals.

Wood. After a January so mild in 1995 I fear the trees might be fooled into budding, early February finally cracks winter's whip. The gauge outside reads –27 Celsius. I know it's cold by other signs. At the several feeders near the house, pine siskins and goldfinches, nuthatches and chickadees fluff themselves into balls and keep their bodies so low to the snow they seem to have lost their feet. Steam rolls off the river like a deep-winter fog, and on still, frosty nights ash trees on the riverbank get coated with ice.

On nights like these, when the smoke from the many woodstoves in the village hangs like ribbons in the air, I am reminded — if ever I needed to be — that I live in the country and not in the city. Woodsmoke in such concentration is not a healthy concoction, and you soon want the wind to clear the air again, but woodsmoke by now smells like home. And when all those ribbons of smoke in the village intermingle, I imagine that the houses and their denizens feel a kind of kinship with each other.

For all kinds of reasons, anyone who lives in the country should have a woodstove. Power outages tend to occur somewhat more frequently in the country and last longer (though in recent years they have been rare here). It's nice to heat and cook no matter the vagaries of Hydro or weather. Our wood-stoves are both airtight Jotuls (pronounced *Yo*-tul), older Norwegian models. The one is upright and black, the Jotul 4 Combi-Fire, which has always reminded me of an Easter Island stone god. The other is a 602B, a small green enamel box-stove with a flat top that can nicely serve as a hotplate.

But perhaps more important, wood is a renewable resource and far cheaper to buy in the country than in the city. A full cord (four by four by eight feet) of hardwood cut, split and delivered might cost $150 in Napanee, three times that in Toronto. Like me, many of my neighbours use wood to supplement heat from other sources. As Thoreau wrote, wood heats you several times — when you cut and split it, when you stack it and move it inside, when you actually burn it.

Entire books have been written on the subject of wood and woodstoves. A free 41-page booklet called *A Guide to Residential Wood Heating*, published by Natural Resources Canada in 1993, offers useful and current information. And there has been a revolution in woodstove technology in the past decade, but let me offer you this primer.

First rule. Never burn wood that has not been seasoned for six months, and ideally a year. Firewood needs to be dried, best done by cutting and splitting: the easiest time to split is either right after cutting or during the coldest days of midwinter. Then let the wood dry, preferably stacked outside in the sun and wind.

Burn the stove hot twice a day for about half an hour each time before lowering the temperature by reducing the volume of air let into the stove. A magnetic thermometer, affixed to the stovepipe a foot or so above the stove, is a great comfort. It tells at a glance how hot you're burning. The thermometer's pointer moves through three broad ranges: yellow (below 200 Celsius) is a smouldering fire. Orange (200 to 450) is a good hot fire. Red (450 and higher) is a very hot fire to be used judiciously.

The enemy is creosote, black flaky stuff that the burning of green wood, especially, creates and then paints on the inside of your chimney. Poorly insulated chimneys or poor air-flow up the chimney also lead to creosote. Regular hot fires help to burn it off; twice-a-year cleaning with brushes helps to clean it off. With new stoves, you may only need to clean pipes once a year. If it's allowed to get thick, creosote becomes flammable and the result is a chimney fire. Ask any firefighter about a chimney fire and — sobered as we were by Bernie's tale — you will burn dry wood and you will clean your chimneys.

If you ever have a chimney fire, you will soon know it. A roaring sound emanates from the chimney — "It's like thunder," says a neighbour who has had three such fires — and the stovepipe crackles and may glow red. You smell tar, and neighbours will observe a Vesuvius-like emission of sparks and flames from your chimney. The best advice is to get out and call the fire department. If it's safe to do so before leaving, toss baking soda into the stove, close the door and shut down all dampers and draft controls to choke off the air supply. You might also spray a light mist of water onto any wood in the firebox: the steam may help put out the chimney fire. Even if you think the fire is out, call the fire department and let them make that judgement.

I have never had a chimney fire, but I have been roused in the dead of night by the smoke detector. It is a call that would muster the dead.

We had been in the house about a month, and we had fire on the brain. We had read books on heating with wood, taken a course offered by the fire department and had the house inspected for fire safety. So when the alarm went off, I bolted awake and my heart was in my mouth.

I raced downstairs to the kitchen woodstove expecting to see flames or smoke. There was nothing in the darkness but a long pencil of light from the woodstove's tiny draft control flickering daintily on the tile floor. All was right with the world. The banshee of a smoke alarm was simply telling the world its battery was low.

To keep the other banshee at bay (in Irish and Scottish

mythology, the banshee was a wailing spirit that warned of impending death), I clean the chimneys. This I do twice each winter, using brushes linked to coupled metal rods. The layout of our house necessitates two stoves — the small one in the north-facing kitchen, which I fire up daily in winter, the larger one on the eastern front in what we call the parlour and stoked only against bitter cold. Cleaning either chimney is not a pleasant task, but neither is it terribly hard. The cardinal rule of woodstove installation is that cleaning be made easy, and thus more likely to occur.

With our kitchen stove, it is a simple matter of climbing onto the one-storey, gently sloped roof and driving the rods-and-brush up and down the chimney a few times. Gravity takes the soot down into the stove. Cleaning the parlour stovepipe is trickier. Because the chimney comes out two floors up in an awkward place on a steep, high roof, I clean it out from below. This time, gravity is a nuisance, and without precautions I will look like a chimney sweep from a Dickens novel and black dust will find every corner of the parlour.

What I do is this: I take the cap off the bottom of the cleanout. Commonly called a T (though it looks more like an L), the cleanout simply means that the stovepipe descends from the ceiling and ends at a removable cap, *then* makes a hard right to the stove. If cleaning the chimney from the roof is not practical, install a T, for a T works to a T.

The cap removed, I insert the brush up the chimney, but only after surrounding the brush with a large plastic garbage bag, whose opening I wrap tightly around the stovepipe and secure with heavy elastic bands. The idea is to contain all the soot inside that bag. The rod, to which the brush is attached, peeks out from a small hole to one side of the bottom of the bag, and as I screw in each new section of rod and drive the brush farther up the chimney, I hear soot falling into the bag. Not, notice, onto my face or the furniture. Minuscule amounts of black dust may escape the hole in the bag and settle on newspapers at my feet, but as a system it works.

Another option is to fit a metal collar, held in place by screws, around the outside of the stovepipe. The collar, in fact, hides a gap in the stovepipe, which gap allows room to manoeuvre when you unscrew the pipe at the ceiling and at the stove. *Or,* failing all of the above, you and half your neighbourhood could simply lift the stove away from the pipe every time you clean the chimney. You wouldn't chimney-sweep very often, though, and we know where that leads.

One other word of advice: ensure that your chimney rain-cap — the one on your roof — has a spark guard around it. The metal mesh keeps large sparks off your roof and serves another purpose. Our parlour chimney has no guard and every spring birds end up in the chimney, and I use a variation on the system described above to rescue them. One year an unfortunate sparrow escaped my bag, and wherever he touched with his sooty wings he left a black reminder, until white ceiling and walls took on a Dalmatian look.

I said wood heats many times. At least twice a year, I truck down to Prince Edward County, to some land we own near Picton, and, with a friend, I cut wood. My back is sometimes not grateful, but I am — for the exercise and for the ritual. We go in the fall, when the bugs have gone.

I once walked the woods on our forty-three-acre property with a forester who taught me a great deal about the diversity of trees there, and which ones to cut to enhance regeneration. Trees the forester later marked with yellow spray paint — trees that lean, or crooked-limbed trees competing too close to a straight tree, for example — end up as firewood in my kitchen. More precisely, they end up in four-foot circular wood-holders made of black tubular steel and fitted with a base. Two came with the house, and almost everyone who heats with wood covets them upon first seeing them.

I like the notion that wood I cut with my own hands warms those same hands in winter. The notion is as circular as those black wood-holders. Sometimes I'll be putting a piece in the stove and I'll come across a slash of yellow spray paint from the forester. And as the wood crackles, I think of where it came from and the day I cut it with my friend David Carpenter. How sweaty we were after, how covered in sawdust and dirt, how I swam in Lake Ontario at Point Petre but Carp had to look on because his dog, Bessie, an enthusiastic but simple-hearted golden retriever, gets distraught when he swims. She worries that Carp will drown when, in fact, Carp swims, as you might expect, like a fish. That piece of wood has all those memories, and I hope not too much moisture, stored inside.

Water. Most people who live in the country get their water from wells. In our case, we take our water from the river (ours is thus called a river well) and deploy a sophisticated system in the basement to filter and purify the water. In winter, the house is prey to all manner of now-familiar and often subtle sounds as the dry heat causes floorboards to shrink and the cracks between them to widen (summer humidity puts them right again), as timbers in the attic creak and as the oil furnace performs its pyrotechnics. But amid all those in-house sounds of winter, the sweetest is still the simplest — the water pump in the basement coming on, and shutting off.

There is a little puckering or pop that a pump makes just before it shuts off. Sometimes it's more like *-ha*. When the sound persists of our water pump pumping, when there is no pucker or pop or *-ha* after about a minute and a half, then my mouth goes dry. I open up the heavy hatch leading into the basement to investigate. And if I then emerge and don old clothes and re-enter the cellar, my red-metal toolbox in hand, the house heaves a sigh, but not of relief. The taps, the toilets, fall silent while I play plumber.

I will save my water horror stories for later. What you need to know here are some basic laws of human physics as practised in the country. 1. Water in the country comes from pumps. 2. When pumps lose prime, people lose patience. 3. When water lines freeze, get on your knees — to your plumber.

Sometimes the pump has simply lost prime. A chance

occurrence, not to be repeated. You undo the nut marked "prime" atop the pump, pour in water, reattach the screw, flick the switch and away goes the pump. But not always. Because if the pump suddenly got thirsty, it got thirsty for a reason.

Alongside my pump is a pressure tank, and on the pressure tank is a circular black gauge. If the sweetest sound in the world is the pop of a pump knocking off after filling up the depleted water tanks, then the sweetest sight in the world is that gauge moving off zero and climbing to 42 pounds per square inch, the shutoff point. When repeated priming of the pump fails to move that gauge, because the pump is pumping air, not water, then your foot valve — at the water source — is stuck open or you have ice in the water line or a dry well or a sick pump. I've had just about all of those things come between me and my water, and the effect has been to make me ever after grateful when I turn on the shower or flush the toilet, and behold, there is water.

We have friends, the Goods, who routinely fill their bathtub with water at the first sign of thunderstorms or ice storms. In the country, a power outage = no electricity = no pump = no water. With the tub full, you can at least dip in a pail and manually flush the toilet.

Did I mention flushing?

The septic tank. One of the things I like about living in the country is that you are made conscious of your own nest, and are thus encouraged not to foul it.

A city person lives in a dwelling with taps and toilets plugged into a massive grid of water and sewer lines. It's a public system, and if it malfunctions one calls city hall. A rural person — no matter how vast the property — typically draws drinking water from a well on one side of the house and flushes waste into a septic system on the other side. The two lines are perilously close to one another, and the rural person has an intense personal interest in keeping the two functional, healthy and apart.

Where I live, you can pay a local guy to come around and pick up your garbage, but most of us make a trip to the dump part of our routine. By composting kitchen scraps, leaves and grass clippings, we eliminate most smelly garbage and need only go to the dump about once a month these days. Each garbage bag has to have an orange sticker, allotted rigorously by the township. In 1996, those tags will cost a dollar each: the more garbage we produce, the more we pay. Glass, newspaper, cardboard, plastic, tin: all go to the dump's recycling bins. No surprise, then, that if you live in a small town, a village or on a concession road, what you flush down the toilet and into the septic tank is also yours to deal with.

Every three or four years, the tank's top must be removed and the contents pumped out. Failure to do so results in the contents coming back up to haunt you. A septic tank is nothing more than a holding tank. Solids eventually sink to the bottom, and liquids run out the top along a pipe and then through perforated pipes set into a field of sand and stone. What comes out the end, if the system is working properly, should be clean water. And while bacteria do break down the solids, the honey wagon must pay regular visits or the whole system will clog.

Well-maintained septic systems can last up to forty years. This is good, because replacing a clogged field or tank can set you back anywhere from $2,000 to $6,000. My uncle Jack Scanlan, a plumber now deceased, once told me that all you need to know about plumbing is that shit runs downhill and pay day is Thursday. The corollary is that when shit runs uphill, *you* pay. Dearly.

I know people who moved to the country expecting to find bliss, not rowdy neighbours next door. The bad news, or so these metropolitans first thought, was catching a rat in the basement; the worse news was that their urban instinct to flush the rodent down the toilet gummed up the septic system, with unpleasant consequences that hastened their retreat to the city.

You can increase the life span of your system by using only white toilet paper. Some people refrain from flushing *any* paper into the system. Your allies in the septic tank are millions of bacteria; harsh toilet-bowl cleansers, bleach and colouring agents in paper are anathema to them.

And if all this sounds too complicated, there's always the privy.

February 4. I have learned, after many winters outside the city, that February is indeed the cruellest month. Winter, I now know, is a long tunnel: January's post-holiday glow offers light from the entrance behind you, March's brightening days let you see light at the other end, and February is that short-dark middle.

Never mind. January's thaw and February's freeze have created perfect ice on the large pond at the conservation area in Newburgh. Kurt has this year discovered the joys of shinny. The pond tugs at him. He tugs at me. I feel the cold. He doesn't. After school and on weekends, we are on the pond.

As Kurt and I played this brilliant cold Saturday, we watched villagers pile old Christmas trees near the pond. Tonight, about a hundred hardy souls are gathered for hot chocolate and hot dogs as Newburgh holds its annual skating party. All those spruces and pines, some with tinsel still attached, go up in flames as they are put to a second use — keeping us warm while the snow drifts down.

A semicircle forms upwind of the gathering flames. Toddlers are entranced by the sight and sound of the snapping bonfire. One sits on a stump while her mother bares her foot and brings it as close as she dares to the heat. Then the wind suddenly shifts and showers sparks on us. Someone screams.

"Oh my God your hair's on fire!"

"Where? Where?"

"It's okay, I got it. It's out."

Nervous laughter. Jokes about moths drawn to flames. We are all eyeing each other, looking on chests and shoulders for sparks, brushing them away when we spot them, turning in circles lest any be missed, thanking the neighbour whose face looks familiar. Familiar enough when preening for fire.

February 18. What a winter this is. Warm again. The Napanee River is flowing freely now, though false banks of snow and ice hang over the briskly moving water. The leaves have been gone for four months, and I desperately miss the sound of wind through the foliage. I cannot seem to connect all these dead-brown trunks and branches with the lordly oaks and maples of summer. I long for green.

What offers at least some consolation are the sounds coming up from the river. The constant sound — aside from the stirring of the falls upriver — is of water sloshing around under ice. I go out to listen in the dark (the better to focus my ears) down at the icy bank. What I hear is strange music, at once modern and ancient.

I hear dogs lapping at their water bowls. Children dropping stones in buckets of water. Rain falling on a tin roof. People clinking ice in their party glasses.

The sounds are delicate and subtle, varied and rich, a measured symphony in which every player seems content to play at the back of the stage all day and all night without ceasing.

River music.

March

THE BEAUTY OF SMALL

In March, the mood lifts with the new light and the longer days. Winter now is more lamb than lion. We are a nation obsessed with weather, and no one takes its pulse more often or welcomes the end of winter more eagerly than country people.

Near the end of March, especially, strong opinions are held on whether IT is done with us yet. Chuck Clark, a gas jockey at McCormick's Country Store — still called McCormick's years after Larry and Reta sold it to Mike and Amy Martin — receives hundreds of opinions daily on this and other weather matters. A typical exchange at the gas pumps may go something like this, and if the customer has lived in the area all his life, as Chuck has (the affable redhead is descended from Samuel Clark), he will speak in the same exceedingly slow, almost Southern drawl:

"G'day, Chuck."

"Bert."

"'Ell of a storm last night, Chuck. But 'at's the last of her. Winter's done."

"Radio says 'nother one comin', Bert."

"Nah."

"Swat it says."

"Yeah?"

"Yeah."

"Damn."

"What can you dew?"

Fair to say that in the country, lot lines are longer. We tend to be accorded more breathing room than in the city, and when the temperature changes our acreages change with it. The river, certain plants, the air, all respond in a way peculiar to March and the promise of spring. We take our cue from the farmers around us: weather is more present in our lives.

City folk, by dint of underground walkways and malls, can sidestep weather to some extent. Living where I do, I have no choice but to look weather in the eye. Each month, then, takes on a character defined by weather. In March, I no longer take winter seriously. A storm may come, and we happily cross-country ski from our porch when it does, but a thaw is sure to follow. The sun streaming through the west windows warms in a way it never could in January.

That phrase "the dead country," meaning way out in the country, must have been coined in winter. In the dead of winter, weeks can pass before I see this or that neighbour; only by tracks in the snow and smoke from chimneys do we deduce each other's continued existence. March shatters that pattern. Villagers go out for longer walks, gab leisurely at the corner with neighbours, end their virtual hibernation. It's as if someone had rung the all-clear signal.

This year, the signal comes on March 14, when the temperature soars to 18. As the snow melts, Kurt and a friend sail homemade boats in village culverts, now raging little torrents. Virginia Thompson and Ulrike praise the sun over the picket fence between our properties. The fence, I see, curves like an old spine and cries out for paint. But who cares on a day like this? We are like that reckless groundhog I spot outside the village standing atop a fence post: far from the ground, drunk on the sun.

Mill Street stirs. Lyle Lawlor gravitates to his spot on the back deck and sits in the light. Doug Thompson, nine inches taller and ten years older than Lyle, finds cause to putter in his workshop, the one that Lyle built. Doug has bad eyes and a wonky ticker, and when he ducked death a few years back (and frightened Lyle half to death), he returned from hospital to find Lyle's elaborate surprise — the old green aluminum garage door gone and in its stead a wall and locking door, a wooden floor below and, thanks to a large south-facing window, a brighter light to squint by.

All over the village, people find pressing business in their yards. Ulrike's thoughts turn to raking and an early spring, but she dismisses the former lest it spook the latter. She sits on our porch — which I see does *not* need painting this year — and feels the wind tickle her bare toes.

This is all well and good, this deeper rural notion of what March means. But why, early in that first March of 1981, was our water pump pumping so furiously and ceaselessly in the basement? Why had taps and toilets become so miserly in their offerings of water? Why did the faucets finally cough and sputter like the *pocketa-pocketa* of an old engine?

Because our water line was frozen.

In Louise Erdrich's *The Blue Jays' Dance,* a lovely book about motherhood, she describes living in a country house when the taps called it quits: "I turned the faucet wide and heard the thunk and yawn of air in the pipes. The hollow sound reverberated right through my body, for I knew immediately that the well had gone dry. As we had no money to drill a well, we hauled water for a month, showered in the school gym, and used the thickets and underbrush for miles around the house."

Erdrich does not recommend the experience, especially during a pregnancy, but she does wonder, romantically, if her baby's appreciation of the natural world was enhanced by her 3 a.m. trips into the night woods where the fireflies sent out "ardent messages," the crickets played "thin riffs" and "surely the night oxygen bubbled into her, blood rich, cool, and dark." Yes. But that was summer in New England, not winter in Ontario. *Thunk and yawn, thunk and yawn* went our taps, toilets and faucets.

That first winter in Camden East gave us weeks of prolonged deep freeze. Around the −30 Celsius mark, I noticed on my midnight walks, the towering old maples out front would start to ache and crack. Not from wind — for it was inordinately still — but from cold, the kind of cold that makes my nostrils pinch if I sniff deeply. The trees made the sound that rusty nails make when wrenched from wood. One step on the pine boards of the porch and they too creaked loudly along their lengths, the sound echoing in the village and up and down the valley. There had been a dearth of snow, and snow, I would learn, is a nuisance to shovel but insulates against a worse nuisance — the frozen water line.

I put out a distress call. We had only been in the house a few weeks.

"Call me if you need anything," our neighbour George Gauld had said. Anyone who could almost singlehandedly haul a bed up two storeys would surely know why our pump was sucking only air. Like most men on Mill Street, he had exited the womb with a tiny red toolbox in his hand. He came right away.

I was too desperate for water — and a toilet that flushed — to stop and think: *Why* did he come to our rescue? Was it because we seemed so young and helpless? Did he feel an obligation, a responsibility as neighbour? Did the need to resolve the mechanical problem answer something deep within him? Looking back on that rescue, and the dozen or so others that followed, I would say it was all of that and more.

During our years in Camden East, my neighbours have responded to two periods of waterlessness in our house. The first, seven days in 1981, was occasioned by freakish cold; the second, three months (!) in 1994, by a freak ice jam that drove the foot valve in the river off its concrete-block moorings and into the river bottom. We thus drew mud, not water, and soon all plumbing ceased. There followed a $200 overhaul of the pump and a near-Arctic expedition to find the foot valve: the ice was a foot and a half thick on the river, and though I chain-sawed through and searched for days in the icy depths with home-made grappling hooks for that errant valve, I could not find it. And so from early January to early April, during the coldest winter in many decades, we hauled water.

Ulrike's office in Newburgh mercifully includes a washroom and a bathtub, though the water is not potable. Saturday-morning trips there to shower and to collect water in fifteen or so ten-gallon plastic containers became part of the routine. It had a certain pioneer feel to it in the beginning, but quickly became a teeth-clenching exercise. I reckon we hauled 3,600 gallons by hand that Endless Winter.

During all that time, Doug gave us drinking water and Lyle did the same, the latter taking several turns at trying to resolve our problem. Other neighbours in and around the village, Maya Jagger and Jane Good and Marta Scythes, gave us the use of their washing machines until we were too embarrassed to ask any more and made the laundromat in Napanee also part of our Saturday ritual. From everyone else in the village who knew of our plight came generous dollops of sympathy.

My hunch is that such altruism can be found in most villages and small towns across Canada. Think, on the other hand, of how city neighbours might respond to a similar plight. In some neighbourhoods, neighbours hardly know each other. Even if they do, would they roll up their sleeves and play plumber? Would one neighbour's woes be felt so collectively? Maybe. Maybe not.

One Friday evening in March, Kurt, Ulrike and I were driving south on the Allen Expressway in Toronto and I had been remarking on the speed of the cars. I was cruising along at 90 kilometres an hour, ten in excess of the limit. Cars passing me left and right must have been going 120. When one such car zipped by me near the end of the expressway, I said aloud calmly

and assuredly, "He won't be able to stop," for the traffic had
bottlenecked up ahead.

The driver frantically swerved left, caught the car in front
and shook it like a dog shakes a slipper, then struck the guard
rail and cuffed it too a few times before finally sliding to a
halt. The woman in front got out to examine the damage,
then strangely went to her own passenger door, opened it and
angrily slammed it before approaching the other car and doing
the same.

To my shame, I did what you do in the city. Did I get out
to make sure this woman was not hurt? Did I roll down my window at least and say I would stop at the next phone booth and
call the police? Perhaps offer my sympathy? Did I suggest that
both drivers just rest in their seats, for both could be in shock?
I did not. I steered for the other lane and moved on. Let the
police handle it.

I thought, How might all this have unfolded on County
Road 4? I am absolutely certain I would have stopped my car
and done everything I did not do in the city.

Why? Why did I swallow my village altruism in the city? In
retrospect, being on a freeway was part of the problem. Though
our momentum had suddenly been arrested, we still felt compelled to press on at the hurried pace of the highway. Besides,
if cars were bent or people hurt or particulars had to be taken
down, tow truck or ambulance or police car would be along
shortly. This is the way of the city.

In the country, there are far fewer of us, with lines of responsibility much fuzzier. In a pinch we make do. A car in a ditch
may get pulled out by a farmer's one-ton before a tow truck
can be dispatched. In the circumstances just described, the
bad news is that on a country road many minutes would have
transpired before official help came; the good news is that we
and others would have stopped. We might have been prodded
by charity, or curiosity, or guilt: had the drivers been local we
might have known them or had friends in common. County
Road 4 seems, therefore, far less intimidating than the Allen

Expressway. None of that should matter though. Next time I will stop, and do the decent thing.

I will take my cue from the country, where my experience has been that neighbours are there when you need them. The greater the crisis, the greater the help that comes.

Others share that belief. Donald Connery, a former correspondent for *Time* magazine, had been living with his wife in the small Connecticut town of Kent for less than a year when their farmhouse caught fire one night in January. As he describes it, "The town came to our rescue ... volunteer firemen swarming about the house, friends running with lengths of hose, strangers donning oxygen masks, shadows chopping through the ice in the pool, the first selectman [councillor] going up a ladder, shopkeepers and artisans disappearing into the smoke ... people risking their lives for you."

When the smoke had cleared, Connery, a city man, was terribly moved and not a little shocked. "It is almost too much to bear," he wrote in *One American Town*, a paean to Kent itself. "Not the fire but the kindness. The involvement. The sheer humanity of it all. This is not what modern man is used to. The drift of the world is to the depersonalized city where the knack of survival is not to get involved. Avoid thy neighbour."

Shelagh Rogers, the backup host of CBC Radio's *Morningside*, tells the story of jogging in the woods near her home in Eden Mills when she broke her ankle. It happened in 1994, not long after she moved into this village an hour's drive west of Toronto, where she had long lived. "I never trusted my neighbours in the city," Rogers told me. "But the day of my accident a neighbour who was also a nurse came over with flowers, she made coffee, she just took control. I felt watched over — for the first time in my life — by a neighbour."

Osha Gray Davidson lived in Mechanicsville, Iowa, for three years while writing a book about rural poverty called *Broken Heartland*. He once found himself in town, far from the laundry he had left out on the line, when a thunderstorm hit. When he got home, the clothes were all neatly folded in a neighbour's laundry basket tucked inside his door.

A survey taken in Mechanicsville revealed that almost half the residents felt their neighbours interfered too often in their business. But 90 per cent also believed that their neighbours would help out in an emergency, and that in the end the trade-off was worth it. "For all the drawbacks to small-town life," writes Davidson, "that sense of belonging to a caring community is what Heartland towns like Mechanicsville have always provided their residents."

On our street, when the choice is between somebody else's problem and your own, it's no contest. I count as a rite of spring, to cite an example of Mill Street mutuality, Doug wrestling with the pump behind his garage where the white picket fence dividing our properties ends. He uses the pump, an old upright model painted aquamarine, to water his close-cropped lawns and Virginia's splendid gardens, and every spring he and Lyle do battle with it. I join in the fray, for I have learned that misery loves company and is mitigated by it. There is undeniable frustration in a recalcitrant pump, but you are not allowed to express it in company, nor would company let you. Grumpiness gets buried in one-liners.

Besides, though mechanical matters usually confound me, I have at least learned the language of pumps. I know, thanks to George, about foot valves, valve rubbers, pressure gauges, lost prime, impellers. I know the surging sound that a piston pump makes when it starts to pump water, the hollow sound it makes when it's moving only air. I know, because Lyle taught me, that a jet pump, when allowed to sit, can rust and that simply rotating the impeller inside (by turning a screw outside) can bring a moribund pump back to life.

But in March 1981, George was the plumber, I was his aide, and ice was the enemy. His diagnosis, borne out later, was ice in the line. Between our piston pump in the basement and the river runs a black PVC pipe below the frost line. The frost went deep that year, and water sitting in the line at the river-bank had turned to ice. I now pile a three-foot-thick layer of leaves there in the fall to prevent just such a recurrence. The standard counter to ice in the line is this: disconnect pump and pipe and feed a garden hose down the pipe's length. Hope that the jet of water eventually breaks through the ice.

The aim is to get the end of the garden hose as close to the ice blockage as possible. You want to create a circular flow of water, so that water pumped down the line hits the ice, comes back up the line, out the PVC pipe and into a pail, which is the water source for your pump. The circle is complete.

It did not work. I tried for days. So did Lyle and a Newburgh plumber named Stan (George's father-in-law, it turned out).

Then George had a brilliant idea: connect the garden hose to the threaded drain valve at the bottom of the hot water tank. This meant that the water shooting down the pipe towards the ice was hot. I tried it that evening, and soon enough the water did not come rushing back. *The water kept on going, past the ice and foot valve and into the river.*

I can barely describe to you the joy I felt at that moment. I was wearing the old clothes hung in the mud room for occasions such as this: tired cords, retired shirt, rubber boots. On the dirt floor of the basement were lengths of garden hose, steel hose clamps, my red toolkit in open disarray, pails of water.

It had been my ritual for six nights to open up the heavy trap door and descend into my own little hell. To wrestle with the hoses — the farther down I thrust the garden hose the more likely it was to crimp, especially if I tried to move at other than a snail's pace. To pass on supper — for martyrs *always* pass on supper. To curse my luck and blue hands — for the water, before George had his hot idea, returned even colder from its encounter with the ice down below. To ascend the stairs later — defeated and smelling worse than before.

What's that expression about the simple things being the best things in life? There is nothing simpler than water. When I reattached PVC pipe and pump as before and flicked the switch, the water surged. I could hear it. I could feel the coldness of the water moving in the poly pipe. I could see the pressure gauge lifting off zero for the first time in almost a week, at first slowly and then with more confidence, before finally clicking off at 42 psi. *-Ha.* We had water.

We also had neighbours.

One of my obsessions, perhaps because I grew up in a raucous home with seven siblings, is quiet. I do love what the Irish call the crack — that playful but competitive verbal jousting around, say, the dinner table, that rewards wit and comic timing. But I also need tranquillity as a counter.

There is no logic in me on this question of quiet, but when the blackbirds gather by the thousands in trees along the river each spring, I actually enjoy the early-morning tumult. I love the drum of heavy rain on a tin roof, wind howling showily through the trees, a chorus of frogs, the call of geese on the wing in the fall.

It is noise from humankind and their machines I object to. When Doug Thompson years ago deployed in his yard an electric bug zapper to kill insects day and night, I less than discreetly passed him articles from *Harrowsmith* pointing out that zappers make no dent on the mosquito and blackfly populations but do harm benign insects such as bees, moths and ladybugs. My aim was selfish: entomology mattered less than tranquillity. To my ears, that snap-crackle-pop of the blue-neon zapper was the sound of elephants dropping from a great height onto beds of dry branches. I hated those elephants, but it took much gumption on my part to complain. How do you tell neighbours you value that their bugger bugs you?

Doug later told me with a straight face that the village church was having a yard sale and that I could probably get a bug zapper at a pretty good price. I felt at that moment a tangle of things: guilt that I had inflicted myself on my neighbour, gratitude that elephant-jumping had ceased next door and that my neighbour responded as he did.

I wasn't always so lucky. Several summers after our arrival in Camden East, a congregation from a nearby village decided to use the hill opposite our house as an outdoor church every Sunday afternoon. They would plug in microphones and speakers, set out chairs and fill the air with gospel music. The aim, to judge by the volume, was to pull in converts from half a mile away. Outside and inside our house, the singing and the sermon rang in our ears. George and I took particular umbrage at this and made our displeasure known to the pastor, who seemed unmoved. But whether the gospelaires desisted a few months later because the crowds were so sparse or because George and I occasionally timed our chainsawing and lawn-mowing to coincide with the singing, I will never know.

Later, someone on the south side of the village felt a similar hankering for audience, for she took to plugging in her guitar and amp and wailing on weekends before she too finally stopped. I doubt that anyone ever complained to her directly about her hurtin' music.

Such antics are dealt with differently in the city. There the tempers are shorter, the cops called quicker. Country people are by and large more tolerant of their neighbours, less inclined to complain for fear of giving offence, and I would venture this stems at least in part from necessity. At some point, you may need those neighbours. It's bad enough to have an enemy in the village, but to have an enemy in the village living next door …

An article in the American journal *The Washingtonian* once pondered the difference between living in the city and living in the country. The author, Patrick Anderson, opined that the city lets you choose your friends and ignore your neighbours. The village, on the other hand, is a lifeboat: "The guy next door might be a jerk, but you have to deal with him because your kid and his kid are buddies, and when your pump breaks down, you'll go to him for water. The good news and bad news about village life are the same: you become intimately involved with the lives of other people."

Country people soon learn caution: if you intend to insult someone, ensure that no one listening is a friend or relative of the target of your malice. And it is one thing for a local to insult another local; quite another for a newcomer to commit that sin.

An hour to the southwest of us in Camden East is Prince Edward County. About one-quarter the size of Prince Edward Island, it is the smallest county in the province, yet people there call it the County, as if it were the only one, or the largest. It is surrounded by the waters of Lake Ontario but for a narrow spit of land. I cross a huge bridge to get there, and so inward-looking and interconnected are people there that I *feel* myself to be on an island.

Only recently has the county been discovered by outsiders, specifically Torontonians. Waterfront properties now trade at what county people believe to be exorbitant prices. Some locals make a lot of money selling their land; farmers looking for extra pasture, however, suddenly find it beyond their range. These days there simmers a mild tension between locals — who can often trace their roots back to the last century — and more recent arrivals.

One Torontonian returned on a weekend to find his retreat trashed; the graffiti sprayed on the walls told him to go back where he came from. Such animosity is rare, but coming to the country can feel a little like coming to an island. You can arrive on the island quietly, or you can come with a lot of loud crashing.

In his book *Far from Home,* Ron Powers tells the story of Henry Kissinger buying a 350-acre property a few miles from the aforementioned Kent, Connecticut. Locals had for years picked blueberries — with the owner's permission — on that land. Kissinger had the bushes uprooted, save for a few that he permitted volunteers to replant on school grounds and back roads.

The vandalism that followed in the area — much of it aimed at newcomers — cannot all be laid at Kissinger's feet, but his imperiousness did not endear him to locals. The new arrivals to Kent responded to the despoiling of their elaborate rock gardens and wrapped-and-staked saplings with alarm systems, set off at all hours by wind and rain and even, as one local wit put it, by the sound of "a mouse farting against the windowpane."

Canadian poet bill bissett wrote a book called *nobody owns th earth* (*sic*), but when a city person comes to the country it is clear — to some locals, anyway — who really owns the earth. Locals do. What follows are suggestions that might make the transition from city to country a little easier.

Listen, just listen. You will find country people welcoming but cautious. It may be a long time before you are truly accepted into the community, and there is no way of rushing it.

Let's say, for example, that you are a woman recently arrived in a small place. You begin to attend the local church and are soon asked to bake a pie for a fund-raiser. You could a) ask why the man of the house wasn't asked to make the pie, or b) make the pie now and the point later. The first option will win you few friends in rural communities where division of labour, especially among older couples, tends towards nineteenth-century models.

This is one legacy of the family farm, and if you come from the city and buy a farm or farmland, you should know a few farm facts. All around small towns and villages, family farms still exist but there remain fewer and fewer of them. When a farm comes up for sale, you might renovate the old house and fix up the barn for horses. You might think of this as urbanites to the rescue.

Farmers will not see it that way. One or two might have bid on that land but could not match your offer. You may rent it to a farmer, but that's no favour either. Farmers are proud and more used to owning than renting from people — especially people who know diddleysquat about farming. Suddenly, the dynamics of landlord/tenant come into play.

No, the family farm is not a happy place these days. The

amount of land being farmed in Canada has not changed significantly since 1941 — it's still about 170 million acres. What has changed since then is the number of farms, down to 280,000 from 732,000, and the size of farms, up from an average of 250 acres to 605. In the 1990s a Canadian farm is lost every ten minutes. In the early 1980s one in three adult male deaths in farm families were thought to be suicides.

So the acreage you bought is often one that a local family sweated over a long time. Being aware of that fact might help keep your foot out of your mouth.

I recently asked a roundtable of smart, sensible and city-born people who had lived in the country for decades what advice they would give newcomers. They all said the same thing — try a little humility. Locals are watching to see: will you adapt to their ways? Or do you expect locals to adapt to yours? You may have money and education; what some locals possess is at least as precious. They own the lore of the place, the stories about the people who live there, and a wealth of expertise. Seek their advice, and ponder it. In the country, there is time for such palaver, most commonly while leaning on and staring into the bed of a pickup truck or over a fence line. This is time well spent.

Learn the local etiquette. In a small community, it is easy to step on toes. At one time in Camden East there were two stores-cum-gas-bars, McCormick's and Hartman's. To whom do you show your allegiance? One neighbour bought his groceries at Larry's and his gas at Ferd's.

Gas might have been a cent or two cheaper in Kingston, but my neighbour felt compelled to keep money circulating in his own community, and farther, to spread it around. It makes economic and social sense to buy locally, to use local carpenters, plumbers, electricians, drywallers. The spinoff may not be immediate but spinoff there will be.

And don't act like Kissinger. When we moved to the village, we learned that the local swimming hole was upriver to the east about a quarter mile. A path on vacant land led past cedars towards a wide rocky shelf sloping into the river. The water was deep here, and rapids just downstream made it inaccessible from the village by canoe or boat. Only locals knew it was there.

Several years later, a For Sale sign went up, and not long after a handsome cedar-siding house. The owner let it be known that he had no problem with locals still swimming there, and we did use the swimming hole for a time, but eventually we felt like the trespassers we were, and we swam elsewhere.

Had he put up forbidding signs and menaced us every time we went there, he would not have endeared himself to anyone. He played it perfectly.

Contribute to the community. Coach a baseball team. Join the parent-teacher association. Neither be afraid to ask for help nor to give it in return. And when there's a crisis, do what most others do. Pitch in, and don't wait for an invitation.

Like many people who have lived in the country a long time, Donald McCaig knows the value of good neighbours. In 1971, he left his job as a copy writer with a New York City ad agency to settle on a 280-acre sheep farm in a remote part of Virginia. In his book, *An American Homeplace,* he writes, "Formal country manners are the lubrication that enable people who don't really care for one another to cooperate in what needs to be done."

"I'm beholdin' ta ya," the cowpoke would say in the old westerns after his buddy had saved his life (by treating the rattlesnake bite/removing the arrow with a bowie knife/pushing him from the path of stampeding cattle). And there is something of that in the small worlds beyond metropolitan life: an endless line of favours owed and paid back.

Alice Munro has a line in her short story collection *The Moons of Jupiter* about a country woman taking in washing and cooking for an ill friend. "Pure generosity," Munro writes. Then comes the kicker: "Pure blackmail." And no doubt some dealings between country neighbours are weighted with motive, but most of my country friends are like me: they *like* their neighbours and depend on them.

Joining the church is another way of plugging into the community. I am not a church-goer, and have never been inside St. Luke's Anglican Church in Camden East. But church and school are the central institutions in small places. Our church hall is a village resource and we would be lost without it. We use it for school plays, concerts, for karate class and meetings of the snowmobile club, it's where our politicians speak and we cast our votes, it's for potluck suppers and church suppers, for toddlers' play and seniors' euchre. Most nights of the week, the church hall lights are on.

Last fall when about eighteen Scanlans came for Thanksgiving dinner, I drove our pickup to the hall and borrowed the extra tables and chairs, cutlery and dishes we needed. The church warden just gave me the key. Anyone moving to a small place and intent on connecting with it will often do so through church or church hall.

When in doubt, try your (pot)luck. There is no easier way to meet your neighbours than to invite them for a potluck dinner. Somehow it all works out, and when everyone brings dessert you laugh about it.

If your house is an old one, your neighbours may have stories about the place and its previous tenants and will delight in telling them.

Trust your neighbours. Often as not, your neighbours think that's what they're there for.

One summer we left for a month's holiday. I paid a friend in the village who was then between jobs to look in daily and to feed our chickens. Normally, Doug next door or Lyle across the street would be given the task, and no money would ever change hands.

We left a front porch light on, something we only do when we are away. I like to think of it as a signal to thieves that no one is home. Our friend either turned it off one day or the bulb burned out. To Lyle, it was a sign of trouble. He called the police, who easily gained entrance by the formal arched front door we never use, and the officer — Lyle in tow — determined after searching the house that nothing appeared amiss.

We all laughed about it upon our return, but Lyle let it be known that looking after our house when we were away was *his* job, or Doug's job, not one to be farmed out to people on the other side of the village. Hmph.

On the other hand, neighbours must earn your trust as you must earn theirs. A friend in western Ontario contracted with a local to harvest timber from her woodlot. She thought, and he led her to believe, that he would take thirty trees. He took two hundred. My friend had not informally checked the woodcutter's credentials with other locals. She will not make that mistake again. Last time I heard, the woodcutter was coming around to discuss terms, or face a lawsuit.

March 2. South-facing roofs are steaming in the sun and the birds are calling out sweetly for mates. But that sun has no business being warm this day, the birds' music seems unseemly. Next door, Doug's old Union Jack is flying at half-mast on his white flagpole. There has been a death on Mill Street.

Marion Estella Lawlor, Lyle's wife, had been canvassing for the Heart and Stroke Foundation, as she did every year. She had just left a house on the eastern edge of the village and was driving on to the next when it happened. Her car drifted slowly into the ditch on the road to Yarker, less than a quarter mile from home.

Lyle was summoned and he went immediately. He held her and kissed her, talked to her in hopes she might hear, held her hands while the ambulance came. But she was gone. At the moment that her heart stopped, she was fifty-seven.

I thought of a day the summer before when the six of us — Lyle and Marion, Doug and Virginia, Ulrike and I — sat on bales of hay in the shade of Doug's driveway. He got beers from his garage fridge and everyone laughed when Doug and Lyle joked that the beer-drinking that always followed their mutual puttering and fixing owed everything to the dust on Mill Street. The oft-repeated lines had worked themselves into a one-act play.

Doug: "Lyle, did you call the township office like I asked you to see about watering the road?"

Lyle: "Doug, I called them twice. Hafta call again."

Doug: "Have you ever seen such a dusty road?"

Lyle: "Nope. Never have."

Doug: "Terrible dust."

Lyle: "Awful."

And each would shake his head and take a slug. Implicit in this one-act play was the theme of allegiance. Doug to Lyle, certainly, and vice versa. But Virginia and Marion too seemed comfortable in their role as Greek chorus. The striking thing about Marion, a friend of hers would tell me at the funeral, was her acceptance of Lyle. Their partnership clicked, it seemed to my observer, because each felt so fortunate to have found the other and therefore made no attempt to remake the other. A rare good match has ended, and the grieving will be long and hard.

At the moment I happen to be reading a quiet, alluring novel by a writer named Howard Norman. *The Bird Artist* is about a man who in 1911 murders his mother's lover, the lighthouse keeper, in the Newfoundland village of Witless Bay and draws a mural as an act of redemption. "Village life, plain village life," the author writes, "is what the ... mural contains. People drying cod, milling about in front of the church, children fishing from docks ... Water, clouds, sky, birds, and no murder taking place — my perfect day."

Life in my village, or at least my village in a certain light, could also be captured on a mural. It might show young lads (as boys are called in the village) fishing from the bridge over the Napanee River, the usual trickle in and out of McCormick's, a jogger in his yellow windbreaker heading east, passing a man and his mother and their collie walking west, and Marion out watering her tomatoes on Mill Street, the garden hose in one hand, a cigarette in the other. As murder would have no place in the bird artist's mural, death would have no place in mine.

Certain courtesies are observed around death in the country. When a black hearse leads a funeral caravan to the graveyard, it is customary for drivers coming the other way to pull over as a sign of respect. I have seen drivers doff hats. When someone dies in a village or small town, even someone not well known to you, you attend the wake. The funeral if you can. Neighbours bring food and drink around to the family, drop off sympathy cards, find words to say.

Food, especially, is thought to bring comfort to grieving rural people. When my uncle Gerard Flynn died in Napanee in November 1995, neighbours and family and friends brought around enough pies and casseroles and cookies to fill both freezers and completely cover a large table in a back room, and still more came.

We mourn the dead but we the living must attend to our bodies. After the burial, there will be a driveway-sized spread of sandwiches in the church hall, served with tea and coffee by the Women's Institute or the Ladies Auxiliary or the Catholic Women's League. Somewhere, someone has decreed that there will be salmon, devilled ham, egg and beef — all served on white sandwich bread cut into tiny triangles. Desserts, on the other hand, share a different geometry. There will be small mountains of brownies, Rice Krispie confections and cakes with shredded-coconut tops — all cut into squares and rectangles. As for the circle, the old-fashioned butter tart nicely fills the bill.

We will bury Marion according to custom. Funeral in Napanee at Wartman's, burial at St. Luke's, luncheon in the church hall.

March 12. I watch as Marion's daughter Robyn and her partner Raymond pass Kurt and me playing ball on the hill this Sunday afternoon. They are on foot and seem purposeful. I knew where they were going. "Say hello from me too," I tell them.

March 18. There is a potluck supper up at the community hall, put on by the Camden East Community Association. But the tone is somewhat muted. We are all still reeling from events of the night before.

At 1:30 a.m., a nineteen-year-old boy hired a cabbie in Napanee to take him to the abandoned ballfield south of the village. There the man knifed the driver in the neck and later in the hands as they grappled. Cut for fifty-three stitches, the driver fled and called an ambulance. The young man walked into the village, then into the home — beside McCormick's store — of aged Godfrey Barr, took Godfrey's wallet as he slept and, finally, Godfrey's car.

The story makes no sense. A creature from TV has entered our domain.

Yet one aspect of the bizarre tale strikes me as doubly odd. How did the kid know that Godfrey never locked his house and sleeps the sleep of the dead? He knew the lay of the land because the village was once his home. When I learn this, I sit silent.

His name was Terry. He was small and lean and surly; a squirrel too wild to hand-feed. His brother was chunkier, even handsome, a likeable boy named Chad. As a seven-year-old, Chad would come around asking for jobs, and several times I employed him in make-work projects, such as pulling dandelions out of the gravel driveway. One day he said he wanted to enter the bicycle-decorating contest at one of our community fairs, but he lacked the resources.

I took an old orange Hula Hoop from the wall of our garage (which is full of such wonders) and bought a few rolls of coloured crepe paper at McCormick's. Ulrike gussied up the bike, wrapped the hoop with some strands hanging loose as streamers, and I then duct-taped the whole thing to the back of Chad's bike. He was clearly pleased with the effect.

Chad joined the others as they paraded their bikes before the judges, and it wasn't long before the hoop fell over. Never mind. He won a prize. They all did.

Where was Terry in all this? He would not weed the driveway with Chad. He would not enter the contest. He remained on the village periphery, and the village probably hoped he would one day go away. Which he did. But one night he came back and a man almost died.

The incident numbs me for a time. I do not feel any less safe in the village. Ulrike will still take her long walks beyond the village whenever the mood strikes. Kurt will still bicycle up and down village roads and along the old railway tracks. We persist in the belief that while break-ins might occur in rural areas, they are the work of "honest thieves" (as one neighbour puts it), not crazies. No, what I feel most strongly is regret. The village shunned this boy, and while he did not harm a villager, he chose the village to vent his anger. The message is clear.

March 26. What a strange year, I think to myself as I walk across the bridge over the Napanee River. One spring, giant icebergs too tall to bypass the bridge stalled here and the river pounded them in its haste to get by. As their number grew, I feared the ice would take out the bridge. This year there will be no freshet, no unleashing of ice.

In mid-March, only tame little icebergs no bigger than pancakes floated down the river as the sun chipped away at the bank ice. Some years there is no spring, just a winter that drops like a rocket, then erupts into blinding summer.

Went canoeing on the river today. Never been out so early. Usually the river in March is still ice-packed or too wild for that first paddle of the year. Saw one beaver. There must be more. They have begun to gnaw at the base of an old bent ash on the bank at the eastern edge of our property.

Is this a tree I simply give to them? A sacrifice to the beaver god? It is an old tree, after all, its bark mostly gone on the south side.

No. I wrap the base of the tree in chicken wire and nail it down. Beavers have a place on the nickel but not in my heart where trees are concerned.

The maples — even the one out front that creaks and groans on the coldest of nights — should leaf out in a month or so.

Yes.

April

FROM VILLAGERS TO GLOBAL VILLAGERS

Every April, it seems, there comes a rain, a soft days-long rain that I associate only with that month. It marks, for me at least, the arrival of spring. This year it arrives right on schedule, more wind-driven than the pitter-patter sort, but as familiar as an old song. The forecast calls for three days of the stuff.

We have many words and phrases to measure rain: downpour, drizzle, shower, thunderstorm; we say it's coming down in sheets, raining cats and dogs or buckets, pelting down; irreverently we say it's pissing out, that rain is heavy, light, monsoonlike, that the rain fell like a curtain. The April rain I have in mind is merely insistent. This is rain to walk in, for it works wonders.

The grass turns from matted brown to springy green. The brave plants — crocuses, rhubarb, chives, asparagus — will peek out from the soil even before that April rain. The others, more cautious, need the long rain as a signal: you can come out now, winter is gone. And so begins their fierce drive for the sun.

In her Pulitzer Prize–winning book, *Pilgrim at Tinker Creek*, published in 1974, the American writer Annie Dillard indulges her great hunger for quirky facts by talking about the immense force of a growing plant, like the larch tree whose root by degrees lifted a one-and-a-half-ton boulder a foot into the air. Dillard delights in telling the story of a farmer who sought to measure the growing power of an expanding squash.

Here she quotes from *The Great American Forest,* which she calls one of the most interesting books ever written: "In 1875, a Massachusetts farmer ... harnessed a squash to a weightlifting device which had a dial like a grocer's scale to indicate the pressure exerted by the expanding fruit. As the days passed, he kept piling on counterbalancing weight; he could hardly believe his eyes when he saw his vegetables quietly exerting a lifting force of 5 thousand pounds per square inch." Throngs of doubters came around to see the exhibit and to be astonished by a mere vegetable muscularly intent on growing.

Spring in the village has some of that vigour. Buds the size of peas appear on the lilacs along the riverbank, the cedar hedge outside my office loses its dark pallor and turns a bright, almost electric shade of green, and you can almost feel the tension as the thousands of red clumps on the maple branches ponder which hour of which day to show themselves as green, blessedly green, leaves.

The air is alive with birdsong as would-be parents begin their frantic nest-making. They sometimes do this in our parlour woodstove chimney, despite the stern black-plastic owl I years ago tied with electrician's tape around the TV-aerial tower to terrify them. From a distance of fifteen feet, the owl stares directly at the chimney and once did a passable job as scarecrow. But years of looking unblinking to the sunny southeast have caused his eyes to turn a pale orange, and birds now pay him no heed. Maybe Canadian Tire, where I bought the owl, sells replacement eyes.

Spring, or at least the first round of nesting, is officially over in Camden East when Kurt no longer reports the sound of wings flapping in the parlour chimney. On the other hand, spring officially *starts* in Camden East when township trucks come along and fill in Mill Street potholes. Our tax dollars at work, for the spring bill always seems to follow a day or so later.

Outside, yard work beckons. We complain sometimes about the work that spring and a spacious yard bring, but we would have it no other way.

We lean on our rakes and gab over fence lines, report on losses to winterkill and beaver teeth. Every spring my dream is to plant more potatoes than last year; Ulrike's is to try the effect of yet more annuals and perennials in her flower garden.

We find any excuse to putter in the sun. Next door Virginia and Doug fill the lattice-and-plastic greenhouse by their garage with bedding plants, and we are inevitably one of the beneficiaries when there is a surfeit of young tomato plants or perennial flowers. In the greenhouse, Virginia leaves on a radio tuned low to classical music: she has read that plants like it. I often marvel at her flower gardens and the dawn-to-dusk vigour with which she pursues the task of gardener and landscaper.

Virginia is much Doug's junior, and her pony-tailed hair, typically under a round and ribboned straw hat, lends a certain girlishness. She and I are alike in one respect: we are both as at home in our gardens as in our houses. We do not dress up for the neighbours. Virginia's garden attire, like mine, tends towards rubber boots, a tea-stained sweatshirt and jeans with peat moss dust in the pockets. When, on rare occasions, she wears a dress and puts her hair in a French roll, she looks like a royalist, and indeed she named several of her children (Henry and Albert) and dogs (the now-departed Duke and Windsor) in memory of bluebloods. (Albert, by the way, went on to become the very fine Shakespearean and television actor Albert Schultz.)

When bedding plants come our way, Virginia will first alert us, then leave them on Doug's work bench by the picket fence. It is where we leave all the stuff — tools and books, flowerpots and plants, news clippings and baking dishes — that passes between our households.

Late in April, a huge white tent shaped like a Quonset hut goes up on Godfrey Barr's lawn right next to McCormick's. Godfrey seems not to mind. Maybe money passes hands, or something is bartered. The tent keeps heat in and frost out; for the next month it will be home to a few thousand bedding plants. Late in May or early June, when night frosts no longer seem likely, the tent comes down and the plants are arrayed outside the store. The scene is like an impressionist painting, dots of shimmering colour that shiver in even the gentlest breeze.

When you plant vegetables the general rule is that you wait until the last frost. Where I live, the twenty-fourth of May has been declared the safe date. But some hardy seeds — peas, lettuce, onions — can go in after the snow melts and the soil is what garden books call workable. I take workable to mean you drive your shovel in the ground and hit neither ice nor mud.

One day in April of 1981, after making it plain by our dumb questions to Allan Carroll that we intended to garden, we came back from a morning in Napanee to find our long rectangular plot (12 feet by 80 feet) neatly rototilled. Allan again looking after the kids next door.

And there was indeed about us the air of city kids let loose in the country: we ran a little farm, or so it seemed at the time. Our first foray into animal husbandry — a fumbling form of parenting before Kurt came — involved ducks. Bernie Duhamel had dropped by one day that first spring with a gift of two ducklings. I remember their marbled yellow-and-brown down, how they peeped when we left them and followed us round the yard, already imprinted on their giant two-legged parents. We put them in the bathtub one night to test their swimming, and they propelled themselves underwater like little furry torpedoes. We sopped up their glee like bread in syrup.

They grew to become Mr. Duck and Mrs. Duck. They were, in fact, brother and sister, but never mind. Allan warned us that snapping turtles would take baby ducks (which seems only fair, since adult ducks prey on baby turtles), so we waited till they feathered out before we put them on the river. They were mallards, the male crowned with a head of brilliant green, the female a muted brown. She grew shy but quacked rather loudly, he grew bossy but spoke in hoarse whispers.

I would bring grain down to the river and whistle to them, eight strong notes one after the other. The water carried the dinner call a long way, because sometimes many minutes transpired before the ducks came steaming up, or down, the Napanee.

We spent hours watching them. The bottoms-up feeding in the mud. The rough love (much splashing by Mrs. Duck, a near-drowning at the hands of Mr. Duck, followed by hours of preening in the shallows before a repeat). The snoozing on the opposite bank, bill resting on the back under a folded wing.

Early one Sunday morning I watched in horror as a fox came down the river road and sent the ducks speed-waddling into the river whence Mrs. Duck sent up raucous calls of alarm. The fox eyed the lost dinner and went off the way he came. Mr. Duck emerged from the water and with his bill low to the ground in attack mode appeared to chase the fox. He was then twenty feet from the safety of the river and closing in on the fox. Had the fox turned around, Mr. Duck would have been dinner. But the fox trotted on, and the bird sauntered back, convinced he had repulsed the enemy. It was like watching *Wild Kingdom* from our backyard.

Protective of his mate and absurdly territorial, Mr. Duck would often nip at people walking along the river road. The targets of his aggression were, mostly, amused. He chased cars, cyclists, mothers with strollers. Mr. Duck was a macho sort and it almost cost him his life many times. That first winter, we unwisely lodged the ducks and our few chickens in the same chicken-house. The resident rooster did not take kindly to the menacing of Mr. Duck, and when we came home one night and went to see how everyone was getting on in their new digs, we were appalled at what we saw.

Mr. Duck looked like a prize fighter in the fifteenth round of a fight better stopped in the fourth. His head bloodied, one eye closed completely, he looked utterly, unspeakably sad. Still he lunged at his assailant. We separated the combatants, and with the aid of time and salve from a vet, he recovered fully from the beating. Putting the ducks back out on the river that winter introduced a new problem: Mr. Duck, never Mrs. Duck, twice got his feet stuck in the ice. Each time someone saw him before we did, rescued him and made inquiries. The phone would ring. "I've got your duck."

In the spring, Mrs. Duck laid eggs by tree stumps up and down the river, finally settling on one close to home on our own riverbank. Her offspring all died but one, victim of a cold, wet spring; one of many duck diseases listed in *Ducks and Geese in Your Backyard: A Beginner's Guide;* or, more likely, Mr. Duck's aimless aggression. The second year, we separated drake from ducklings, and eventually — Mr. Duck having courted his sister, his daughter and one newcomer — the bevy grew to twenty-two. That number included two domestic ducks from who knows where that had joined the flock and, for a time, a magnificent wild male mallard. I loved the sight of them, the way they came when I called them. Eight strong notes would be met with — well, a few hundred quacks.

That fall, the ducks (save the original pair) went the way of all domestic fowl. It broke my heart to do it. In fact, I didn't do it. I farmed out the job and have never raised ducks since. Oftentimes we have raised fourteen or so chickens for meat, and the job of slaughtering them is a sobering one. But I never felt affection for chickens as I did with the ducks. We gave Mr. and Mrs. away to farming friends, who reported back years later that while Mrs. Duck was a good mother who aged with grace and dignity, Mr. Duck finally succumbed to a fox. It was not clear who was chasing whom when the end came.

When we Mill Street ranchers were not consumed with the fate of our various fowl that spring, we were fussing in the garden. We gardened by the book(s), which we took out and read in the plot itself. I remember measuring distances between rows with a ruler, stretching string neatly between stakes to mark our plantings, fixing the empty seed packets to the stakes to tell us what was what. In time we gardened more casually and ceased fretting about inches. I measured by rubber boot lengths, let old peat pots mark the rows, and the paper packets — which bleached in the sun and rain anyway — were replaced by a touch of professionalism: a garden plan organized according to some basic principles of companion planting, recorded on paper and fixed to a clipboard. Ulrike's idea. A garden at a glance, and kept for future reference so we could see which varieties fared best.

During most of the 1980s, Ulrike and I worked in Kingston and slotted the yard work around jobs — me at *The Whig-Standard,* Ulrike, a graphic designer, freelancing for various newspapers and magazines in Kingston and, increasingly, the book division of *Harrowsmith/Equinox.* In the fall of 1988, I left my job as literary editor at *The Whig* to work as the book producer at CBC Radio's *Morningside* in Toronto. It was to be a trial year. We found a tenant for our house in Camden East and became, with two-year-old Kurt, tenants ourselves in Toronto. But the village soon yanked us back: early in 1989 Ulrike was offered the job of art director at *Harrowsmith/Equinox.*

By that summer, I had left the CBC to co-author a book called *Riding High* with Canadian equestrian Ian Millar, intending later to freelance. But by January 1990, I too was working at the magazines up on the hill. Astonishingly, we had both found rewarding work in the village.

It was the best of times. We walked two minutes to work. Along to the bridge, up the hill. Kurt went to the day care centre at the four corners. Camden East was quite literally the centre of our universe. By my reckoning, I had about 1,217 salad days — more than most, I figure — before the lettuce just got too bitter to swallow any more.

The magazine's corporate masters in Toronto could make no sense of us, nor we of them. In time the best of times — for Ulrike and me, and eventually for just about everyone on staff — became the worst of times.

In April 1993, Ulrike and I departed the magazines within two days of each other. Suddenly neither one of us had a regular job. Naturally, we skipped the country. With Kurt, we went on a holiday to the south of Spain, as we had planned to do in any case, and rented a villa with Canadian friends for a month. In the short term, Spain was the answer to everything.

Annie Dillard suggests in one of her essays that if you want to write about summer, do it in winter. She reminds us that Ibsen wrote of Norway from Italy, that Joyce conjured Ireland from Paris, that Mark Twain wrote *Adventures of Huckleberry Finn* in Hartford. Dillard herself may give a barefooted impression when she writes about nature, but in truth she is pretty well glued to a desk that faces a blank wall or overlooks a tar-and-gravel roof. Implicit is the notion that distance sharpens the focus. It seems I had taken her advice.

In a walled Moorish town called Tarifa, at the very confluence of Europe and Africa, Spain and Morocco, I wrote in longhand about a chestnut gelding who lived across the ocean. I was then embarked on another book, a biography of Big Ben, the horse ridden by the aforementioned Ian Millar. The fierce winds of Tarifa seemed to blow all our troubles away. The old Williams mansion, the village of Camden East, that country called Canada, all receded. They were places on a map.

Eventually we went home, to tag-team joblessness. The Camden East door, which had so benevolently opened, was now closed. And even were our old jobs available in Kingston, it would have seemed a backward step.

Living in the country was as good as ever, but would we have to pull up stakes and move to Toronto to find work? It seemed at first we might have to, and we gave the city option some thought. But then things just fell into place. The two of us now blend contract work, telecommuting (using technology to bring work into a home office) and freelance work — in both Kingston and Toronto. We are modern-day Paladins. Have computer, will travel. The village is where we live, the global village is where we work.

The Luddites were early-nineteenth-century rebels who trashed machinery when they saw it creating unemployment and inferior products. My kind o' guys. Only in 1994 did I purchase my first colour television and my first fax machine; my computer is so old, so pre-Windows, that when I take it in for repair, the techies all gather round it as if it were an Edsel.

I am, I admit, a reluctant driver on the so-called information highway. But even I marvel at how information technology can let me live in the country and connect to the city. The brave new world of telecommuting has pitfalls, but much potential too.

Distance matters less now. Why move people to work in the city when you can move work to people in the country? Many observers, and lots of data, suggest that cutbacks are fuelling the economic decentralization of North America. The dominion of the office, and of the city, is crumbling.

In the spring of 1995, *cutback* was the operative word. The federal government would lop 45,000 jobs, Bell Canada 10,000, the CBC up to 4,000. Every provincial government and most corporations downsized and rightsized, obsessed over balanced budgets and deficits. Bodies were flying.

No place seemed safe, no job secure. The anxious class, as some call it, grew by the hour. The whole effect was to put masses of people in motion. They switched careers. Went back to school. Moved. Took their severance pay and started up businesses.

On *Morningside,* Peter Gzowski noted in a 1994 program that one in eight Canadians now work for themselves, that this number would increase dramatically in days to come, and that in 1995 about 45 per cent of Canadian homes would likely support some kind of working space. It seems we are becoming a nation of small entrepreneurs and telecommuters. Even those with regular jobs feel the tug of change. Never has work been so portable, never have so many office workers been so tempted to do at least some of their work at home.

In the United States, the numbers are staggering: in 1992, 25 per cent of the work force claimed their homes as their primary office space — a 12 per cent increase over the previous year. The data on what some call the New Economy suggest that 18.3 million Americans — two-thirds of them women — operate home-based businesses. The U.S. Department of Transportation estimates that the number of telecommuters will rise to 15 million by the end of the decade. And for the first time in thirteen years, the unemployment rate in rural America dipped below that of urban America.

A *Morningside* roundtable on self-employment and small business included Sally Banks, herself the operator of a home-based business. She is a freelance writer, editor and broadcaster. In a sense, Banks says, the home-based business marks a return to the previous century, when most people farmed or operated their own enterprise. She concedes that their modern counterparts are in many cases "reluctant entrepreneurs." But some are acting on lifelong dreams, trading corporate stresses for a simpler life that allows more flexibility and more time with their families.

Banks quite rightly sees herself as a self-employed business person. The label has changed, but the constant in her life has been place. A place, that is, in the country. If you call Banks at her Calgary number, the call is automatically forwarded to her actual address an hour and a half northwest of the city. She lives on a quarter section at the end of a dead-end road near Sundre, a town on the Red Deer River. The closest village to her house is Bergen, which consists of a Quonset hut housing the general store, plus a gas station, a few postboxes and a telephone booth. The sign reads "Welcome to Beautiful Downtown Bergen, aka Paradise."

"I love what I do," says Banks. "It allows me to live in places like this. Surrounded by wild things and quiet. I draw sustenance from it. I look out my window and I see spruce. There are moose, deer, elk, coyotes and wolves around here. I can't imagine living in the city — although there are times I do wish I could order Chinese food or a pizza."

In Denver, Colorado, an independent and nonprofit think-tank called the Center for the New West believes the future is bright for many of the 2,400 nonmetropolitan counties in the United States. The theory is that knowledge workers — consultants, freelance professionals, writers, analysts and others — are looking to get out of cities and into small towns or open country. The center's president, Philip Burgess, is calling the 1990s "the decade of the micropolitan boom in America."

Corporations and governments steadfastly gouging their employee rosters are saying to some of those who remain, Want to work at home? And home could well be a place in the country.

I spotted this ad in a magazine. A large house with a glassed-in porch occupies the right side of the ad; a glorious sunset the other. The mood is of peace, contentment and solitude. It's a Bell Telephone ad to promote teleworking — using technology to work at home and connect with the office. The copy reads: "Since Jennifer moved to the corner office, the company's outlook has never been brighter."

The ad would have you believe that employees and employers both benefit. "Chances are," the text reads, "Jennifer is happier working from home. And her improved morale should cheer her employers. Teleworking can boost an employee's productivity by 30 per cent. It can help cut overhead and travel expenses, reduce real estate costs and assist in attracting and retaining key employees."

Doug Glover, associate director of business development at Bell Canada, helped launch the telework project in 1994, and by 1995 it involved some two thousand Bell employees in Ontario and Quebec. Across Canada, says Glover, two to three million people are working "remotely" — that is, working either full-time in a home office or only coming into a business office a few days a week. He expects those numbers to increase dramatically as companies go on downsizing and the number of contract employees, also known as consultants, keeps growing.

Treasury Board president Art Eggleton told a teleworking conference in Toronto in 1994 that federal civil servants could save taxpayers hundreds of millions of dollars by working at home. He sang teleworking's praises. With fewer cars on the road, air quality improves and the risk of accident declines. Employers report reduced turnover. Productivity gets a boost, sometimes a rocket boost: at the Canada Mortgage and Housing Corporation, teleworking bureaucrats report an increase in productivity of 73 per cent. (Do bureaucrats work that much harder in the home office? Or did they do precious little at the office office?) Productivity gains reported in other studies of home office workers range from 10 to 40 per cent; home workers are apparently happier and less inclined to book off sick.

My own experience of working at home — writing books and magazine articles on contract — has been mixed. I value the quiet of my book-lined office. How I managed to write anything in the chaos of a newsroom seems astonishing to me now. To get the mind flowing, I crank up Miles Davis or Wynton Marsalis or the Talking Heads on the stereo. I have lunch on the deck in good weather, go for afternoon runs from spring through fall. But some days I feel lonely and housebound and by the end of most weeks I crave company beyond the village and a beer with fellow freelancers.

We contract employees may be happier than our office-bound confreres; I frankly hope we're healthier. No work, no pay. Insurance for solo flyers like me to cover disability or chronic illness is expensive.

Tied by unseen umbilical cords to an office and yet removed much of the time from it, staff employees who telecommute are somewhat different creatures. Their number is growing because the boon to employers, especially in real estate savings, can be enormous. IBM Canada believes it will save $5.7 million over the six years ending in 1997 by reducing its downtown office space requirements through a national teleworking program — or flexiplace, as they call it. In 1995, two-thirds of IBM Canada's six thousand employees had the capacity to telework through portable or home computers, and thousands did just that. At Xerox in the United States, a similar program called Work from Anywhere will eventually involve all sales and marketing reps — up to four thousand people.

Teleworking is much more common in the U.S. than in Canada. American Express, Ford and General Motors, Sears and General Electric, among others, have telecommuting programs. Five states, worried about pollution from commuter traffic, have passed legislation *obliging* companies of a certain size to offer the work-at-home option to their employees.

And employees have warmed to it. The average full-time worker who drives thirty minutes each way to the office would save $5,000 a year in car maintenance, gasoline and parking by working at home. Lunch at home is far cheaper than lunch at that trendy Italian place near the office. And when you work at home, you don't need to buy as many power suits. You can work in your pyjamas or stark naked if you like. Some American studies suggest that working at home — when you factor in all the benefits listed above — is akin to a 20 per cent pay hike.

I scanned numerous articles on both teleworking and managing a home-based business, and those who had experienced either were mostly, but not always, positive. Here's a sample.

"I'm more mentally comfortable. I'm more rested and I have less stress. And I don't get caught up in office politics."

"I have few interruptions — with the exception of my dog."

"I get more done and I'm more efficient. I'm pleased with it, and I think my managers are too."

"Having a home business is almost romanticized. In some respects, it's even harder working at home for yourself than it is for an employer. Remember that when you own your own business, suddenly you have to do everything — be your own janitor, secretary and PR person. You're in charge of your own In basket, and that's a shock for a lot of people."

The biggest advantage for the employee, though, is the personal one. When my son comes home from school at four o'clock, I am there. To inquire about his day, to read to him, to play catch or hockey with him. Working at home has disadvantages, and I will come to them shortly, but the great bonus is wider contact with your own family.

So many households, especially in the city, revolve around lunatic schedules that devour time. Dad doesn't get home till six-thirty or seven, depending on freeway traffic; mom's home at 5:45. Babysitter minds kids till then. Supper may be a pit stop at a fast-food place. Mom drives this one to music lessons, dad takes that one to basketball. Mornings are even more manic. Every day is a frantic day. By Friday evening, the parents are as lifeless as cold toast.

Working at home gives back some of those lost hours. You tend to eat healthier meals because there is time to plan and prepare, to make that salad and that home-made dressing. There is time to go for a run before your children come home from school. Time to get involved in your community.

I coach my son's baseball team in the summer because I like working with children. And because I have the time. It may mean, if I am facing a deadline with a writing project, that I start work early that day or work late. My schedule often seems pressing, but I like its rubbery aspect, the way I can twist it when I need to.

Because I now do much of my work at home, my son can see with his own eyes what I do for a living. He knows first-hand about writing, editing, interviews, deadlines. It's one thing for a child to hear dinner chatter about an office the child seldom sees, or colleagues the child will never meet; another thing entirely for the child to watch and hear the work get done. Work becomes less of a mystery, more a part of the family fabric.

Home offices may even benefit community life. Here's a new term I like: technotribalism. The thinking goes like this. Instead of trading gossip at the office coffee-machine, perhaps you the teleworker or small entrepreneur have lunch with a neighbour in your smalltown diner. There may indeed be a swapping of gossip, but on home ground it may also include

local fare — the school and whether it's any good, town council and the issues that face the neighbourhood and the town.

Most people live in one place and work in another, sometimes hours away. When you live and work in the same place,
your allegiance to that place may grow. A conversation in my
village, outside McCormick's in April when rumours of quarries
abounded, may well have gone something like this.

Graham: "Hey, Judy, how's it going?"

Judy: "Pretty good, Graham. What do you think of that
quarry business?"

Graham: "What quarry?"

Judy: "Big developer, Lafarge Cement in Bath, wants to
make a fifty-acre quarry out of that old limestone pit north of
the village that no one's used in decades. The province wants
to freeze the land all around it — eleven hundred acres. They
want to set it aside, maybe quarry it too. Could go on for centuries, Graham. Big forty-ton trucks roaring through the village from dawn to dusk, noise and dust and diesel fumes. And
I won't be surprised when wells run dry and our houses are
worth a hell of a lot less … I don't like it, Graham, don't like
it one bit."

Graham works in Kingston as a machinist, leaves early in
the morning and comes back around suppertime. Judy works
from a ceramics studio in her home that faces County Road
4, the main north–south road. When the giant forty-ton trucks
roll through, laden with crushed rock, her windows would
rattle, she would feel and smell the trucks as they climb out
of the valley. Graham would miss the convoys and think the
quarry poses no threat. Judy would set him straight.

But working at home introduces lots of problems too. The
career-minded, the ambitious, may find it impossible unless
kept to one or two days a week. Many offices are still run like
the court of the sun king, and if you are not there to pay
homage, to see and to be seen, then in the eyes of some managers you barely exist. That seems to me an antiquated view,
but I understand it because I also understand the value of

human contact: phone/fax/modem is not the same as huddling over coffee and looking into someone's eyes.

I have worked at three media organizations where the atmosphere was charged with purpose and a high degree of professionalism. *Morningside, The Whig-Standard Magazine* and *Harrowsmith* were extraordinary places to work, with a deeply felt sense of collegiality and a great appetite for fun. I don't miss office politics. What I do miss — and working at home can't provide it — is that sense of creative collaboration. Home alone is fine, but so is team play, and if I had my druthers I would spend half my time at one, half at the other.

The full-time teleworker, critics warn, is open to abuse, some of it self-inflicted. Theresa Johnson is a researcher with the Public Service Alliance of Canada in Ottawa. Her fear, especially for women who want to work at home, is this: "They may end up being mothers all day and data processors at night. The double day, as some people call it, is the endless day. Is this progress? The tradition of home work is steeped in oppression and piecework and exploitation. We can't ignore the history." The home, not as quaint electronic cottage, but as electronic sweat shop.

Johnson concedes that working at home may indeed allow people to spend more time with their families and even to live in the country if they desire. But she wonders whether work itself will prove more alluring to some individuals than family time and walks in the woods. Johnson cites one study showing that civil servants with computers in their homes worked an average of two and a half hours longer per day than their counterparts without home computers. "The workaholics would work nine to five," she says, "then go home and fire up the computer."

More than anything, Johnson worries that the teleworker is an isolated worker, a tele-unit. Forget solidarity forever when the work force is scattered. Collective power, she says, would soon erode: "Employers love telecommuting. It raises productivity. It lowers costs. And our members are very interested in it. But you'll have to pardon my cynicism when employers say they're doing this for the workers. They've never done that before."

Teleworking, Johnson says, has not taken off quite as quickly as the federal government had hoped. Senior managers want it, and workers want the option, but middle managers balk at having workers out of sight.

Finally, while technology may allow you to choose where you work — away from the city, away from the traditional office — only those with education, sufficient means and computer skills will have that option. The new world order, if that's what it is, has nothing to offer the illiterate or the blue-collar workers reeling from plant closures.

Mixed blessing though it may be, technology does permit the home to become a place of work. Meet some of those who have tried it, not all of them willingly.

Leon Livingstone was forty-four and working as a chemical process engineer at a pulp mill on Cape Breton Island. The eighth-generation family farm was close by, at the village of Judique, not thirty minutes from where he worked. And though he wore a shirt and tie to his office, Livingstone connected to a life on the homestead that took in farming, fish and lobster, bees, fruit trees and blueberries. He did all this according to a time-honoured schedule determined by the seasons, and so his contact with his extended family was regular, even ritualistic. They fished for lobster in July, picked blueberries in August, harvested apples in October.

Then one day in January 1994, he got laid off. "Now what?" Livingstone said to himself. He could not bear to leave the island. On the other hand, he could not stay. He had three children, and their education would cost dearly.

Livingstone found work off the island, but work that let him stay where he was. A company in Fredericton, a six-hour drive away, hired him as a consultant. It so happened that the man who hired Livingstone sits on the board of New Brunswick Tel, and NB Tel leads all other provincial phone companies in gearing up and rewiring for the information highway. "He's very modern," said Livingstone of his new boss. "He said, 'You can live where you are. Use technology.'"

Livingstone spent about $15,000 on computer hardware and software with video capabilities that allowed him to see and hear his co-workers in New Brunswick. They could each call up the same technical drawings on their computers and discuss design changes. On a nail by the computer he hung a knotted tie and slid it on whenever he had to teleconference.

"I had the best of both worlds," said Livingstone. "I used to get out my putter and put while I tried to think. I was there when the kids came home from school. I got more involved in their lives."

Alas, it did not last. After a year and a half of being an at-home consultant, new clients insisted on face-to-face meetings, the job entailed more travel, and the carrot of a permanent job dangled before him proved too hard to resist. When I last talked to him, Leon Livingstone was pulling up stakes for Fredericton. "I'm sad about it," he said. "My kids will always see Cape Breton as home." He'll be back.

Shelley Tanaka writes and edits books; she wrote in 1993, for example, *The Disaster of the Hindenburg,* which, along with books on the *Titanic,* was a favourite of Kurt's for years. Shelley's partner, Keith Abraham, designs books.

They work together in a west-facing sun room of their old country house, she facing inward towards her computer and fax, he looking out over his light table to cedars and jays, maybe a circling hawk. The nearest neighbour is a mile away.

"On nice days," says Abraham, a stocky British expatriate, "we can put on the answering machine and go for walks. In the winter, we cross-country ski, we skate on the pond." Tanaka, who often wears an impish grin and is inclined to mischief, reflects on their previous life in Toronto (where rat races are now held for charity, proof that the city has a sense of humour after all): "We didn't have two nickels to rub together. It was dumb." In 1988, they were both working sixty-hour weeks, felt impoverished by their mortgage, hardly saw their daughters, Claire and Jessica — then seven and four respectively — and paid $1,000 a month in day care fees.

They considered a move to Kingston but got discouraged by the price of houses. Then one day Abraham spotted an ad in the newspaper, something about "the rolling hills of Newburgh" forty-five minutes northwest of Kingston. They sold their Toronto house for $250,000 and bought a 115-year-old clapboard farmhouse on two acres of land for $118,000. "It's palatial — to us," says Tanaka. "We didn't know it would work out. But a week after we'd moved in, we felt as if we had never lived anywhere else." Suddenly, they were mortgage-free. The financial pressure was off. It's a point they come back to several times in our conversation.

Tanaka connects to Toronto publishers via phone, fax, modem and courier, going in to Toronto about once a month for meetings. The Napanee train station is twenty minutes away; Toronto's Union Station is two hours down the tracks.

"One reason we moved to the country," says Abraham, "was to work less. The financial pressure in the city was considerable. Here, our requirements are low. Overall, we've dropped down. It's a lot better life, a quieter approach. We're much happier."

Jessica and Claire are not fussy about long bus rides to school, the limited choices on television and the fact that, as Claire puts it, "you can't just walk down the street and — boom! — there's a friend." But on the whole they too are happier. They made me a list of both likes and dislikes about living in the country, and on the plus side they wrote: "We have pets. A bigger house. More friends. Bigger yard and more places to explore."

Much like our house, theirs sprawls. Their high-ceilinged kitchen features a long harvest table and the light pours in from all directions. The living-room couch and chairs face a big black woodstove and the shelves in that room are heavy, as you might expect, with books.

Like all freelancers, Shelley and Keith are loath to turn down work for fear of a dry spell next month or the one after that. But the dry spells rarely come: both work long hours, yet they can at least embrace a more relaxed pace if they desire it.

"We still love living in the country as much as ever," says Shelley, looking back on their time here. "You can lose a lot of hours in the week driving kids to friends' houses and to music lessons, and maybe in ten years I could see us moving to Kingston. But Keith loves it here. He would die here. He loves long walks in the forest with the dog. People visit us from the city and they reinforce the nice things. They love it and we say to ourselves, yes, we are right to be here."

Arthur Black, host of the CBC Radio program *Basic Black,* for years lived in the village of Fergus near Guelph, west of Toronto, working from home two days and then going into Toronto the last three days of each week to do the show. By the time these words of mine are in print, Arthur Black will have settled into a new home on Saltspring Island, B.C., and he will commute as before — but this time by ferry. For a long time, Black has viewed the city as a good place to work but a lousy place to live. "Going away for the weekend?" people would ask Arthur on a Friday. "No," he would reply, with no small amount of smugness, "I'm going home."

From late 1993 to mid-1995, I was a half-time producer with the CBC Radio program *Writers & Company,* and my office at the broadcast centre in Toronto was just down the hall from Arthur's. I took the train in Monday afternoon, bunked with Ulrike's parents and returned Wednesday evening. And like Arthur, I connected to the city when I was not there by fax, telephone and courier.

A great many people — entrepreneurs, writers, editors, stock brokers, consultants, accountants, word processors, architects, auditors, insurance agents, lawyers, real estate agents, social workers, translators, urban planners, programmers and graphic artists — can do something similar if they set up an office in their homes and live within a certain radius of the city. That radius, these days, could be a hundred miles or more.

April 29. A kind of spring fever afflicts Ulrike one way, me another. In the mud room, under a grow light almost as wide as her outstretched arms, Ulrike is tending plants in peat pots: zinnia, lobelia, cosmos, larkspur, hollyhock, nolana, squash, marjoram, basil and many more. The room calls to mind the hothouse: the smell of damp earth, the sight of green shoots pushing up towards the light, the hum of fluorescence. Soon the natural light from the west window will be enough to take up the task. Soon Ulrike will put the pots outside for a few hours, then longer each day, to harden them off.

My own spring instincts take us outside, on this last Saturday in April, to our land in Prince Edward County. The provincial Ministry of Natural Resources still encourages land-owners to plant trees by offering seedlings for about a dime. For five years now, I have taken up their offer. My eventual goal is to make a forest out of a ten-acre field, but sometimes I wonder whether natural regeneration would be quicker. One year a young farmhand was working the combine for a farmer who rents three fields from us: he missed our orange markers and lopped off the tops of several hundred seedlings. Drought and weeds menace young trees. Deer may eat the leaves; mice may girdle the bark. But a dime a seedling is peanuts, and peanuts is what I pay myself to tree-plant.

Most years it rains on us, the planters — Ulrike, Kurt and a pal, maybe a young lad hired from the village, myself. The little black truck has been known to get stuck in the field, requiring the intervention of a farmer's tractor. But I do not begrudge the rain; it is just the headstart the seedlings need.

This time the sun comes out and we are almost warm as we cut into the big brown bags the seedlings come in, take off the rubber bands encircling the tiny trees, drop them into buckets of water in our wheelbarrows and set off across the field. You can plant a seedling in about twelve seconds. The adult drives the shovel down, then forward, the small person drops the plant into the wedge, both heel it into place, then it's on to the next. Today we plant five hundred trees; in other years we have planted as many as a thousand: white and Norway spruce, red and white pine, black locust, walnut, red oak, poplar. Every year I want to plant more; every year Ulrike reins me in.

A Chinese proverb urges us in our lifetimes to plant a tree, have a child, write a book. They are all acts of faith.

May

VOICES OF THE RURAL RENAISSANCE

Larry McCormick was for decades the villager's villager. Along with his wife, Reta, he was the proprietor of McCormick's Country Store until 1993. When Hartman's General Store folded early in the 1980s, and the village school not long after that, "Larry's" became the central institution. A place to post notices, get the news along with groceries and gas, complain about the weather. Sort of a neighbourhood pub without the beer, just Larry's coffee. With every gas purchase you got a wooden nickel the size of a loonie, entitling you to a free coffee. But I always found Larry's coffee an acquired taste, and free or not, I never acquired it.

What I did acquire was an abiding respect for Larry. Every town and village should have someone like him. Now in his fifties, he has a barrel chest, cauliflower ears and a voice powerful enough for the stage. From the porch of our house, the four corners is about 150 yards away. A fair distance for a voice to travel. Larry might have been with a customer, speaking normally, but his voice sailed up and over the roof of his store and effortlessly reached our porch. I never minded.

I welcomed the voice of the town crier as I would the sound of birds at dawn — which was about the time Larry got up.

Despite his size, Larry McCormick is a darter. He hates to stand still and thus his nickname, Buzzie. Some claim, with affection, that he has never finished a sentence in his life. My theory is that Larry was privy to so much insider information that he would start a sentence and halfway through wonder if that was supposed to be common knowledge, then cut to another thought and the same thing would happen. The result made him sound like an appliance short-circuiting.

So Larry, at Larry's, with patrons and staff coming and going, he turning his head this way and that and habitually pushing his glasses back with his middle finger, may have sounded like this: "G'dayneighbour / Don't worry about those Blue Jays, they'll be fine once Jack / Say, I was talking to Jimmy Hinch the other day and I guess he wants to sell that land down by / Looks like we're in for a little rain, but / Saw Jim Lawrence last night. Sure miss him. I guess he's going to be starting up a new / Thanks, Fred, same to you! We can always use the / Jeff, when you get a minute if you could move some peat moss out to the / That cedar hedge of yours is looking real good. And speaking of wood, I hear the township may cut down all those trees over on ..." I always left a conversation with Larry a little winded, as if I had been running uphill.

According to legend, Larry gave away more merchandise than he sold. In the fall, when his brown bins were full of Prince Edward County apples, he would spot you gassing up and in one of those great paws of his would be three Macs, to be dropped in your lap or back seat with a "G'dayneighbour" before he ricocheted somewhere else. Every day was a good day; every weather brought some gain. He was village-proud in the way that others are house-proud.

They were trusting sorts, Larry and Reta, and the lines of credit they offered to people stretched far. Probably too far. Newburgh singer-songwriter David Archibald wrote "The Ballad of Larry and Reta" and sang it at a roast to mark Larry's passage from storekeeper to member of Parliament. One verse goes:

> If you *wonder* why they're lookin' like nervous wrecks
> Givin' credit to their customers, riskin' their necks
> They're the only ones who would take my cheques
> The Bank of McCormick is a beauty, by heck.

Larry was a divided man: his mind was always casting about for ways to make money, his heart was always telling him to give it away. Several years before we came to the village, he raised buffalo in the field opposite our house, convinced they would attract tourists. Then it was metal detectors. He was a prospector too, and I figured that if he ever struck it rich on one of his northern tramps we would *all* be rich.

In the mid-1980s Larry and Reta started selling greenhouse plants, shrubs and trees. If I bought, say, peat moss, tomato plants and birch trees, Larry bestowed on me his own bizarre system of discounts. One discount because I worked at *Harrowsmith*. Everyone at the magazine got that. Another discount because I lived in the village. The neighbour discount. Then he shaved something off that to round the number. McCormick math.

He and Reta placed potted geraniums on stumps along the riverbank by the river road, larger ones at the four corners. It was a privately undertaken beautification campaign that said to the village and anyone passing through: "This is ours. Isn't it something?"

Larry periodically dispatched the young lads who worked for him to comb the hill and village roadsides for litter. He sometimes hired roughnecks-in-the-making and gave them responsibility. They always seemed to respond. Bins of apples, his nursery trees, hundreds of annuals and perennials were all left outside at night from spring to fall. If there were thieves in Camden East, they left his stuff alone. "What goes around comes around," Larry would say. And so it did.

Discreetly, he would drop off baskets of apples to the school, to the *Harrowsmith* office, to the day care, to families in the village who had dire need of them. Kids called him the Apple Fairy. He sent out trays of coffee for firefighters at house fires. He knew everyone, everyone knew him. Villages do not have mayors. But Larry was, for all intents and purposes, ours.

When fire took a house in the area, Reta — a tiny Newfoundlander infused with quiet outreach instincts — placed a brown envelope on the cash counter with sparse details of the tragedy. Reta never mentioned it unless you asked, but you couldn't buy milk without seeing the envelope. In the worst cases, Reta organized showers. The idea was to bring to the community hall on the appointed evening furniture, clothing, toys, appliances to help the fire victims rebuild their lives.

Larry and Reta have moved on to a life in federal politics, but McCormick's Country Store remains, a general store and seasonal clock. Bedding plants there confirm it's spring, fresh corn that it's midsummer. In September the apples come, and even as I write this the thought of that first Mac, exploding with flavour, wet with juice, more than a little sour, fills me with longing. In October, a hay wagon piled high with pumpkins occupies a spot near the four corners; straw men and women, witches and ghosts take up their positions under the store's awning, signalling Hallowe'en. In November, shelves are lined with green lace-up swamp boots and reversible jackets and hats — camouflage green on one side, fluorescent orange on the other — to announce hunting season. Rows of cut pines and spruce along McCormick's northern flank say Christmas is close. And winter is with us as long as the bins outside are full of birdseed in fifty-pound bags. Bedding plants take their place in May, and another year has gone by.

I like the rhythm of Larry's, connected as it is to the seasonal round, to the life of farmers, and that of gardeners — farmers writ small.

I drop by the store early in May to get my supply of Yukon Gold seed potatoes. Everything about these potatoes appeals: the yellow colour, the bold flavour, the way they store long into winter. There is an unspoken competition among country gardeners to see who will grow the first ripe tomato. Greenhouses are built, plastic covers brought out at night. Plants put in early, frost risked. But as much as I love a fresh tomato, it is the thought of new potatoes that stirs me to wheel my wheelbarrow over to Larry's in early spring to load up.

In the country, May is dedicated to gardening. Virtually all my friends in and around the village plant flowers and vegetables. We do it on a scale that truly does distinguish us from city folk.

A few of my city friends also grow vegetables, but they complain of tiny plots shaded by neighbours' trees and overrun by squirrels and cats. Country cats are less drawn to gardens, I find: too many mice in the fields, too may snakes and birds to hunt. As for squirrels, they abound in the country too, but usually pass on garden fare because other food is so abundant.

Our own garden is an organic garden: we shun any use of pesticides and herbicides and did so long before joining *Harrowsmith* magazine, then emblematic of approaches natural and practical. Fifteen years of vegetable growing and everything I have read about organic gardening have convinced me of its wisdom.

Our plot of soil, I now know, is a veritable jungle of barely seen and unseen cultivators. A tablespoon of that alluvial soil may contain more bacteria than there are people on the planet. Tiny worms called nematodes perform the useful task of breaking down humus, dung and compost, and there may be as many as 20 million such creatures in a square yard of soil. Moving up in the hierarchy of size, we come to the earthworm, which Charles Darwin dubbed nature's ploughman.

The last book he wrote, *The Formation of Vegetable Mould Through the Action of Earthworms,* published in 1881, was a virtual hymn to that creature. The book was the British naturalist's attempt to grapple with a mystery that had long confounded him. Rocks in a meadow will disappear over time. Darwin wondered: did gravity pull them down? Or did the earth mysteriously rise up to cover them? Darwin conducted experiments to prove to himself — and to science — that with the help of worms the earth did indeed rise up. Here he is writing about a field he had observed for three decades:

"For several years, it was clothed with an extremely scant vegetation and was so thickly covered with small and large flints (some of them half as large as a child's head) that the field was always called by my sons 'the stony field.' When they ran down the slope, the stones clattered together. I remembered doubting whether I should live to see those larger flints covered with vegetable mould and turf. But the smaller stones disappeared before many years had elapsed, as did every one of the larger ones after a time; so that after thirty years, a horse could gallop over the compact turf from one end of the field to the other and not strike a single stone with his shoes. To anyone who remembered the appearance of the field in 1842, the transformation was wonderful. This was certainly the work of the worms, for though castings were not frequent for several years, yet some were thrown up month after month, and these gradually increased in numbers as the pasture improved."

Darwin calculated that one acre of garden soil contains 53,767 earthworms, weighing 356 pounds. These cultivators can move in one year 7.5 to 18 tons of soil per acre. In the garden, worms concentrate nutrients such as calcium, potassium and phosphorus into compounds more easily accessible to plant roots. The castings the worms deposit on the surface return to that surface, and to your vegetables, nutrients otherwise lost through leaching to the subsoil. And earthworm burrows are a boon to soil drainage, aeration and structure.

When you spray poison on your soil, you may ruin that ecology and, claim many scientists, the soil itself.

Having said all that, you should know — if you plan to move to the country and garden there in a major way — that not all tiny creatures are as benevolent as earthworms. Aptly named flea beetles, specklike black bugs hard to see and impossible to catch, will make your plants look like someone took a tiny shotgun to them. Cutworms, those cursed little loggers, will fell your young tomato plants and other seedlings. Slugs will devour your lettuce and cabbage and leave slime trails behind. Colorado potato beetles are just as voracious, and so disgusting as spotted red larvae and later as striped beetles that even normally omnivorous chickens will not touch them. Rabbits, groundhogs and deer can also be a scourge.

The Harrowsmith Northern Gardener, a classic written by the magazine's former gardening editor Jennifer Bennett in 1982, offers benign counters to them all. Along with many others, that book and its 1996 version, *The New Northern Gardener,* transformed me. I was a rank amateur; I am now a rank amateur who knows a thing or two but mostly wants to grow Yukon Gold potatoes.

The previous owners of our house had left behind a vegetable plot that ran parallel to the river. We had planted a sandbox-sized garden in Nelson and had been amazed when the lettuce and carrot seeds actually grew. But that plot was playfully small and forgiving of amateurs. The bare plot that stretched out before us in Camden East in the spring of 1981 seemed of professional dimensions. A daunting prospect in every way.

Where did you buy seeds? What kind? When did you plant? How deep? How close in the row? What went next to what? We had as many questions as there were varieties of tomatoes in the fat Stokes seed catalogue we borrowed from Allan and Coral. The Carrolls, who had farmed and gardened all their lives, had the answers. We soaked up their knowledge like blotters.

Looking back on that apprenticeship, I realize how much I now know and should share. I have set out below a few tips (Larry's Laws), with the really important stuff at the top.

#1. When gardening in your rubber boots, *always* wear your pantleg over the top of the boot, else clods of earth will get inside the boot and dirty your socks and, later, your house.

#2. In case you forget rule #1, *never* wear white socks when you garden.

#3. Rubber boots by the back door is the mark of the country house, what distinguishes it from the city house. Boots slip on and off easily, thus saving time when you go out — to dump the compost, fetch firewood and feed the chickens, then come in, then go back out again for the compost pail you forgot outside. Thus, there is rule …

#4. The worse your memory, the smaller your rural property should be. Our garage is on the west side, the house's back door on the east. Some days the spread seems too big, my mind too small. At 10 a.m. on a Saturday I may exit the back door intent on one thing. Dig potatoes. But a dozen yard jobs present themselves en route to the garden and start tugging at me, like puppies at my pantleg, and pretty soon it's 5 p.m., I'm dog-tired, sliding off my boots at the back door and a little light enters the brain. Dig potatoes.

In time, Ulrike and I specialized in the garden. I took more of an interest in vegetables, while she developed a passion for flowers and landscaping. She remembers that first year going over to Coral's flower garden and seeing a poppy. "This was before I gardened and could admire the delicacy of a poppy," she says. "Poppies are common in country gardens, especially the bright orange ones. At the time, I associated poppies with the drug that some varieties produce. I innocently, but jokingly, asked Allan if their poppies produced opium. Next time I looked, they were gone."

What does the story say? It speaks of Allan's innocence — he would never have made the link between a flower and a drug. It says that he valued what neighbours thought. And it says that Ulrike had a great deal to learn about flowers and about country manners.

Not everyone who moves to the country warms to it as I did. There are those who find the isolation — especially in winter — unbearable. They find too much nonpaying work (maintaining a huge house and property) and too little of the paying kind. They find life in the country dull and the trip to a decent restaurant too much like a Himalayan trek. Walks in the woods, hanging out at auctions, the view from the porch don't cut it. They pack up and go back to the city.

I can tell you what *my* village is like, and how it suits me, or not. I can offer what I take to be home truths about life in small places, but each place has its own quixotic character, which may, or may not, be to your liking.

The people whose lives are sketched below *did* warm to country life, some sooner, some later. They are voices in what has been called the rural renaissance.

Four bearded men are sitting in Adirondack chairs arranged in a circle. This day in March 1995 seems so uncharacteristically warm and sunny that it's hard to feel anything but grateful. Michael Riordon has a white and red beard. My own beard seems much like his, though mine is more red than white. His partner, Brian Woods, owns the most dramatic beard: a black number with white trim. My friend David Carpenter sports fresh brown stubble. The topic of conversation is the country and how we came to it.

Almost a decade ago, Michael and Brian grew weary of a cooperative housing venture in Toronto. "One day," they said to each other, "we will move to the country." They had in mind the Canadian Shield territory around Parry Sound, a few hundred miles northwest of Toronto, but that was before they discovered Prince Edward County.

The two men had camped in the county at Sandbanks, a provincial park notable for its beach and high sandy hills, and idly made inquiries with a realtor. There is, of course, no such thing as an idle inquiry with a realtor. The last property they looked at, off Chuckery Hill Road, was in lamentable shape and lacked an indoor toilet, but the house and sixty acres of woodland could be had for $30,000.

On that day in 1987, Michael and Brian went for a walk in the woods by the house. Someone had cut trails. Dense woodland opposite and around the house put the neighbours out of sight. It was like a trick with mirrors: the feel was cabin-in-the-forest; the truth was you-can-jog-to-town.

They moved almost immediately. Then a kind of terror set in. Terror on all kinds of fronts.

Would two freelancers find work? Brian, a tall, lanky fellow with thick black hair who could be cast in a film as a serene Mennonite leader, is a cabinetmaker. He found construction work right away. Not work he especially liked, but work. Michael, a soft-spoken, fair-skinned man whose large eyes give him a look of surprise and amusement, writes plays and books and journalism; he had worse luck. One of the brothers who live down the hill, locals from generations back, once asked him about his line of work.

"I'm a writer."

"Oh," came the reply. Then a pause. "I never met one of them."

The silence and the isolation closed in on Michael. "I wanted some of the dewy-eyed stuff about moving to the country to happen," he remembers.

Certain rural realities began to sink in. "The big difference," says Brian, "was water. That was a real issue." Michael elaborates: "It's interesting to hear weather reports in the city. Rain is always bad. Here, rain means your well will fill up and your fields won't dry out."

And eventually the dewy-eyed stuff did come. "You become much more aware of the seasons," says Brian. "You begin to notice that you are part of something bigger than you are. In the city, you are indoors a lot. Here you are outside a lot — gardening or cutting wood." While we talked, the sounds were of chickadees, of water running past us in rivulets as the last snow in the woods melted, and of a wind chime somewhere behind me.

After the move, six months passed before Michael found freelance work and got comfortable looking at the world from Chuckery Hill Road. When he goes back to the city now, he feels assaulted by the noise. "It's so *demanding* of the senses. Here, a lot is going on but you can hear specific things."

Michael has written a fourteen-part drama series for CBC Radio. Called *The Middle of Nowhere,* the series centres on an insurance-agent-cum-sleuth living in a small town and was inspired by the author's own experience of country life. "One of the points I wanted to make with the series," says Michael, "was that what happens outside cities matters." Alice Munro, Timothy Findley and the late Robertson Davies, all writers intimate with small places, would agree.

Michael has come to value local knowledge, like the fact that the brothers who live down the hill know the place intimately, played there as boys, know the paths in the woods and where the wild ginseng grows. "One of the good things about living in the country," says Michael, "is the relative stillness and unchangingness — save for the seasons. So much unlike the city, where things are disposable and fashion changes. It's a comfort that within a certain range, you know your surroundings."

Theirs has become a modest but inviting property. The workshop outside, almost as big as the house itself, reveals — by its quality tools and their precise arrangement — that Brian is a cabinetmaker of the first rank, and a neatnik. A measure of the pair's worries about finances is that the first thing they built and poured all their money into was this workshop. An indoor toilet, on the other hand, would be close to a decade in coming.

The roof of the house is a strikingly green steel affair; here and there on the new cedar siding a dart holds a strip of red ribbons in place — a benign and efficient way, says Brian, of discouraging woodpeckers from wreaking havoc. On the uphill side of the house, the owners point out proudly, the foundation has been laid for a bathroom.

Inside, the house proves to be small but cheerfully lit by natural light. Brian's handiwork is everywhere: a cherrywood bannister and bookshelf you want to run your hands over, freestanding pine closets in the upstairs bedroom. City friends with aspirations of moving to the country come to this place and pronounce it perfect. Then they add with a note of surprise, says Brian, "And you don't work." And we — all four of us — laugh.

"I'm fifty-one," says Michael. "I have arthritis and I've been told that one day it might be disabling. This place requires a lot of physical work: we heat only with wood, we garden. It's *good* to be doing it. But somewhere in the back of my mind is, What will happen when I can't do all this stuff? People ask us, 'What do you *do* in the country?' We work."

We work with our hands, with our bodies. We welcome winter, if at all, for the respite it offers from yard work, but by spring we are like dogs tugging at our leashes, yearning to get outside and work in the yard. Yes, that's what we do in the country. We work.

Tim Moore runs a Toronto-based $70-million corporation, A.M.J. Campbell Van Lines, out of Chester, Nova Scotia (pop. 3,000). He seems an ebullient sort who can sound one minute like the corporate man he is and the next all folksy and down-home with just the hint of an acquired Maritime accent.

Now fifty, he left Toronto in 1987 for the small town where he and his wife, a Maritimer by birth, had spent their honeymoon. "They were taking bets in Toronto," he says. "They didn't think I could make it. But I was a school teacher once. And I've always had this affinity for the country, for the water, for small places. In the city, you're always going about 150 miles an hour; it's very stressful. Here there is serenity, tranquillity, peace of mind. You have extra time, and so I pace myself differently."

For Moore, home and work are an eight-minute walk apart. Home is a three-acre place at the tip of Chester Peninsula, with a majestic view of Mahone Bay and several islands in the sea. Work is an office in town, where a laptop computer keeps him in touch with his colleagues. He also travels two weeks in four, but the plan for 1996 is to spend three weeks a month in Chester and only one week on the road. "I run a major corporation," he says, "but on *my* terms. What I see is people looking to get out of the big city yet still have some involvement."

Moore observes that a move to the country often occurs to people in their forties, when they have, as he puts it, "paid their dues." Timing, as in everything, is all.

The only drawback to the country/city link, Moore believes, is that to be out of sight is to be somewhat out of mind. As it becomes affordable, he will turn to teleconferencing, enabling him to see and talk to colleagues via computer.

In the meantime, Moore is active in his community and sails on the ocean with his two teenage sons. "I'm far happier now," he says, "than I ever was."

Dorothy Pot has lived in Rossburn, Manitoba (pop. 650), with her husband, Bill, and their three young children since 1993. Home used to be Oshawa, a city thirty miles east of Toronto. It would be wrong to say that their previous life in Oshawa was hell and that their current life on the prairie is heaven. Wrong, but close.

Ask Pot why they fled the city and the word *safety* comes up. Crime was high in their old neighbourhood. Her daughter narrowly avoided abduction on one occasion by fighting off her attacker. The children sometimes came home with forms granting the school permission to administer thyroid gland medication in case of nuclear accident at the two power plants nearby. The cost of living devoured their savings. Traffic was too fast, too slow, too much.

Then one day they spotted in the *Toronto Sun* an ad that extolled the fresh air, pure water, low crime and cheap housing "where the prairie meets the mountain." The newspaper followed up with articles of its own.

Dorothy remembers saying to her husband, "There's no place *this* good." But they were intrigued. They left the kids with relatives and took ten days off to drive out and investigate.

At the time, Bill managed a building supply centre; Dorothy was a reflexologist, a natural therapist who works on points of the nervous system through the soles of the feet. Among the stumbling blocks to the move were the weak employment prospects in smalltown Manitoba and the strong objections of the junior Pots.

Bravely, perhaps recklessly, they decided to move. When they arrived on November 10, 1993 — Bill piloting the moving truck, Dorothy the car — there were six townsfolk at the house to help them unload. Strangers bidding welcome to Rossburn.

Two years later I asked Dorothy Pot, "Are you happier in the country than you were in the city?"

"Big time," she says without hesitation. "My marriage is better. There has not been one sorry moment. It doesn't mean we'll live in Rossburn for the rest of our lives, but the small town is our calling now. Once you've had a taste of this …"

Which is not to say that the transition was effortless. Dorothy strikes me as an effervescent but open sort, not the kind to put the best face on a bad move. If she is gleeful about the place she now calls home, she is also forthright about the snags along the way.

The children, for example, were extremely angry at being uprooted. Now aged eight, ten and twelve, they left behind friends and grandparents and cousins. If, as Dorothy says, "Bill and I became each other's best friends," that was in part because they had to present a united front to the children. Within six months, the kids made new friends and peace was restored. In fact, when they revisited Oshawa in the summer of 1995 they experienced sensory overload and could not wait to get home again.

The Pots sold their semidetached house in Oshawa for $125,000 and bought a sprawling place in Rossburn for $15,000. Needless to say, they were then mortgage-free. Employment required a little more imagination. Like many rural people, they took on several jobs, half-time and part-time, since full-time ones are scarce. Eventually, Bill bought a woodworking business, started driving ambulance on the side, and when I last spoke to them he was running for town council. (He lost by four votes.) Dorothy has set up reflexology clinics in her home and in two nearby towns and helps Bill in the shop when she can.

On the down side, Dorothy must contend with –30-degree winter weather that lingers for weeks. When the kids took on a paper route, Mom drove them around all winter. And breaking into the community was hard. "You are an outsider, and the fact that you're coming from the east hangs over you. Locals are naturally leery. They've seen so many come and go and their attitude is 'Let's see how long these ones last.'"

But Dorothy's list of pluses is much longer. "The fresh air is fabulous. Low crime. The freedom the kids have is incredible — they're gone for hours and I'm not worried. The schools are better, smaller, with a lot more one-on-one instruction. Manitoba is not flat here but rolling and green; Riding Mountain National Park is fifteen minutes away. Everybody knows everybody else and if you want to know what's going on you just go to the coffee shop. It's wonderful, hard to describe. Some days I feel like we're the only ones living on the planet."

Lindsay Beaudry once stood at the epicentre of the Toronto magazine scene. Between 1982 and 1987, she was the art director of *Toronto Life* before leaping to the *Globe and Mail,* where she designed that newspaper's *Toronto* magazine. She dressed the part. Loved the work. Hated the workplace and its attendant pressure. The expression "life is too short" stuck in her throat like a bone.

She and her husband, John, who managed a typesetting business, suddenly felt tired — of the city, of the upscale house they kept renovating, of the pace. In 1990 they sold the house and went to live in Lindsay's mother's cottage three hours northeast of Toronto. It was a gutsy move, for neither had work.

"We decided," said Lindsay, "that something would come up." And it did. The Beaudrys took a course in building twig furniture and from there fell into the business of making high-quality bird-feeders and functional bird-houses. I was later struck when I went to their studio by how elaborate and immense some of the latter are: clients typically send a photograph of their house or cottage, which the Beaudrys then replicate in precise detail and colour. In a converted driveshed, John cuts the wood and assembles the bird-houses; in her studio, Lindsay paints them.

The two were drawn to the Haliburton area because it is known as an artists' enclave, and now their gothic farmhouse on twelve rocky acres near Lake Kashagawigamog ("the lake of long and winding waters") is part of a studio tour that links them with nineteen other artisans working as potters, silk painters, wicker workers, jewellery makers and canoe builders.

In a typical day, Lindsay will work on bird-houses, then "take a horse break": they have three miniature horses and may one day breed them. She may dry flowers (another enterprise) and finally work on book design. She recently bought a computer and a modem, enabling her to design books for a Toronto client.

Among the benefits of living where they do is a greater connectedness with nature. "We help a neighbour with her maple syrup. She calls up and says 'The weather's good!' and we go. We drop everything. It's a priority. So life is scheduled more around the elements. I love the gardening; John likes chopping wood and going for hikes and making home-made wine from our own crabapple, plum, blackberry, strawberry and dandelion."

The Beaudrys are forty-four years old but sound younger. Life's an adventure again. They call themselves cash-poor but rich in other ways. Life beyond the city got them more involved in the community, John in amateur theatre, Lindsay in therapeutic riding for the disabled, both on the local volunteer search-and-rescue team.

Like country people everywhere (even, these days, like multinational corporations) they barter. Lindsay recently helped a neighbour with haying. "It was *so* romantic walking in the fields with the tractor." ("For about ten minutes," John pipes in.) "But later I never felt so exhausted in my life." In return the neighbour tends the Beaudry cats and horses when necessary and ploughs their driveway in winter.

Through the Internet, their sense of community has expanded. With other crafts people all over the United States, they exchange information on building bird-houses.

It all sounds idyllic. Is it?

"There have been bumps," Lindsay concedes, mostly to do with generating work and income. "But we love it. We were in Toronto yesterday at a crafts show, and it was nice being there, but as soon as I see that Entering Haliburton sign I just want to shout 'Yippee!'"

Sometimes, when metropolitans move to the country, they fairly reel from the new pleasures they find there. Still fevered when I spoke to them this past summer were a family who had just moved into a century farmhouse a few miles away from my own village.

We had tea and fresh strawberries and brownies in their backyard as the sun was setting in the river valley below. A three-year-old boy, Qasim — like a puppy unleashed in a park — ran around the sprawling yard and insisted I see his newly acquired pet rabbit. Mackenzie had been rescued from death row in his sister's classroom.

Almost six, sister Ayeila fussed over the dogs, a giant collie who came with the house and a brown lab, a neighbour's dog who hoped I would forgive him his dog breath and toss him a brownie. Lindsay, thirteen, joined her parents, Jennifer Nichol and Laeeque (pronounced Lake) Daneshmend and all talked about the Country. They had been in the Country precisely seven weeks.

Jennifer, most animated of them all, was born in Montreal,

but she had had enough of the city, of separation politics. She had always wanted to live in the country, had stoked that dream for years by subscribing to *Harrowsmith*, and now that she was here, she seemed quite flush with it all.

"The first morning I woke up at six," she said. "I looked out the window and saw a layer of trees down in the valley and a layer of mist, and then another layer. I ran downstairs and woke up Lindsay and I said, 'Look at this.' It was *so* beautiful. Every day is like a gift. I love the air — it's so clean you can almost eat it. You can see the stars at night. And when we first moved in — people seemed to know when we were coming and a fair bit about us, I guess the previous owner had told them — neighbours brought muffins and cookies and home-made bread. One neighbour brought his rototiller over and tilled the garden."

What they left behind, in their eyes, was bad air, paranoia and concrete. At Ayeila's school in Montreal, a computerized surveillance camera had to recognize any parent or guardian come to pick up a child at the end of the day, because a ten-year-old girl had been molested in the school by someone off the street. They felt unsafe in Montreal, and so left it — but not entirely. The Internet links them to family and friends.

Laeeque Daneshmend, now a professor of mining engineering at Queen's University in Kingston, has no regrets about leaving the city. "There were school-age kids holding up other school-age kids at the Métro station near where we lived — for their jackets. We lived next door to someone for seven years, and we'd say hello in the morning, but that was it. I never got to know his name."

When Laeeque and Jennifer first walked into the old Manion farm — the Manions had lived there for sixty-five years — they felt a great tug from the red-brick house built in 1884, with gingerbreading over the porch and about ten acres of sloping land that rises, finally, to a heavily wooded ridge on the south. Beyond the property line lies a duck pond and marsh, and the land's owner has given his blessing to their treks to watch the birds and animals that gather there.

From the house you can see for miles to the north, a great plain unfolding where ten thousand years ago the glaciers scraped off so much soil in places that only stunted junipers grow there now. The Napanee River valley looks from here like a deep wrinkle into which the land on each side tilts; only there, on its banks, do the majestic maples find what they need. I live in that valley, downriver, and the feeling up here on the heights is quite different, open and windswept. A medievalist might have chosen to build his castle here, for the dust of advancing armies would herald their arrival long beforehand.

In 1976, at the age of thirty-six, Sharon Butala left the city of Saskatoon to live in the southwest corner of Saskatchewan. As she describes it in *The Perfection of the Morning: An Apprenticeship in Nature,* she left behind family, friends and job, taking only her hope that it would all work out: "I was both rather proud of my own daring and a little appalled at it; the image of a burning bridge was strong in my mind, and I stoked the flames gleefully, with a feeling close to triumph." You're making a big mistake, friends told her, and Butala at first agreed. It took her three years to realize that this remote ranch in the Old Man on His Back range of hills near Eastend was where she was meant to be.

The Perfection of the Morning is a very personal, very moving book about a woman who left the city — "where the only constant was steady but, nonetheless, gutwrenching change and the resulting mad scrabbling for position." Clearly, the book struck a chord. *The Perfection of the Morning,* first in hardcover and then in paperback, seemed rooted on the *Globe and Mail*'s bestseller list.

We talked one early-summer afternoon in a Toronto hotel where Butala was staying before giving a reading. Tiny, clear-eyed, at times forceful but never taking herself too seriously, she talked about the things that she loves, and hates, about cities, about small towns, about living where she does, in one of North America's great inland deserts.

Butala believes passionately that place matters a great deal, and that humans can discover much about themselves by spending time alone in nature and simply watching and listening. Her advice sounds airy but is solidly grounded in her experience, and she is far from alone in thinking it. For your own health and that of the place in question, she urges, establish a relationship with that place, accept its beauty. For it leads to wonder and gratitude.

By place she means a place in nature where humans are few and wild creatures feel a certain freedom to roam — in her case, the high plateau around the ranch. The rolling hills of the forbidding Palliser Triangle are arid and treeless and cut here and there by coulees, where the animals find refuge.

Sharon Butala loves the city for its bookstores and cinemas and conversation, but when I spoke to her she had been in cities for five days and she was desperate to get home.

She loves to walk, and so I asked her, What's the difference between walking in the city and walking in the country? "In the city," she said, "you walk on asphalt or concrete, rarely the soil itself. The city has a hum all the time. It's like a living creature. You can't see the sky. It's unsafe at night, you lose the stars. It's not real solitude. You can't escape the fumes and all that is needed to run a city."

Butala is under no illusions, certainly no romantic ones, about the country. She lived the first four years of her life in the bush of northern Saskatchewan and then in Melfort, vowing never again to live in a small town. "For me," she says, "the impulse to leave the city is driven by the belief in the healing power, in the *sanity* to be found in a natural environment."

Just as we broke off, she told a story about a wrinkle, and how the country ironed it out, and it summed up neatly and concisely all that she said. My question was this: Are you physically healthier for having lived in the country?

"I don't know the answer to that question," she began, "but I think it's largely a case of how much drinking and smoking I might have done in the city that I don't do in the country, and just not having that constant steady pressure. I know when I left the city to marry Peter I was getting a wrinkle, a strange wrinkle in my forehead. Well, within a few months of being married to Peter and living at the ranch, that line was gone. It's gone. It was a sort of curve from constantly walking around all keyed up."

George Orwell possessed what a friend of his called "country eyes." The friend was Kay Ekevall, and she met Eric Blair (his real name) in a bookstore called Booklovers' Corner. You can find all this in *Remembering Orwell* by Stephen Wadhams. Orwell and Ekevall would take long walks on Hampstead Heath, and this is what she remembers of those hikes:

"A lot of walks we went on. He knew an awful lot about the countryside, and he would notice birds or animals and point them out to me. He'd say, 'Listen!' and he'd tell me what bird it was singing. By the time I saw them they were gone! And different trees — he knew the names of plants. I found it fascinating. I would say to him, 'What tree is that?' and he would always know what kind of tree it was ... I've met a few people like that who have what I call 'country eyes.'"

Country eyes. Every summer, Peter Good — he and Jane live a bit over a mile away but they are neighbours in every sense of the word — take anyone interested on a birding walk through their 125 acres. It starts at 6 a.m., and the rewards are twofold: more birds than I ever imagined, and the classic Good brunch that follows. Peter is one of those naturalists able to tell the bird by its song, and often by its location — high or low in a tree — and finally, by its shape and colouring.

It's a way of seeing the world that native people once universally possessed, a knowledge that our forebears would also have known. You can lose it entirely in the city; the country will give it back if you work for it. Peterson field guides are a boon to those who walk in nature and wonder, What is it I just saw?

May 14. At midnight, I sit on the bottom stair of the stone steps to the river, as quiet and still as the flat rock itself. Times like this, the river feels ancient. The moon is rising and full, with a ring of white light around it so bright that the stars are in hiding. To the right I see a fleeting movement — a great bird, a great blue heron — lifting its bulk out of the water and moving upriver, the sound of its wings lost in the gurgle.

Two days ago, Ulrike went walking in the woods and got too close to a hawk's nest. The bird circled, complaining loudly all the while, before making a series of attacking swoops that came within a few feet of her head. She left in a hurry.

Robertson Davies, in his novel *What's Bred in the Bone,* tells of great horned owls at the turn of the century mistaking fashionable hats featuring black and white plumes for skunks. He describes what happened to one of his characters: "As Mary-Ben strolled musing in the vice-regal shrubbery, an owl swooped, seized the hat, and soared away with it — and with a considerable portion of the wearer's scalp in its terrible talons."

My heron, Ulrike's hawk, Davies's owl — from indifference to menace to pure savagery. Nature's range. Sitting on the step by the river, it is not nature's indifference but the human kind that troubles me. I can feel such contentment here, but if the big trucks and the quarry come, the place will change utterly and so will my feeling for it. At times I feel alone in my outrage over that possibility. Six months ago we quarry-bashers were a company of great horned owls, fearless and cocksure. Now we are circling like the hawk, hoping by threat alone to drive out the enemy. The final step would be to pack up and leave, maybe upriver, with the heron.

These are my thoughts as a brief flurry of cars crosses the bridge, sending harsh light rippling down the length of the painted railing so the bars glow green in sequence, like neon sticks.

May 15. In the late afternoon, as I planted potatoes — Yukon Gold, always Yukon Gold — I saw a light on the river I had never noticed before. The water glowed aquamarine, at least in the shallows near the bridge. Were there moss-covered rocks in the water? Why had the rocky shelf I know to exist there gone sea green? I kept staring, and staring brought an answer: the grey light on this day of intermittent rain was coming through the aquamarine railing on the bridge. Last night it had been neon green; today diffuse light through the railing casts a glow on the water. Fifteen years of living here and I had never stood in this spot on a day with this light to see how it worked on this river.

By 8 p.m. the sky has turned the colour of a bruise and, by contrast, the day's rain has turned every living plant within sight a luminous shade of green.

June

THE PRICE YOU PAY FOR COUNTRY LIVING

The village is stirring again, as if someone has taken a stick to an ant's nest.

In mid-June, the first heat wave hit. It felt like a great glass bowl had been set over the village and clamped down tight so no air could enter. Kurt fashioned a solar oven using a cardboard box and aluminum foil. I felt like the cheddar he put in the oven and set out in the sun: sticky and flat. Even the birds seemed uncommonly quiet and shade-bound. Ah, but the village was hot for another reason. In the Chinese calendar, 1995 was the year of the pig, but for people in Camden East it was the year of the quarry. We had another tempest in our teapot.

I have grown to hate the tempests, to love the teapot. The village has a reputation for coming together and getting things done. When the board of education closed down our village school in the early 1980s, the village roared (as an ensuing chapter will describe). Local, even national, media chronicled our battles, kept our profile high.

To fight the school fight, to launch a new day care, to counter the quarry — all require a certain spirit, which is common in small communities. That's the up side of country life. The down side is that sooner or later a metropolis may look to dump its garbage or a chemical company its toxic waste on rural land that someone calls home. The county may want to close your little school, the government to nix your post office, a roads engineer to chop those century maples, a cement company to dig a quarry nearby the size of Prince Edward Island.

Some of those most outraged about the prospect of a quarry just north of the village have formed HOWL, an acronym for Hands-off Our Water & Land. The issue is esthetic in a way: a lunar crater would be visited upon our landscape. Like a cancer, a seven-acre quarry would become a fifty-acre quarry, and the way paved for many quarries more. That's because the province has declared its intention to freeze, essentially, the land all around. Blasting could go on for centuries. Forty-ton tandem trucks would descend into the village every few minutes laden with crushed limestone. The noise, the dust, the fumes offend us. We worry about the safety of our children, about property values, about wells near the quarry, about the village we call home.

I do not like the odds in this match. Goliath is an alliance of Ontario's Ministry of Natural Resources — protecting, in this case, a resource of rock — and Lafarge Canada Inc., one of several multinational cement companies eyeing the rock. David is little Camden East Township and the village of Camden East, and some of those who value both are HOWLers.

Among them are Duane Williams, the longtime reeve ousted in the '94 election. Jane Good, the former teacher and *Harrowsmith* gardening editor now back in education. Fred Galbraith, the septuagenarian farmer up on Bethel Street. Jeff Adams, a professor of physics at Queen's University who came to the country and found a monster-in-the-making literally next door.

Back in March, HOWLers hoped for a large crowd at an information meeting in nearby Centreville. Alas, the day brought black ice and treacherous driving: several school buses landed in the ditch that afternoon. Still, 125 people packed the hall to listen as the MNR and Lafarge indulged in damage control. A traffic expert assured that there will be negligible noise from the trucks. A hydrogeological expert promised that wells near the quarry will never run dry. A blasting expert, like a smiling doctor holding a needle in his hand, said we won't feel a thing.

The three-hour meeting had shape and momentum, like a wave building as it makes for the shore. The gum-chewing guy from the cement company introduced a linked set of speakers, like a train — the company lawyer, the bureaucrat, the three experts, a landscape architect who called the quarry a win-win situation. But this was a train going nowhere.

"You guys just don't get it," said a woman from the back. "We don't want the quarry!" Another woman said with great feeling, "It makes my blood boil!" Politeness turned to impatience and finally to hooting. The gum-chewer, who no doubt had witnessed this anger many times before and who seemed even bored earlier, buried his head in his hands. Near the end, the lawyer for the township rose to ensure that he had all our concerns collected and written down. He was Tim Wilkin, a bespectacled young guy in a suit, but he was our suit, and we cheered him.

It felt good to express some of that anger, but we took no comfort in the hard questions posed and the feeble answers offered. To the company's promise of bottled water if her well ever ran dry from quarrying, a woman shot back, "And what if Lafarge has gone bankrupt by that time?" No answer, just smiles from the suits.

"If the quarry comes," I tell Ulrike and Kurt at supper one evening, "I can't live here any more." I take their silence as tacit agreement.

Ulrike, in fact, takes a let's-wait-and-see position. Kurt, disinclined to gamble and less wed to the house than to the area, would sell. But the two choices have been inflicted on me, and I resent them both.

The village, the river, the place we call home — I feel protective of them all. But my dream of a peaceful life in the country, I know too, is rooted in quiet. Noise drove me from the city; the noise of quarry trucks would drive me from the village.

There is the place as you dream of it, then there is the place as it is under a harsh light. What follows is a long, hard look at the down side of life in little places.

Privacy. If you guard yours, maybe life on the concession roads and in villages and small towns is not for you. Let me show you how quickly word can travel. One afternoon in June, Ulrike ran out of gas a few miles outside the village. It was not the first time; the truck's gas gauge doesn't work. Lyle's son-in-law Raymond spotted her on the roadside and did as I would have expected: he drove Ulrike to a gas station, waited while she got a can of gas, drove her back and stayed to ensure the truck would start. I knew all this even before Ulrike got home because Lyle told me about it from his deck as I was walking up the hill for milk.

"So," I said to Ulrike when she got home, "you ran out of gas again?" Her jaw dropped. The village telegraph: Raymond to Lyle to me.

I wish my old computer was that fast.

Villagers know by the truck parked outside your house what work is being done and who is doing it. The year we lived in Toronto a woman rented our house and became alarmed when Marg Kelly, the postmistress, making conversation, wondered how work was going on the new furnace. Our tenant reacted as if someone had been scanning her medical file. She was not long for the village.

Because homophobia and gay-bashing are threats everywhere, Michael Riordon and Brian Woods paused to think before moving from the city.

"One of the major and unique complexities of living in the country," says Michael, "is that it's more conservative and therefore more dangerous. We are not free of fear." He describes how one night in the winter of 1994, at about one o'clock, he heard a knock at the door. A man said his car was stuck on the hill; could he use the phone to get help? While Michael pondered the request, another man came to the door. A little later two more came. The four friends in the car knew, as Michael did, that having strangers at your door after midnight invites paranoia. Like the thirteen dwarfs come to visit Bilbo Baggins, they came one or two at a time lest their number overwhelm.

Michael trusted his instincts. The men, all local, shuffled in, tea was served while they awaited the tow truck, and the mood relaxed. The strange thing was this: both Brian and Michael were almost certain the four men were gay, and no doubt signals went the other way too. But no one broached that subject.

The irony for Michael Riordon and Brian Woods is that when they lived in Toronto, both men were openly gay and active in the gay rights movement. In the country, they feel it wiser to swallow that stance. They even debate whether to post an NDP sign on their lawn at election time, fearing that it might draw unwanted attention.

But that guardedness is about to end. Michael has just finished researching and writing a book called *Out Our Way: Gay and Lesbian Life in the Country.* He criss-crossed the land by bus and was surprised by what he found.

"I heard only a few horror stories," he says. "The notion of gay-bashers in pickup trucks and shotguns — that's very American. I did encounter gay and lesbian people who left where they grew up. They left small towns to go to the city. They were exiles from the country. Some went back to the country and were stronger for being part of a community of gay people. The smallest number of people in my survey — because they hid themselves — were gay people who stayed in small towns but who lived discreetly."

Writing his book will mark the end of living discreetly for Riordan and Woods. The book is an act of courage. In the city,

where neighbours may hardly know one another, anonymity
guarantees a measure of freedom. And so gays flock to cities.
In the country, anonymity is impossible, and privacy, though
possible, is hard won.

One car, one truck. If you live in the city, and both you and your
partner work, you can sometimes get by with one car. You can
also get by with no car at all, using bicycle, public transit, cabs
and car rentals. Not so in the country. Most of my friends and
neighbours in the country have both a truck (to haul wood and
garbage and manure) and a car (to haul people and groceries).

Public transit is largely unavailable to rural Canadians. Since
cars are cheaper than houses, I would rather face a hefty car
payment than a crippling monthly mortgage, but the fact
remains: owning two vehicles doubles the cost of gasoline,
insurance and repairs.

The other, more sobering, aspect of living in the country is
that because you must drive longer distances and spend more
time on the road, you heighten the risk of accident. A University of Alberta study published in 1992 showed that rural drivers are two to three times more likely to die on the road than
someone living in Calgary or Edmonton. The death rate among
males over sixty-four was 60 per 100,000 population, compared
to 25 per 100,000 in the city. The most vulnerable drivers
were males fifteen to thirty-four: they recorded 73 deaths per
100,000 compared to 28 for their urban counterparts.

Rural drivers, the study noted, tend to be less cautious on
roads they know well and more cavalier about using seatbelts.
Ageing and hard-pressed farmers contribute to the death rate,
but the most significant factor is the dearth of emergency
services in remote areas.

I still love driving in the countryside, all those barns and
pastures to admire, not to mention the always open road.
Highway 401 seems soporific by comparison. I once asked the
Swedish writer Lars Gustafsson, then living in Texas, if he minded the heat. "It can never get too hot for a Swede," he replied.

Likewise someone raised in a city can never get enough open road. But the more I drive country roads, the greater the odds that one day I'll meet someone coming the other way.

Wild kingdom. Long before the farmers, long before the first peoples, were the animals. All are a pleasure to watch. I have sat drinking coffee at the harvest table in the kitchen observing a huge snapping turtle meticulously digging a hole in the garden and laying a dozen or so golfball-sized eggs. From the same vantage I have watched an otter in winter dive down to the river bottom, rouse frogs from their winter sleep and cast them up on the shelf of ice, to be eaten later slowly and casually.

Sometimes the animals come closer. Not all are welcome.

In the city, raccoons are a nuisance around garbage cans. In the country, raccoons eat your chickens. Mink eat your chickens. Foxes and coyotes eat your chickens. The solution is industrial-strength fencing and vigilance, but even then, most of my neighbours on concession roads have lost fowl to predators.

One night a few summers ago I spotted a raccoon *inside* our chicken run and on his way into the chicken-house: a cartoonist would have added a white napkin around his neck and a knife and fork in his hand. My just-in-the-nick-of-time arrival (to close the chicken-house hatch for the night) spooked him. In the dark, by flashlight, I fortified the run — and especially the section of chicken wire the varmint had lifted off the nails. As I hammered in the dark I marvelled at the strength of raccoons. Thereafter, I shepherded the chickens through the hutch and into the chicken-house at dusk, made nightly checks and left a light on by the garage door, but I was always surprised in the morning to find all the hens still there.

Dogs sometimes acquire a taste for chicken blood too, a happenstance that will strain to the limit relations with neighbours. Shelley Tanaka and Keith Abraham once decided to do the country thing and raise chickens. They built a pen, bought three dozen chicks, and within a month the birds had feathered out somewhat and seemed to be flourishing. Then one day the would-be chicken ranchers returned from a day in Toronto to find what looked like Kleenex strewn around the yard. Their dog, a normally eager-to-please black Lab, languished on the lawn a little too proudly. The plan is to try chickens again, but to take certain precautions.

Even cats are not to be trusted. We once bought a dozen chicks, kept them in our chicken-house on straw bedding under a red heat lamp, and one sunny day in the spring left them outside on the grass in a portable pen. We later found all but one decapitated by, we surmised, a cat's claws. The only creature sillier than a chicken is a chick. The chicks were safe had they only stayed inside the cage and not stuck their necks out.

Where was that cat when we needed it? I speak now of rats and mice, and I know of no one who lives in the country who has not encountered one or the other. In the fall, they typically seek warmer lodgings for the winter. You will hear a familiar scrabbling in the walls at night (I am amazed that such tiny creatures can make such elephantine noises) and then you must act. Live and let live is a country maxim, one much put into practice. It is not a good idea with rodents. They breed.

In the fall of 1993, I was catching an unusually high number of mice. I was then working in Toronto for a few months as a producer at *Morningside*. One day, casting about for program items from the country, I telephoned Jane Good. "What's new?" It seemed that mice were. Mice on the biblical scale. For three weeks, Jane had caught on average five a night. Traps on the basement stairs were springing like corn in a hot-air popper.

I put together what *Morningside* calls a drive — host Peter Gzowski talks on the telephone to several guests in succession. From Jane, from a mammologist and from an exterminator, the radio audience learned the following: that the countryside around Kingston, and even the city itself, had been visited by a plague of mice that fall; that such explosions in mouse populations occur cyclically, generally every seven years; that a chemical found in certain grasses favoured by mice had acted as a signal to the mice to go forth and procreate; and finally, that while peanut butter works well as bait in traps, so does chewy candy.

On the subject of rodents, talk to your older neighbours. They will advise you.

Meanwhile, I must add one new note of caution on the subject of mice. In May 1993, an unsettling cluster of deaths occurred in the American southwest, and later in the Canadian west. Victims complained of flulike symptoms, then rapidly fell prey to asphyxiation. By November 1995, some 124 people in twenty-four states had contracted the disease, of whom 61 died. In Canada, there have so far been twelve cases, four in British Columbia and eight in Alberta, resulting in three fatalities.

Dr. Harvey Artsob, a virologist at Health Canada's Laboratory Centre for Disease Control in Ottawa, believes that hantavirus — carried by mice and spread by mouse feces, urine and saliva — is the culprit. He advises caution around all mouse droppings, black rice-shaped pellets: "If you see *any* mouse droppings, widely wet the area down with disinfectant." A 10 per cent solution of household bleach in water will do nicely, he says. As an added precaution, don plastic gloves and wear a mask; wipe the area clean and discard the cloth used. Do *not* sweep or vacuum the area beforehand, since you risk inhaling the virus.

Disturbingly, the virus seems widespread in deer mice from the Yukon to New Brunswick. On the other hand, and for reasons not yet well understood, exposure to the virus remains rare. Still, caution around all mouse droppings seems the wise course.

The other creature you might encounter around old country homes loves mosquitoes and attics equally, so that to have one or more of these creatures as tenant is to be equally grateful and dubious. Laeeque Daneshmend et al. of Yarker seemed delighted to be in the country, and their giddiness had another source: their house is the first one they have ever owned.

But what, they asked me as we toured the place, is that strange smell upstairs? Might it be bat guano?

Sure enough, as I was leaving at dusk, bats were dropping from the confluence of chimney and roofline like fighter pilots taking off from an aircraft carrier. One every thirty seconds. We counted nine and from the roofline I heard a familiar noise, like little smooches. Bat calls. I suggested they telephone a bat-buster I knew of in Kingston. No stranger to bats, I once chased one in the bedroom for half an hour with a laundry basket.

In the morning, Jennifer called me back to get a telephone number, and to add: "There's something I forgot to tell you, and it's this. I feel closer to God in the country. I'm a laid-back believer" — she and Laeeque are both Muslim — "but here creation is all around me." Maybe closer than she would like. Already a mouse had leapt from a kitchen drawer, a rather thick milk snake (that's *snake*, not *shake*) was found sunning on the porch, and the horses in the field across the road were relocated after a colt filled his nose with porcupine quills. The bat-buster, who came to the farm one night and sealed up all the entrances when the creatures were out hunting, evicted by his estimate seventy-five to a hundred bats.

Dial 911. The country doctor, black bag in hand, who rode out in cutter and buggy to deliver babies and tend the sick is no more.

Doctors and hospitals can seem far away when you live in the country. I once drove Ulrike, who was in much pain and distress, to hospital in Kingston, normally thirty minutes away, but we chose the worst blizzard of the winter to make the trek. It was one of the longer ninety minutes of my life. Another time, Kurt knocked heads with someone at the day care and suffered a concussion. That too was a stressful drive. He vomited on the way to hospital, where I was assured he was fine, then vomited on the way home. Many people I know around here have put in a stint as ambulance driver.

When Ulrike was pregnant with Kurt and his arrival seemed imminent, we sought to avoid a back-seat-of-the-car delivery by making an arrangement with two friends in Kingston. The mother-to-be sat in one of their living-room chairs amid a vast crinkling sheet of plastic (in case her water broke) and the four of us conversed, more or less normally, until the time came to drive to hospital, then five minutes away.

If medical help for outbackers seems far away, it looks about to recede even further. The crisis in rural health care has been building for decades. The problem, from the doctors' vantage, is burnout. Family physicians are expected to take turns working long, sometimes twenty-four-hour, shifts in the local hospital's emergency department. But the cruel hours and low rate of pay for country practice in general, and emergency duty in particular, have riled them, and in several small towns in Ontario doctors have taken the dramatic step of withdrawing services.

In 1994, a group of frustrated family doctors formed the Society of Rural Physicians to press the matter. Its then president was Dr. David Fletcher, in Mount Forest in southwestern Ontario. "This is a war," he said at the time. "If we're going to have a rural Canada we have to do something now. Five years from now will be too late." Significantly, Dr. Fletcher now practises medicine in the city.

Many country doctors are doing the same. Some who remain are refusing to handle births, in part because of costly malpractice insurance and the added stress inflicted on their own family lives, and partly because expert backup help may no longer exist. That's because overworked and ageing anesthetists and general surgeons are leaving too. As for psychiatry, the Ottawa region has 252 psychiatrists; all of northern Ontario has just 49.

If you are considering a move to the country, ask if obstetrical and emergency care are close by, and whether the nearest town has a doctor. You might also inquire about the availability of midwives, now licensed in several provinces. American hospitals are courting doctors across Canada and offering them dream tickets — free rent, more money, weekends off, paid medical insurance and six weeks of paid vacation a year.

In desperation, several Alberta towns put up billboards in 1994 to advertise their medical needs. The sign outside Milk River, sixty miles southeast of Lethbridge, read: "Wanted: Two Doctors." Last I heard, the sign had been changed to "Wanted: One Doctor." Blackfalds, north of Red Deer, also got a doctor the billboard way. A rural county at the southeastern edge of Ontario posted a $1,000 reward to anyone who persuaded a doctor to practise there.

In November 1995, the Ontario government agreed to pay rural and northern doctors $70 an hour to work in emergency departments, and if that incentive fails, restrictions may be imposed on doctors to cope with the rural shortfall. The government may insist, for example, that new graduates at least start their careers in the outback.

Generally, the farther from cities you go, the worse the health care gets. Consider these numbers: almost 25 per cent of Canadians live outside major cities, but only 10 per cent of physicians do. It makes a certain amount of sense to concentrate specialists in cities, but even the generalists are underrepresented in the countryside. Only 17 per cent of the family doctors and 4 per cent of specialists live in rural areas, and that includes communities with populations as high as ten thousand. The result is that in cities, which may indeed have *too many* physicians, the doctor/patient ratio is 1:425. In the country, it's 1:1,275.

On the other hand, some surveys suggest that country people feel a greater satisfaction with their family physicians than city people do. Why? Because there is often a tighter link between the doctor and the community. At the clinic in Tamworth, for example, doctors typically see four generations of one family, the clinic operates very much as its own emergency department, and yes, they still do house calls.

As for specialty medicine, that usually means — for Kurt

and Ulrike and me — a trip to Kingston. And Kingston can be a long way away when a blizzard drops down like a curtain.

... *But not a drop to drink.* Water from the well is cool and clean. Or is it?

More than thirty years ago, biologist Rachel Carson wrote *Silent Spring* about the danger of pesticides, but she had water in mind too. Carson wrote of water as a collective and wide-ranging resource: "Seldom if ever does Nature operate in closed and separate compartments, and she has not done so in distributing the earth's water supply. Rain, falling on the land, settles through pores and cracks in the soil and rock, penetrating deeper and deeper until eventually it reaches a zone where all the pores of the rock are filled with water, a dark subsurface sea, rising under hills, sinking beneath valleys. This groundwater is always on the move ... It travels by unseen waterways until here and there it comes to the surface as a spring or perhaps it is tapped to feed a well ... All the running water of the earth's surface was at one time groundwater. And so, in a very real and frightening sense, pollution of the ground-water is pollution of water everywhere."

If you live in the country, odds are you will rely on ground-water: nearly 40 per cent of Canadian municipalities use groundwater; 65 per cent of Canadians drink it. When Agri-culture Canada widely tested rural Ontario wells in 1992, the results were shocking. Nearly 40 per cent of 1,300 wells tested were found to contain unacceptable levels of one or more con-taminants: nitrites, nitrates, fecal coliform bacteria and herbi-cides. One of the most commonly used herbicides is atrazine, a suspected carcinogen, and typically sprayed in corn fields.

The old way, my grandfather's way, of defeating weeds and insect pests in the fields was crop rotation and cultivation. Some farmers are going back to those methods, but they are time-consuming and require the purchase of new cultivating machin-ery. Given the cruel realities of farm economics, I can hardly blame farmers for sticking with cheaper sprays.

But sprays, I am convinced, are deadly. We rent our land in Prince Edward County to a farmer, a man I like and respect. But where he planted corn, he said he had to spray, had no choice. At first I only insisted that the spraying observe a 100-yard perimeter around the casing of a well we had drilled in anticipation of one day building there. But as I learned more about atrazine and groundwater, I dug in my heels.

The farmer now gets use of the land for free, but in return he must respect our declared moratorium on spraying. That means no corn, and no atrazine on our land. Just clover and hay.

The threats to well water in small towns, villages and beyond are both insidious and ubiquitous. There are, for example, an estimated 200,000 underground petroleum storage tanks in Canada, of which 20 to 25 per cent are either leaking or suspected of leaking. Once into an underground aquifer, gasoline has an amazing ability to travel great distances. Among the other enemies of clean well water are fertilizers, road salt runoff, landfills, livestock waste and graveyards. Some well water is sulphurous and foul smelling; some water is overly hard and foul tasting.

There is nothing like the taste of pure water cold and clear. Just be sure it's pure.

Three longs, two short. Will the information highway stop short of your dream home in the country? Is rural Canada about to pay a lot more for the telephone than urban Canada?

For most of this century, Bell Canada, with the blessing of the federal government, had a virtual monopoly over telephone service. The only catch was that Bell was supposed to provide universal service, even to remote and rural areas. It could do this by using profits from its lucrative long-distance service to offset losses from local service.

But in the early 1990s, in the wake of similar developments in the United States, the federal regulator broke the long-distance monopoly. Suddenly, companies such as Unitel and Sprint wanted a piece of Ma Bell's long-distance action. The telephone wars had begun. And questions were raised: Are Bell Canada and the provincial phone companies still obliged to service the boonies? When the dust settles, will the real losers be rural customers?

Evidence from Britain suggests that telephone competition, as opposed to monopoly, has meant that rural users now pay 25 per cent more for long-distance calls than urban users do, while technological improvements tend to occur in urban, not rural, corridors.

On April 11, 1995, the headline in the *Globe and Mail* read: "Bell Seeks Rates Based on Cost: Businesses in Toronto, Montreal Would Pay Less for Phone; Rural Clients Would Pay More." The *Toronto Star* quoted Bob Blake, the mayor of Dunnville, Ontario: "It's another crappy load," he said, "heaped on small-town Ontario." The article pointed out that in some rural areas local charges could double in only two years.

It's the long term that should concern rural Canada. If country people are seen as unprofitable millstones, if the regulator ducks while the telephone giants swing at each other, if "universal access" to the telephone comes to matter less than "global competition," then we rural diallers will indeed become poor country cousins.

The Ontario Federation of Agriculture entered the fray in April 1995 and accused Bell of betraying its rural customers in favour of city and corporate clients. "Left to Bell," said federation president Roger George, who clearly has an eye for metaphor, "rural Ontario residents will be nothing short of road kill on the information highway."

Even senior Bell officials warn that the country cannot expect all the techno-bells and whistles coming so quickly to the city. Doug Glover, associate director of business development for Bell in Toronto, says that teleworking "increasingly allows people to work beyond the city fringe. A new technology called integrated services digital network, for example, allows you to send a fax, talk on the phone and receive high-speed data all at the same time. But that new technology is not yet available in rural areas. Competition" — between Bell and all the other telephone companies — "will slow down the development of rural equipment."

Among provinces, New Brunswick is clearly the leader. The entire province is plugged into the Internet. All of Saskatchewan has been connected with modern fibre-optic cable, though rural users do pay more for the privilege. Manitoba is well on its way, and so are British Columbia and parts of Newfoundland. Elsewhere in Canada, it's hit and miss.

Finally, there is this little insult that city-minded phone companies inflict on some of us outback folk. Many companies have replaced receptionists with voice mail. "For customer relations, press one, for widget repairs, press two ..." Some companies have a little tag at the end — "If you're using a rotary phone, hold and an operator will be with you shortly." Other firms offer no such option; to them, rural callers do not exist and cannot connect. A computer-generated voice comes on at the end and tells us politely to go away.

Cabin fever. I have never encountered cabin fever, that madness induced by long winters in the true north, so I am being loose with the term here. What I mean to suggest is that small places, especially in winter, can begin to close in on you. And despite all my affection for the country, there are times when I crave the big city. Toronto beckons: a café on Queen Street, a favourite bar on the Danforth, that Hungarian bakery on Bloor.

I lived as a boy for six years in the northern Ontario town of Nakina, for almost three years in smalltown British Columbia, and for the past fifteen years home has been an eastern Ontario village. But for almost half my life I lived in the city of Toronto.

My heart is in the country, but I am a city boy, and the list of things I miss is not short. I sometimes miss the adrenalin of the city. Working at *Morningside,* for example, made me feel at the very centre of things; my home office in Camden East feels more like the periphery. The city imposed work discipline; at home I have to muster it myself. Some days I feel a little lost, as if the world is unfolding elsewhere — in city offices, schools, malls, busy street corners. Anywhere else but here.

If I have so far celebrated the sense of community I feel in my village and on my street, anyone moving to the country should know that *small* can also mean suffocating. You are fortunate if you have such neighbours as mine, but there is no shortage either of the cranky and the just plain strange. Imagine *them* as neighbours in the tight confines of a village.

I know a man who lives in a village north of mine who sleeps with a gun under his bed. Call him Bill and his wife Eleanor (B&E). Eleanor had once given damning testimony at a trial, and the close-knit family of the accused, perhaps in anger, perhaps prophetically, had threatened retribution one day. Years later, a family moved into the house next door to B&E. You can guess who the family is related to.

Something else may contribute to the feeling of being cramped, and that is the natural caution of people born in the country. The village and environs, for example, are not uniformly opposed to the prospect of a mega-quarry in their midst. Opposition, for the most part, comes from people like me: come-from-aways. Many of us are educated, hold strong opinions and feel no compunction about expressing them. Not so true locals. They worry about getting on the wrong side of neighbours, who might drive a truck, or whose brother-in-law drives a truck.

In Eden Mills, Ontario, most locals in the township want the town's old bridge torn down and the main street widened, as council wants. Most newcomers — and the village is full of newcomers — are appalled at the thought of losing the heritage bridge and devastating the main street. Taken to its extreme, the argument goes like this. Locals say, "You new people are romantic tree-huggers and we resent you, your money and your belly-aching." Recent arrivals counter, "You born-and-breds have no sense of history or the value of your own community."

It's a classic battle, and as much as I would like the bridge preserved, I don't want newcomers winning all the battles either.
Because the oldtimers *are* the community.

In Camden East, few people really want a mega-quarry next
door. But you can draw a line here just like the one in Eden
Mills. Relative newcomers (who value the place as it is and who
dread the noise of trucks) rank among the feistiest opponents;
some locals (inclined to welcome trucks if they might mean a
few jobs) are indifferent or in favour.

And so a rift divides locals and newcomers. You may cher-
ish your new community yet feel apart from it. I wear gum
boots out in the garden and plug into my community in myriad ways, but I will never talk like a local or think like a local
or sit at McCormick's trading hunting stories with the locals.
I will never see the village in the same way as, say, Reeve Jim
MacDonald, who was born in a frame farmhouse outside the
village, never match this farmer's knowledge of the place, its
geography, its people. "This is a gap," says my neighbour Bev
Smallman, "that will never be bridged."

There are class and territorial distinctions here as everywhere. Aside from close neighbours, my country friends —
with some exceptions — tend to be city-born, educated and
like-minded. I go to their houses, they to mine. I work alongside the locals, I value their company and their counsel, but
in the metaphorical and literal sense, I will not likely see the
inside of their houses, or they mine.

Hoping they'll forget to remember. Author Stuart McLean tells the
story of a new-to-town garage owner — let's call him Fred —
who got too involved in conversation and forgot to add oil to a
truck's crankcase after an oil change. The truck did not get far,
the story sure did. Fred's fear was that he would henceforth
be called Forgetful Fred and that this one slip would cost him
his business.

Small places have long memories. In the early 1980s, after
we had lived in the village a few years, someone had a notion

of installing a video games/pinball emporium on the site of the old village school. This struck me as less than wise use of a valuable community resource and I went to township council offices in Centreville one Monday night and spoke on the side of those against the proposal.

The proponent, it turned out, was a terrier known for his savvy with engines, and for his temper.

Council had much the same concerns about a pinball emporium as its opponents did, and rejected the idea. As he walked out of the hall with his solicitor, the terrier stopped, fixed his gaze on me and said, "I'll get you for this." And strode on.

For some time I was sure the terrier would make good on his threat. How easy it would be one night to smash my windows, or worse. He never did. But at a time like this, the anonymity of the city suddenly appealed.

Mono vs. cosmo. "One of the things I miss about the city," says Brian Woods, "is the diversity. I enjoyed the city's cultural and ethnic mix, the kind of exchanges that were possible. This place is *so* white."

When Kurt was small, and we were visiting the city, we had to discourage him from staring and pointing at people of colour. In Camden East and Napanee, our usual haunts, people only came in one colour as far as he could see. And you have to wonder if country demographics will stay as they long have been: mostly white.

Disturbingly, sociologist Stanley R. Barrett found that racism plays a role in some people's decision to move to the country: "One of the striking revelations of [my research]," Barrett writes in *Paradise,* "was the discovery that a motivation (in some cases, the main motivation) for moving away from the city for some people was simply to escape from an environment that included a large number of visible minorities."

Canadian census data suggest that while many people are leaving the city, their places are being taken by immigrants,

largely from cities themselves. You wonder whether that trend
will continue and where it will take us. With more racists sent
packing to the country, might cities become better places?
Would us ruralists wish the racists had stayed put?

All that labour, all those labour-saving devices. Lot lines, remember,
are longer in the country. I count it a privilege that even in
the village, houses are far apart, lots often huge and heavily
treed. It means, on the one hand, more privacy, more space.
On the other hand, the lawns can be massive. Our lawn is not
huge by country standards, but my old Lawnboy mower still
needs seventy-five minutes to do the job. In early summer,
when lawns grow quickly, it can be strange *not* to hear a lawn
mower or weed-trimmer within earshot. The sound of lawn
mowers, big riding lawn mowers, is the sound of summer.

And because houses in the country are often rambling old
farmhouses — hard-to-heat old farmhouses — the other sound
you will hear in spring and fall is chain saws and mechanical
wood splitters. In winter, snowmobiles are the machine of
choice. Many country people *like* machines, as labour-savers
and as antidotes to boredom.

Most villages and small towns are quiet places, but purists
who think the country is noise-free should think again.

June 12. Another of the preconference conferences about the
quarry-in-the-making. This is a tangled issue, requiring three
sets of suited lawyers, one for the cement company, one for
the Ministry of Natural Resources, one for the Township of
Camden East. The township lawyer pleads before the chair-
person — a Madame Dhar, from the Ontario Municipal Board
— for two separate hearings to help unravel the issues.

I like Madame Dhar. At one point, after our lawyer's impas-
sioned plea, the audience of about forty citizens (not bad for
a Monday afternoon in summer) breaks into applause. Madame
Dhar, who has the manners of a principal, briefly shakes her
head and waves her right hand. The warning says, "Don't even

bother doing that again." We don't. She is cool, down to earth, and as fair as I might have hoped.

The time has come for ifs, ands and buts. If the ministry gets its way and eleven hundred acres are set aside in reserve; if the cement company gets the fifty-acre quarry it wants; if the monster trucks come ... then all our buts will have been for naught. The hearing slated for the summer of 1996 will decide the fate of our village. Those who oppose the mega-quarry make dark jokes about the sign they want to put up if the trucks come: Welcome to Camden East, Home of the Biggest Pit in Canada. Others suggest that the word before *Pit* should be *Damn,* or even *Goddamn.*

June 21. Seems like a month of sun days. The river is balding at the banks, and rocks long immersed in fast-flowing water are drying in the sun. In all my summers here, I have never seen these rocks above water or the current so lethargic.

At night, the crickets call to their pals. The June bugs — their wings like little motors — make headlong rushes at our sliding-door screen in the kitchen and then hang there by the dozen. The black sky is salted each night with stars, and from the river wafts the sweet and ancient smell of damp earth. For me, it is the smell of summer.

June 28. No rain for eighteen days. The field across the way has turned a mustard yellow, the grass burnt and prickly and dry, though the dandelion leaves remain doggedly green. The river is a rock garden and looking every day more like ... a mere creek. The other day canoeists came down the river and had to get out and haul their canoes over the rapids and many shallows.

Strawberries — our own and at Paulridge Berry Farm down the road — have come and gone. In the absence of rain, a short season.

A few weeks ago, the Anglican priest — a jolly ex-military man whom everyone calls Father Ed — came to dedicate the

Mill Street garden that honours Marion Lawlor's memory. Near Lyle's work shed and expanding on Marion's own plot, it is mostly Doug and Virginia's doing, but many village gardeners, Ulrike among them, have contributed plants to it. Early in the proceedings, Virginia took the twenty-five or so villagers present on a tour of the garden, describing each plant and who had donated it, how this or that plant was one of Marion's favourites. Her garden had become a village garden.

There are peonies, lilies, baby's breath, irises, roses and a host of others. Nearby is a spruce that Marion once backed over with her car and it grew horizontally for a while; we had a good laugh remembering that.

We all stayed longer than we intended. Lyle kept filling our glasses with wine, kept foisting cheese and crackers on us. "Sure is nice to have neighbours," he told each one of us as we left. "Sure is nice to have neighbours."

Father Ed struck the right note in his blessing, for it looked to the heavens as his collar would have him do, but it was down to earth too, and I remembered how shaken he had been presiding over Marion's funeral, how genuine had been his eulogy.

In his blessing, he spoke of the flowers as God's handiwork, and how we should be grateful for them. At one point he said that Marion was dead. Not departed, not gone from us, not in a better place, but dead. Lyle and his daughter Robyn stood facing Marion's garden, clinging to each other tightly in their tears, like two reeds in the wind.

July

BOOM AND BUST IN
SMALLTOWN CANADA

In July 1994, staff at *Harrowsmith* magazine began to pack up.
By August, the Williams mansion that had been the magazine's
home almost since its inception in 1976 had all but emptied.
Harrowsmith the country magazine would henceforth be published from an office tower in Toronto. *Equinox*, its sister publication, would be gone by September. Left behind to maintain
a presence while a buyer was sought for the building were two
copy editors, one for each magazine.

What a silly, sad arrangement. The two women, Charlotte
DuChene and Lois Casselman, seemed forlorn in that suddenly ghostly building overlooking the village. They were like
Charlie Brown, whose worst fear — the family moves without
telling — had been realized. Yet Charlotte and Lois saw the
absurdity: they shared an airy space on the ground floor and
invited each other out to lunch by dropping a notice in a metal
Memos box. Office gossip, though little remained, got dropped
in as well for their mutual titillation.

In February, the mansion was sold (to become, one day,
a bed-and-breakfast), and Charlotte set up a home office and

continued her long-distance liaison with *Harrowsmith*. A sign, you might say, of the times.

When the magazines pulled out, Camden East lost a little, well, a lot of the tiny glory in which it had so long wrapped itself. The home-of-*Harrowsmith* claim to fame had vanished. Several dozen people in the area lost work, and the proud limestone building at the corner, the former *Harrowsmith* bookstore, lay despondently vacant. (By 1996 it still had not sold, despite its "new" price — the victim of recessionary times and rumours of quarries.)

This was boom and bust on the village scale, but the story of the coming and going of *Harrowsmith* is not necessarily a sad one. I offer it as an illustration of the possibilities for small, even tiny, places. How ludicrous: putting out a national magazine from the middle of what some people call nowhere. With the magazine's departure, a circle was completed, and if the end seemed inglorious, the same could be said for the beginning.

When I was still on staff at the magazine, in 1991, *Harrowsmith* prepared a landmark issue — #100 — and it seemed appropriate to include there the history of the magazine. I volunteered, more out of personal curiosity than anything. The legend of the hick magazine that could was too tempting a subject: in 1978, in only its first full year of existence, *Harrowsmith* won the prize for overall excellence at the National Magazine Awards. I wanted to get it all down before it was too late. War between staff in Camden East and corporate headquarters in Toronto had broken out. Blue jeans against suits, and we know who wins most of those battles.

The history assignment took me to Charlotte, Vermont, where the founder of the magazine had relocated in the late 1980s after selling *Harrowsmith* and *Equinox* to Telemedia Publishing. He had gone on to launch two other magazines and yet another publishing house. James Merton Lawrence, then forty-four, doodled as we talked; Mozart played in the background. "I've always worked to music," he told me. "Studies show that your IQ goes up in the presence of music. I need all the help I can get." A shy man, even with people he knows, he looked up only occasionally from his doodling to make eye contact.

In 1976, Lawrence was a police reporter with *The Whig-Standard,* and he had observed that some thirty thousand Canadians subscribed to an American publication called *Organic Gardening and Farming.* Why not, he thought, aim a *Canadian* magazine at those people? Here the story takes on a Cinderella quality, but instead of wicked step-sisters, a pumpkin carriage and magic slippers, we have a farmhouse kitchen table, a green Volvo station wagon and a shoebox.

The Volvo served as collateral for a $3,500 bank loan to produce the first issue, assembled by James, his wife, Elinor, and cronies around the kitchen table of their rented farmhouse near Camden East. In the shoebox were collected the names and addresses of 707 people who had responded to James's ad in *Organic Gardening and Farming.* That first issue featured an article about growing organic vegetables and kissing supermarkets goodbye, hence its cover of a green tomato on which someone had planted a red kiss. The magazine was called *Harrowsmith* after a nearby village whose name James found "euphonious."

The first trickle of letters mocked the name of the magazine and James prepared to fold his cards. His back-of-the-envelope calculations had told him the idea would fly; he sombrely began to use another envelope to calculate loan repayments. But then the party-line phone (nine shared it at the time) began to ring: James didn't get the ten thousand subscriptions he hoped for, but forty thousand. Bigger digs were in order.

The magazine's second home was the old Farmers Bank building at the four corners in Camden East, site of the nearest post office and a wee local library. As I wrote in my piece of the old building, "Lawrence first entered its side door: the front door was blocked by musty rugs and a wooden wheelchair.

Home to bats and pigeons, the second storey — once a dance hall with a curtained stage running east to west — had an eight-foot-wide hole in the ceiling. The place offered no running water, no toilets therefore and only when the library was open — Wednesday evenings and Saturday mornings — did the furnace come on." Township council told James that if he fixed it up, the place was his rent-free.

Locals thought James was crazy but admired his chutzpah. If he wanted to be so foolish as to try to publish a national magazine out of the middle of nowhere, well, it was at least *our* nowhere. Larry and Reta McCormick of the general store across the street granted James et al. washroom privileges. Even gave them their own key.

Harrowsmith staff, many of them, were city-bred, and here they were living in the country for the first time. They had questions. How do you heat with wood? Raise chickens? Keep bugs off garden vegetables? Fix the water pump? The magazine answered those questions, so the tone of articles was practical where appropriate and always encouraging: you can do it yourself, here's how. Its humour was wacky, its journalism investigative. Small was good. Big was bad. Energy was alternative all the way. The magazine was eclectic and simply reflected its young and spirited staff. During the next decade, *Harrowsmith* and *Equinox* would win more than a hundred awards for editorial and graphic excellence.

James's editorials made readers feel part of something important — a new way, an alternative way, of seeing the world. But they were folksy too, chronicling, for example, the tribulations of then-postmistress Hope Hartman as she struggled with the biggest little post office in Canada, handling up to a thousand pieces of mail a day. The magazine put the village on the map, and plugged readers — some living in cities but dreaming of a place in the country — into village life. Readers took a proprietary interest in the magazine, as if all belonged to a private back-to-the-land club, and feuded in a friendly way in the Letters pages.

But, oh, there were dark days. On a Friday in February 1977, as I told the story in the anniversary issue, "the office ran out of firewood, the first of many dominoes to fall that day. Lawrence and Barry Estabrook, his first employee, borrowed a brand-new pickup truck from a woman in the mailroom and loaded it with green, wet slabwood from a nearby mill. A sleet storm delayed them. It took longer than promised to unload the truck. This was unfortunate because its owner — who had just been fired by the business manager for some infraction — was in tears and desperate to go home. The wood refused to burn. The magazine was far past deadline and without hope of paying the printer anyway."

In 1979, the magazine moved to its last home in the village, what everyone called the mansion. James loves fine old things, and this house had once been very fine indeed. Lorenzo Dow Williams, whose progeny still live in the village, built the place in 1881 with California gold rush money. The story is told, without corroboration, that a woman being courted by two men had promised to marry the one who built her the finest house. Lorenzo's seventeen-room mansion featured a mansard roof, elegant dormers, black shutters at every bay window, and white keystone accents on red brick. Alas, Lorenzo lost the hand of the woman he loved.

Like the Farmers Bank building, the mansion had fallen on hard times. Incredibly, someone had been raising chickens on the third floor and the other two floors were the domain of feral cats and black mould. Lawrence restored it to its former glory, seeing himself to every detail. One employee told me of staining the baseboards six times — and stripping them six times — until James finally approved the seventh stain. The employee told the story fondly, which says something.

James Lawrence, according to co-workers, was a benevolent dictator, a cool patriarch. His editing, said former colleague Michael Webster, later editor of the magazine when I was on staff, "could be a size 13 workboot right in the middle of your manuscript. Other times, it was a word here, a phrase there."

A longtime editor at the place, Frank Edwards, described how the mansion and the magazine melded: "James was the magazine was the building was us."

Hard to imagine it fracturing, but that's just what happened on November 17, 1981. James called it Black Thursday and what followed the Year of Living Dangerously. His marriage with Elinor was dissolving bitterly and the launch of *Equinox* loomed only days away. James arrived at work to find himself fired, the locks changed and the mansion thick with security guards and lawyers hired by Elinor.

Who was in charge on the hill? It seemed Elinor was. James called editorial shots, but the law recognized documents that revealed Elinor as majority shareholder. Eight staffers associated with *Equinox* followed James out the door. From the old Women's Institute building across the river, they set up a new office with government-surplus desks, just as they had done in the early days of *Harrowsmith.*

The ensuing battle for control was fought for more than a year in the courts, in the pages of *The Whig-Standard,* and indeed in media across Canada. Everyone in the village followed it, like some homegrown soap opera.

On the north side of the Napanee River, new bodies were hired to replace James's departed disciples. *Harrowsmith* staff hung a dartboard featuring grotesque cartoons of the other side's villains. On the south side of the river, *Equinox* staff did the same. Chance encounters at McCormick's between disparate staffs were hideously awkward.

Villagers, too, had divided opinions and sympathies. On the night of Black Thursday, a local entrepreneur declared his own sympathy: he located James and dropped $10,000 in cash in his lap. "Pay me back when you can," said the angel and left. He still prefers official anonymity on this matter but many in the village know who he is.

James and Elinor finally settled out of court on Christmas Eve, 1982. Elinor got an undisclosed amount of cash; James got the two magazines but not before paying out half a million dollars in lawyers' fees, severance packages and wrongful dismissal suits. Naturally, James housecleaned on the hill when he and the old guard reinstalled themselves.

They ran an office like none I had ever seen. The *Harrowsmith* test kitchen meant a free lunch and fresh muffins for mid-morning snack. When staff had babies, they brought them to work in bassinets. In a babysitting pinch, staff brought their school-age kids to work. Tom Carpenter, who occupied a second-floor office next to mine, brought his black Lab to work every day. Leke (pronounced *Lake*-ah, a Norwegian verb that means to play) would make her rounds, selecting now this office now that one to snooze in; at noon she retrieved tennis balls and the sticks we threw in the river. Friday afternoons in summer were often devoted, variously, and in this order, to barbecues, volleyball, Trivial Pursuit and single-malt scotch — the latter kept in editors' desks year-round, there being no bar nearby to retire to.

The thirty or so staff in the mansion often walked the village at noon, grabbing an ice-cream cone at McCormick's and feeding cone ends to the fish cruising the current below the bridge. For mansioners, the village school put on a special production of its Christmas pageant, and pupils walked up to show off their Hallowe'en costumes. The mansion was a village within a village.

And when Telemedia, a Canadian communications giant, bought the two magazines from James in 1987, the spirit of that old guard — its values and instincts — and even some members of that old guard still governed the mansion. The coming of corporatism to Camden East had the makings of disaster: some mad scientist had taken a new head from the city and stuck it on a body that belonged in the country. The result was Frankenstein-like in every way. The head gave orders; the body balked. What ensued was war — wars of words, memos, personalities. When *Harrowsmith* considered an ad from Atomic Energy of Canada in 1991 — to get the measure of how heretical that seemed, imagine *The Catholic Register* advertising abortion clinics — suits in the city said yes ("of course") to the idea; blue jeans in the village said no ("hell, no").

To my amazement, the magazine endured in Camden East for another three years, with bodies periodically flying out the door — from "downsizing," "restructuring," personality conflicts, resignations and firings — right to the end in 1994, when the For Sale signs went up.

The magazines had given the village of Camden East much to talk about, had given the village a degree of self-importance not felt here since the days of Squire Clark. Their loss brought it down a notch or two.

Why, then, should anyone move from the city when small-town Canada, as evidenced by Camden East, is dying?

'Cause it ain't necessarily so.

Small towns in Canada are literally and figuratively all over the map. Some are struggling to stay alive; others, in the shadow of metropolises, are trying to control the dizzying pace of growth. Many other places — blessed with heritage architecture, pleasant locale, imaginative entrepreneurs and reasonable proximity to cities — have avoided either extreme and have simply flourished.

Futurists who long ago predicted the demise of cities have the usual amount of egg on their faces; but the yolk is also on those who keep predicting the death of towns and villages. The truth likely lies in between: if large numbers of computer-linked workers choose to leave the city for smaller places, as polls say they would love to, what does this mean for the future of cities? And of rural areas?

Jan Fedorowicz looks to the past to reveal the future. What he sees looming is tumultuous change and cities in disarray. All because the computer changed everything, especially the rules.

Fedorowicz lives in Ottawa and works for the most part out of a basement office connected to the world. The day I spoke with him I could hear his young children playing upstairs, and after our conversation he joined them for lunch. Earlier, he had been looking over some slides with a client — in Paris. Fedorowicz also speaks Polish and does translation for Polish banks. "I am," he says, "a global businessman."

A publisher of business materials and manuals, he has also been a communications consultant to the federal government. And what he tells government is to prepare for a sea change. Fedorowicz previously taught early modern European history at the University of Western Ontario in London. Here is how he sketches the old Industrial Revolution and the new computer revolution.

"Nothing as dramatic has ever happened to compare with the change that technology will introduce," he says, sounding very much the lecturer. "Technology will undo the consequences of the Industrial Revolution. That revolution said that people with capital would attract workers to their place of work. And so people working at home — that is, the farm — came to town where the factories and the work were. You went to where the machine was. Everything was geared to that model. It affected transportation, housing, where you place shops. All that is going to change. Our social model is no longer relevant. It's an extinct model, this notion of 'I'll grow up and work for someone.' Now it's 'What kind of job can I create for myself?'"

Fedorowicz looks at the numbers of home-based workers and he sees dramatic movement — from corporations, from cities, from the old model. "I work from my cottage north of Ottawa," he says. "And if there were good schools in that area, I'd live there as well. All this change is a good thing for small places. Giant office towers will empty. Cities will become ugly and dangerous." He chooses a movie metaphor to make his point: cities will be as they are in *Blade Runner*.

I cannot imagine Ottawa in *Blade Runner* terms. Craig McKie can. Former editor-in-chief of *Canadian Social Trends* for Statistics Canada, he teaches sociology at Carleton University and he believes that the world around the corner will have a decidedly Edwardian look, with a wealthy upper class, no middle class and at the bottom a great many poor personal-service employees. McKie is convinced that, for better or worse, "the boulevardian life" is coming. Like Fedorowicz, he sees the Industrial Revolution giving way to the Internet revolution.

McKie foresees more people, the computer-literate anyway, leaving cities and moving to where they would prefer to live. "Already I telecommute to my students at Carleton," he says. "There's no real reason I could not do 80 per cent of what I do in Ottawa from the house we own in Chilliwack, B.C."

And, like Fedorowicz, McKie refers to the current model of society as if it were already defunct. He cites the mind-boggling growth of the Internet: 50 million users worldwide and growing at the rate of 10 per cent per month, in some places 10 per cent per week.

The impact of the computer revolution on jobs, McKie figures, will be dramatic. "More and more employers are saying to themselves, I can employ someone and pay them fringe benefits, supply a workplace, paper, phone and the conventional work setup, or, I know a guy living in Kingston and I can contract him — at 50 per cent of a regular employee's rate and with no commitment for the future."

In his book *The End of Work: The Decline of the Global Labor Force and the Dawn of the Post-Market Era,* Jeremy Rifkin observes that American corporations are eliminating more than two million jobs annually. Their Canadian counterparts are doing the same: the *Globe and Mail* was reporting in August 1995 that only 14 per cent of Canadian corporations intended to hire new people in the year ahead. The sour economy explains some of that, but it is also clear that technology destroys jobs even as it creates others. Voice mail and bank machines, for example, have displaced untold numbers of receptionists and tellers. Rifkin believes that "workerless factories and virtual companies loom on the horizon." He quotes Wassily Leontief, the Nobel Prize–winning economist, who warns that with the introduction of increasingly sophisticated computers and robots "the role of humans as the most important factor of production is bound to diminish in the same way that the role of horses in agricultural production was first diminished and then eliminated by the introduction of tractors."

Rifkin forecasts that by 2045 only 20 per cent of Americans will have full-time jobs. Somewhat optimistically, I think, he argues that all those people squeezed out of the Darwinian market economy today will be absorbed by what he calls the social economy of tomorrow. They will become not so much *consumers* as now but *citizens,* working in community day care and geriatric centres, art galleries, community gardens and coaching kids' soccer teams — all this paid volunteerism funded by a value-added tax on high-tech goods and services.

But however rosy or wrong Rifkin's crystal ball may be, he does touch on an attitudinal shift towards work that may have a bearing on that other shift — of people from city to country — and, ultimately, on the future of small towns everywhere. Rifkin cites surveys suggesting a disinclination to make sacrifices for work and a desire to devote more time and energy to personal needs and family lives. That *quality of life* mantra again.

British and French studies make much the same point: young people, especially, want a life. They have seen what workaholics their parents were and want no part of it. A British public policy think-tank produced a report called *Generation X and the New Work Ethic* showing that young people want control of their lives and a "life friendly" work culture.

Less is more, the saying goes, and as the North American economy reconfigures and decentralizes, as we ponder the notion of the four-day work week and sharing what work there is, as more people flee the city for the country, small places could well be the beneficiary. David Pecaut, a vice-president with the Boston Consulting Group's Canadian operation in Toronto, thinks it's a golden opportunity. His company, with thirty-seven offices around the world, offers strategic advice to multinational corporations everywhere.

Pecaut — he on the cell phone driving home from work at 7:30 p.m., me in my home office taking a break from grass-cutting — remarked that while he personally likes living in Toronto and sees a bright future for cities, he also observes centrifugal forces at work in cities. "I do see a move to smaller communities. There is now a wider range of occupations, even in remote communities, all enhanced by telecommunications. The pressures on cost in urban areas — though they dip in recessionary times — are high over the long term. For companies, the cost of labour, the cost of living, are high in cities. These are tremendous pressures."

This, says Pecaut, explains why a small city such as Moncton has become a major call centre, or what some refer to as a "back office." Call your credit card company to query a charge and you may be routed to virtually anywhere on the continent, or off. The American Airlines reservation office operates out of Barbados. South Dakota, as remote a state as there is, has become home to the giant Gateway Computer firm, with more than five thousand new jobs in the past decade. The Sioux City, Iowa, area where Pecaut was born once housed a meat-packing plant, a General Motors plant and a Zenith factory — now all closed down. What took their place in the regional economy were Gateway jobs just across the state line in South Dakota.

"This is an extreme example," concedes Pecaut, "but look at the list of high-tech companies in out-of-the-way places. I credit the low cost of labour and people yearning for small-town life."

Many large corporations have snuggled into small places. Kellogg's is in Battle Creek, Michigan. GM's Saturn is built in Maury County, Tennessee. The L.L. Bean empire is run out of Freeport, Maine, Exxon out of Irving, Texas. Wal-Mart's headquarters is in Bentonville, Arkansas. In Canada, the McCain empire calls Florenceville, New Brunswick, home. Alliston and Cambridge in Ontario have become the homes, respectively, of Honda and Toyota car plants.

It's also worth noting that small towns have long been home to small manufacturers. A Canadian firm, the Nautical

Electronic Laboratory, ranks as a major player in the production of AM and FM radio transmitters, with a 25 to 35 per cent share of the global market. Since 1969, home base, aside from a subsidiary plant in Bangor, Maine, has been a plant in the village of Hackett's Cove, Nova Scotia.

Meanwhile, in 1992 there was *Forbes* magazine, in an article on the virtual workplace, suggesting in a headline that you "sell your urban real estate, buy land on the exurban fringes, invest in telecom companies." Why? "Because electronics is changing our world faster than anyone thought possible."

The article described a flurry of movement — by both corporations and workers — from cities to small towns. A \$3.2-billion shipper resettling in Liberty Corner, New Jersey. An investment firm opening a branch in Covington, Kentucky. A computer software company with four hundred employees setting up shop in a restored country inn in Marlow, New Hampshire. Junk bond analysts for a Chicago brokerage firm now living and working where they want to — in Montpelier, Vermont. "As the jobs disperse to the corners of the earth," the authors of the piece wrote, "the biggest losers will be the tax collectors and landlords in the old centers of employment." In New York City over the past thirty years, for example, the number of residents has remained the same but the number of full-time private-sector jobs has dropped by 19 per cent.

What is astonishing about small towns in Canada is how, on average, they manage to hold their own. Ray D. Bollman is a research economist with Statistics Canada and the editor of *Rural and Small Town Canada,* a collection of essays published in 1992. Bollman collects mountains of data, some of it conflicting. "What do you want to prove?" he once asked me mischievously. "Do you want to show that people are moving from the city to the country? Or vice versa? Because I've got data to support both contentions."

Bollman warns that small towns beyond Canada's urban shadow have a rough road ahead. But he is also amazed at the doggedness of little places. "We learned," he and his co-author wrote in their own essay, "many things we did not know before ... Overall, we were surprised that the trends in rural Canada were essentially level. In one sense, this is alarming, because we know some communities are closing down. In another sense, a flat national average suggests that if some communities are declining, others must be growing."

Bollman warns that the migration of people is difficult to chart and the definition of *rural* is elusive. What is known is that 7.8 million Canadians live in rural areas or in towns and villages with fewer than five thousand people. But contrary to prevailing opinion, the rural population of Canada has remained astonishingly stable. What has changed is its make-up: in 1956, 49 per cent of rural Canadians lived on farms; in 1991, the figure was 13 per cent.

But if, as the data suggest, many Canadians are moving out of cities and into smaller places, that is sometimes because the towns are actively seeking homesteaders. Retired people all over North America are selling their city houses and buying country properties. The Napanee branch of the Canadian Imperial Bank of Commerce, I see, displays several large posters that celebrate a certain kind of dream. In the black-and-white photo are a smiling fifty-something couple, he in check flannel shirt and holding a mug of coffee, she in hand-knit sweater and sitting on stick furniture. The caption reads: "We see enjoying our retirement relaxing by an open fire ... along a Rocky Mountain river."

About four million Canadians will retire in the next ten years, and many small towns are vying for their buying power. Some rather unlikely places are becoming retirement havens.

Elliot Lake in northern Ontario, best known for its uranium mines, started luring seniors from Toronto — a six-hour drive away — in 1985 with new houses at $40,000 and apartment rents at $250 a month. Mining companies had built the units in anticipation of a mining boom. Worse than the boom that never came was the bust that followed: in 1989, four thousand jobs vapourized. The town faced extinction. Now it thrives, thanks in large part to oldsters.

If you call Retirement Living, the nonprofit company in Elliot Lake that rents to seniors, you might be put on hold for a minute. A chirpy voice backed by elevator music speaks of Elliot Lake's "smalltown charm and big-city services." When I called, 93 per cent of the company's 1,520 units were occupied.

General manager Richard Kennealy said the town is going through a period of economic renewal. Of the town's 14,000 residents, 3,600 are over the age of fifty; a town once teeming with young miners and their families has gone decidedly grey. In the past two years, private developers built some eight hundred homes for seniors and sold them all. Demand has pushed the price of homes for seniors into the $35,000 to $55,000 category. The appeal, says Kennealy, is lifestyle, the secure and pleasing environment (three thousand lakes within a ninety-mile radius of the town) and of course much cheaper housing than can be found in the city. Rents these days start at $315 a month.

"It's not so much that they're fleeing the city," says Kennealy. "Elliot Lake is a place to go *to*. The pull of the natural setting is strong."

The Canada Mortgage and Housing Corporation looked at small towns as retirement communities in a report published in 1991. The report's author, gerontologist Nancy Gnaedinger, observed that many seniors in North America are moving to small towns for reasons that will seem familiar: to escape high costs and "to get away from the pace of the city, to slow down. There is also a yearning for a sense of community and neighbourhood, associated with small towns. Many retired persons simply seek good clean air."

"Senior settlers" in Elliot Lake feel secure in their neighbourhoods, strangers nod hello on the streets, some pensioners have even been "adopted" by nearby children who have had little contact with older people.

I talked to several seniors in the town, and they concede

that distance from relatives is problematic, as are the long winters. "By March," said one, "I've just got to get out it's so claustrophobic." Most, though, are very much plugged into the community.

"The safety factor is important," says Carlie Bennett, executive director of the Renaissance Centre in Elliot Lake. "People who are ageing prefer a more controllable environment. A small mall as opposed to a huge mall where you can forget where your car is, no expressways to worry about, the fact that your doctor is ten minutes away: all this is very comforting." On the other hand, between 5 and 10 per cent of seniors from the city cannot adjust to northern isolation or comparatively meagre cultural, shopping and dining amenities and they go back. Even those who do stay will often return to southern cities every six weeks or so; in summers, the traffic is the other way as families come up to visit grandparents.

One sour note here is that the government of Ontario seems bent on deregulating bus service, and if that happens, about 170 small towns in the province may find themselves with sporadic or no bus connection to cities, and often no train or plane service either. Seniors in these places who do not drive may be more isolated than ever.

Officials at Transport 2000, a lobby group advocating public transit, observe that even under regulation hundreds of small towns have lost bus service. Small bus operators have expressed interest in filling the gap, but will they?

For the benefit of municipal leaders hoping to lure seniors to their towns, Gnaedinger listed three noteworthy Canadian examples: Lunenberg, Nova Scotia; Summerland, B.C.; and Elliot Lake; and an American model, Roswell, New Mexico, whose circumstances curiously mirror those of Elliot Lake. The airforce base closed down and the town suddenly had a surplus of modern, inexpensive homes. Once again, seniors filled them.

In the United States, about 35 million people will retire in the next ten years, and many smalltown politicians have taken note. "A quiet revolution is altering American living patterns," reads an article entitled "Small-Town America Wants You" in a 1992 issue of *New Choices*, a magazine aimed at seniors. Some states now fund programs to help communities trace high-school graduates, the better to ask them back for their sunset years.

Except for the Plains states, rural America is rebounding, thanks in part to seniors. Of 190 nonmetropolitan counties designated as retirement destinations, 99 per cent gained population between 1990 and 1994. Most of these counties lie in the sunbelt, coastal areas and upper Great Lakes regions. Counties that sell recreation are also growing. Of 285 such designated nonmetropolitan counties, 92 per cent gained population between 1990 and 1994.

Even a few new people can revitalize a small place. The Canada Mortgage and Housing Corporation estimated in 1991 that twenty retired couples can contribute anywhere from $540,000 to $1.1 million annually to a local economy.

But seniors alone will not secure the fortunes of small towns in Canada. Little places will only endure if the people who live there care enough about them. In 1992, I attended an international conference in Goderich, Ontario, that gathered academics, bureaucrats and community workers to ponder the future of small towns. And while I heard the usual dire predictions (the emptying of rural Saskatchewan is especially alarming), I also heard — and this surprised me — many heartening examples of communities doing for themselves.

Winkler, Manitoba, seventy-five miles southwest of Winnipeg, seemed on the ropes in 1967. The population of 2,500 was ageing and the town's two key industries were vulnerable and offering only seasonal work. But by 1992, the population had almost tripled, and thirty-six new industries employed 3,500 workers. Civic pride rose, the outward flow of young people was stanched.

I later asked Henry Wiebe, the town's longtime mayor and the architect of the transformation, how it happened. "We started," he said, "by saying we wanted homegrown entrepreneurs. We formed an industrial-development corporation and offered interest-free loans to people with good ideas." Those notions became actual enterprises — manufacturers of travel trailers, precast steel buildings, windows. "The key," advised Wiebe, who is now president of the Winkler Economic Development Corporation, "is for the community to get together, to roundtable and decide what direction it wants to go, based on the value system of its members."

Nelson, B.C., lost in succession its small university, its art school and its single-largest employer, a sawmill. When we left town in the summer of 1980, after living there for almost three years, we felt ourselves to be literally fleeing a volcano. Mount St. Helens, three hundred miles away in Washington, was spewing volcanic ash, and the black dust was drifting as far as Nelson. It seemed like a metaphor for a town with no future.

But Nelson fought back. The film *Roxanne,* starring Steve Martin, was shot in the town, which afterwards became a favourite location of Hollywood filmmakers. I remember watching *Roxanne* with Ulrike in a Toronto cinema in 1987, the two of us gesturing and whispering as we recognized streets and landmarks and even people we knew from our time there.

These days the mood is far more buoyant. The Kootenay School of Art, where Ulrike had studied, was re-established by a citizens' coalition. The university campus became an English school for Japanese students. Vancouverites have discovered the glories of this historic community built on a mountainside overlooking Kootenay Lake with fabulous skiing, and especially powder skiing, at Whitewater half an hour away. The real estate market, at rock bottom when we left in 1980, was riding a wave in 1995.

Rossburn, Manitoba (pop. 600), was losing its young people in 1993. The town had empty houses, no pharmacy, no doctor and, it seemed, no future. By 1995, ten new families had moved in, along with a physician and a pharmacist. The turnaround came when a Rossburner trying to sell his farm noticed he got quite a few nibbles by running ads in southern

Ontario. Why not, he urged, promote the town the same way? Town council agreed, and their half-page ad in the *Toronto Sun* resulted in a year's worth of media attention. Even CNN liked the story — Little Town on Prairie Toots Own Horn in Big City. From more than five hundred inquiries came a fresh infusion of blood into the town.

The newcomers, many of them semi-retired, are drawn not least by the town's affordable housing. You can get a small two-bedroom house for less than $20,000, a large three-bedroom for $45,000, a lot for $1 if you build within a year. With real estate that cheap, you can imagine how town council at first balked at paying $2,000 for a newspaper ad. But clearly it paid off, and now other small towns on the prairie are trying the same tactic.

It is the fate of small places such as Nelson and Camden East to rise and fall. My hope is that they resist both the booms that would mall-ify them and the busts that would empty them. "You will be safest," wrote Ovid almost two thousand years ago, "in the middle."

July 1. The tradition of Canada Day fireworks, established by Larry McCormick back in the early 1980s, continues on the hill across from our house. For this day in the year, the village takes on town dimensions.

At dawn, the flea market stalls are set up on the hill and yard sale tables spring up throughout the village. I pay $2 for a nearly new pine-and-glass bird-feeder and twice that for a lemon meringue pie: St. Anthony's Church is selling barbecued sausages and desserts as a fund-raiser. For the kids there are face-painting, pony rides, a dunk tank and a huge rubberized maze that shakes like jelly from the fan that keeps it inflated and from tykes gleefully bouncing off its interior walls.

By midafternoon, there are few empty spaces left on the hill, a checkerboard of blankets and lawn chairs. All of us face the bottom of the hill and a makeshift stage — a hay wagon with a blue-tarp roof and backdrop draped over a metal frame. Larry McCormick, MP, is up on the stage wearing the whitest shirt I have ever seen, the reddest tie I have ever seen, and in his shirt pocket a small Canadian flag on a stick. A gifted amateur band then takes the stage, followed by the pro, Cheryl Hartin, wife of Bob, the village mechanic. She belts out her country songs, all recorded in Nashville, at this our tiny Woodstock.

At dusk, I look out from our upstairs window at two thousand or so faces. I count about thirty-six green-neon glow rods, some curved into halo shapes by their tiny owners. When darkness falls the rockets fly. The hill looks like an amphitheatre full of people watching a B-movie, *War of the Worlds,* perhaps. "Ooohhhh," they cry as the rocket ascends, "aaahhhhh" when it blossoms and the cannon shot pierces the air.

I like to be here for this spectacle, not out of love for fireworks, but out of concern for real estate. Ours. The fire department is on site, monitoring the whole thing, but the rockets sometimes go off over our house, not the river as they should, and the sparks rain down on our roof. Within seconds of the explosion, I can hear debris trickling through the maples like shrapnel. This year, perhaps reflecting lean times, the fireworks display is mercifully short.

In the dark, blankets are rolled up, lawn chairs folded, and a few thousand people head for home. By midnight, all is quiet.

In the morning the only evidence of the day before will be the stage — which Bob and sons will dismantle — and a few disappointed gulls fighting over too few cold french fries.

July 2. I finally hear the loon on the river that Virginia Thompson has been talking about. The poor fish must be easy targets for loons and herons, so shallow and clear is the water. From the bank I can see almost every inch of the bottom and most of the fish. Wells are going dry in this drought. "When is it going to rain?" everyone asks. "It's never going to rain again," I say.

July 23. It finally does rain, an all-day soaker. The grass on the hill greens up visibly, the corn in the fields sweetens mightily, and the river rises an inch or two. The land heaves a little sigh, as do we.

August

LIFE IN THE SLOW LANE

In August 1994, I began to teach Kurt, then seven, how to stern a canoe. Since he was a year old, he and I have been canoeing up and down the Napanee River, mostly between rapids upstream of our house and those at the western edge of the village. We canoe to see the fish lazing in the shade of the bridge, the painted turtles sunbathing on logs by the marsh, the thick-as-my-wrist water snake curled on the riverbank.

They have come to tolerate our presence, the resident creatures: the osprey that perches on the white ash over the deck, the blue heron that hunts for fish and frogs along the opposite riverbank, the downstream beaver that brazenly circles our canoe to look us over before finally losing nerve — or interest — and slapping the water hard with his tail and disappearing, as if down a hole in the river. Wild ducks — mallards, buffleheads, mergansers — only occasionally cruise our section of the river, but upstream in the reeds we see them often and the sight of the red canoe soon flushes them.

Kurt has lived all his life in a village, all his life on a river. He is no Huck Finn, but he is close to nature in a way that I never was as a child growing up in suburban Toronto. Watching him captain the canoe with a friend in midsummer, I was struck by his competence, for he knew — as he and his pal Andrew turned and reversed — not only his own strokes but which instructions to issue the bowman. By comparison, I learned to stern on a rented canoe at a marina when I was sixteen and almost drowned the same day when a storm caught two hapless buddies and me out on Georgian Bay.

The country, it strikes me, offers no better playground for the very young. Like all parents, we sometimes hear the dreaded "There's nothing to do …," but for the most part Kurt loves where he lives and — quarry aside — any mention of selling the house on the river elicits the same response: if we want to move, we should feel free to do so. He is staying, if not in this house then in this area. The teenage Kurt, perhaps, will find the village a cage. But for the moment, he is happy on the Napanee.

When he was still a baby and fighting off sleep by day, I would walk him in a snuggly, always to the bridge, across the river to the north side, then up the river road towards the falls. There, at the ruins of the old mill, I would rest my back against blocks of limestone within feet of the cascading water.

The sight mesmerized and soothed my infant son, as did the sound. The Napanee River, except in spring, is mild, but where the river narrows or goes over even a little falls, the current is of the no-nonsense variety. The water here dips and turns back on itself, as if debating whether to continue or go back. The action, so contrary and circular, conjures salmon fighting current by vaulting it. All that motion creates foam and a gurgling mantra. If you close your eyes you can hear the river saying "hush-hush-hush-hush-hush …"

In minutes Kurt would be asleep and I would return from the falls and mime to Ulrike — my thumb closing slowly on my forefinger — that her son was out. Then I too would want to nap. The river had done its work.

Years later, Kurt would return to that spot with his pals and toss sticks upriver of the falls to observe their fate in the foam. The river is a place to skip stones. The river is for walking in, and on hot summer days there is nothing like donning old runners (we save them by the bagful for just this purpose) and going river walking, a staff in hand for balance on the stony bottom. The river, of course, is for fishing: we have a photograph of Kurt when he was not quite four, clad only in red swim trunks and black rubber boots, sitting in a tiny blue camp chair, his focus on the red-and-white bobber. The chair is in the river, a few feet out from the bank, and the boy seems utterly at home as he faces the current. Kurt and friends fish from the bridge, catch frogs in the creek near Larry McCormick's house, explore the ponds alongside the old railway tracks north of the village.

Such are the summer days of a child in the country. His nights are fine too. Occasionally in winter we see the vibrant colours of the northern lights, and on clear nights, especially moonless nights, the stars. From the darkness of the deck in early winter we can see the Northern Cross in the Milky Way and what seems like a million other stars. An astronomer friend in Yarker, the author Terry Dickinson, puts it closer to four thousand.

A neighbour, Anita Grant, is a walker who thinks nothing of marching the mile from her house north of the village, even on the coldest days of winter. She tells of city children who were actually frightened the first time they came to her house and saw a night sky full of stars. How many such children, she wonders, can there be?

Mark Twain was born in the village of Florida, in Monroe County, Missouri, in 1835. The village was then home to 100 people, and in his autobiography he makes the justifiable claim that his arrival increased the population of the village by 1 per cent.

For two or three months every year until he was twelve, Twain lived on a farm outside the village with his uncle, whom he adored. In a piece he called "A Heavenly Place," Twain remembers it: "I can call back the solemn twilight and mystery of the deep woods, the earthy smells, the faint odors of the wild flowers, the sheen of rain-washed foliage, the rattling clatter of drops when the wind shook the trees, the far off hammering of woodpeckers and the muffled drumming of wood pheasants in the remoteness of the forest, the snapshot glimpses of disturbed wild creatures scurrying through the grass — I can call it all back and make it as real as it ever was, and as blessed."

Twain wrote that in 1907. Almost a century later, country life still holds much of that promise for little people. Kurt is gone for hours at a time, bicycling in and around the village. Village eyes watch over him. I remember one time a visiting child fell off her bike just outside our house, and within minutes three other neighbours and myself were out there with ice and wet cloths, a bandage and heaps of sympathy.

But since Twain's time certain modern realities have asserted themselves. Like working parents. Like day care.

Day care, like almost everything else, is often cheaper in the country — $24 a day for preschoolers in Camden East versus $36 a day in, say, Kingston, and $40 in Toronto. But there is less of it and consequently parents drive farther to get to it. Jane Wilson, for example, lives in Langruth, Manitoba (pop. 100), and grew so frustrated by the absence of day care that she not only helped launch a centre there in 1990, drawing on volunteer labour, but she also formed the National Coalition for Rural Child Care to press the matter. In one national survey of 1,740 parents who live in rural areas, half said they had to travel ten miles or more to find suitable day care.

In a pinch, country parents do what Ulrike and I did during the early months and years of our son's life: you create ad hoc arrangements with friends, neighbours and others you trust. I remember some very satisfying arrangements (such as Kurt's time with Jane Good, then home with her own young son) but I also remember that there were *many* arrangements.

After Ulrike and I helped a neighbour in Yarker establish a nonprofit day care in Camden East above the library, Kurt spent his days there for several years. Two after-school arrangements with neighbours followed. Eventually, my own and Ulrike's work schedules became so flexible that usually one of us was home to greet him after school.

It is the fate, I have learned, of all parents to be chauffeurs. In the country, where population is dispersed, you may have to drive far in order that your child study the trumpet, participate in organized baseball and hockey or simply play with a friend. To an eight-year-old, friends are everything. Most of Kurt's friends are classmates who live in nearby villages and points beyond, typically a five- or ten-minute drive away, so there is a steady traffic between our houses.

The courtesy is that if one parent drives the child to the other's home, someone there handles the return trip. In the city, friends often live in the neighbourhood. In the country, you drive and drive and drive.

The one advantage of all that driving, as Jane Good once pointed out to me, is that you have far more control over who your child gets close to. I have come to know not just my son's friends but their parents. I get inside their houses. Invariably, our paths cross and recross. We end up coaching together, serving on the same fund-raising committee, fighting a quarry or two.

Still, it bears repeating that *cosy* is not so far from *claustrophobic.* Little places limit our choices in almost everything, and that includes friends. Good ones may be few or at least far between. When Kurt was seven, a boy of ten took an interest in him. At first I saw it in a positive light: Kurt is precocious, the older boy has *such* good taste, etc. But the boy, who was small for his age, delighted in wild behaviour, and his antics fed Kurt's. The tandem required constant monitoring.

How to discourage the friendship? He came home on the same bus as Kurt and his impishly sweet little face would be there at the screen door minutes later. He didn't come right out and say, "Can Kurt and I go down to the river and torment snakes/hack at trees with your axe/generally raise Cain?" But that was invariably the result. By gentle and persistent dissuasion, Ulrike and I managed to derail the pairing.

I once asked Kurt if he had any regrets that his classmates, who move as a unit from grade to grade in his small school, would be his pals for years, with little chance of turnover or new blood. No, he has none. And my hunch is that he will remember his childhood growing up in a village with great affection.

I then asked a group of nine- to fourteen-year-olds — Kurt, plus the three sons and daughter of close friends who live nearby on large acreages — to list the best and worst things about living in the country. Number one on the negative list was "Far away from friends"; number four was "Far away from everything." Trick-or-treating is harder, TV reception limited, "You live in places people never heard of" and "For entertainment we watch the clouds go by."

On the plus side, "Lots of space" topped the list, along with more freedom, wildlife, fresh air and peace, plenty of free skating, "It's easier to find a Christmas tree" and "Chances of getting shot in a drive-by shooting are significantly lower."

I wonder what those same kids will have to say about the country five years from now when they have joined the ranks of teenagers.

The singer Joni Mitchell grew up in Saskatoon only two blocks from the open prairie, and I have heard her say in a radio interview how much she loved as a teenager just walking out to an aspen grove — to smoke cigarettes, of course, but also to watch the birds, the flowers, the scudding of the clouds. "I was always," she fondly recalls, "poking around out on the prairie."

American author Ron Powers catches a similar feel in his book *Far from Home: Life and Loss in Two American Towns*. Again, there is this notion, a young person's notion, that the greatest thing about a small place is the free space around it. Powers

grew up in a small town, the same one that Mark Twain grew
up in — Hannibal, Missouri. Writing about the hold of smalltown life, Powers remembers how connected people were to
each other and to the physical town itself. The gathering force,
ironic as it seems, was the void — "the earth, vast and unpop-
ulated, beyond our town's borders, the tilled and electrified
vestiges of wilderness."

Perhaps the free space beyond the town beckons most when
the town seems surly. Yarker once had a reputation for rough-
ness. We had friends there who moved out because their sons
had been singled out for abuse by a few village teens. This
kind of intimidation happens all the time in the city, but is
perhaps more easily skirted in those larger confines. Harder to
do in a village.

A woman I know, the mother of two imminently teenage
daughters, has a word of warning to parents who look longingly to the country as a refuge for themselves and their young
children. "I think a lot of city folks are so entranced with the
idea of their kids making forts in the bush," she says, "that they
fail to consider the all-too-soon reality of teendom."

By teendom she means the lure of "field" or "bush" parties,
drinking and driving along concession roads (or horn trips, as
they are called), the frustrations that teens face in trying to
earn spending money, and the shock when they move to the
big city for work or further education. My friend is city-bred
but loves living in the country; she is, though, bracing for a
rough ride through her daughters' teenage years.

Another friend, who spent his own teenage years living outside a small town in the Ottawa Valley, recalls why field parties
— or quarry parties, as he called them — were so alluring. "I
remember the boredom," he says, "the impossibility of seeing
new movies, the fear of doing anything that would mark me as
different." He remembers the great things too, like space and
nature. But the quarry parties offered him a chance to cut
loose against the sense of confinement that teenagers feel in
small places.

My friend David Hutchison grew up in nearby Napanee, then, as now, a town of five thousand. The train, mercifully, stops there a few times a day. The people are friendly, the town boasts impressive Victorian architecture, but ...

David's stories about growing up in Napanee call to mind that adage about familiarity breeding contempt. He's in his late forties now, teaches English at a Toronto high school and has cultivated an eccentric profile. Among other things, he is a wine-taster of merit — he is the so-called master vintner in our grape-growing co-op, and we often work the fields together. As a boy, what he liked about Napanee was getting *out* of Napanee, into the fields and forests around the town.

He remembers with utter clarity returning to the town in the late 1960s with his York University leather jacket and his long hair in a pony tail. As he was walking along an aisle in a grocery store he felt a sharp tug on that tail from behind. David spun around to face a woman, a teacher (not, note, one who ever taught him) from his old primary school, who said in a voice full of disappointment and rebuke, "So. It's come to this, has it?" Imagine what familiarity bred such contempt.

Two Canadian authors I much admire, Sandra Birdsell and Sharon Butala, happen to have grown up in small prairie towns. Both also hated growing up in small prairie towns.

Birdsell now lives in Winnipeg, and she remembers her arrival there like a flowering. For too long, home had been Morris, Manitoba, a small town south of Winnipeg on the Red River. She was the daughter of the town barber, one of eleven children, and she remembers the character-denying tag the town gave her: she was one of Roger Berthelet's daughters. That was all. "One of Roger's."

And contrary to the mystique that surrounds small towns, Birdsell never saw the place as particularly safe. Country manners, she felt, tolerated not just eccentricity but incest and child abuse. "The code of small towns is simple but encompassing," the American writer John Irving wrote. "If many forms of craziness are allowed, many forms of cruelty are ignored."

Birdsell wrote two collections of short stories about small towns and family tensions, all collected in *Agassiz Stories*. Her novels, *The Missing Child* and *The Chrome Suite*, similarly can be seen, in part, as cautionary tales about young adults living in small places.

For her part, Sharon Butala grew up in Melfort, Saskatchewan, and she vowed when she left it at the age of thirteen "never never never never" to live in a small town. "My maiden name," she told me, "was Le Blanc and nobody could pronounce Le Blanc. I wasn't the only one whose name was mispronounced. All the Ukrainian kids had the same problem. And it made me furious. I just thought, 'How could people be so bloody stupid?' There was a lot of meanness among the kids — not to me especially but to each other. I can't even remember any more all that I hated about it."

But it's not that simple, and just as chinooks can make you forget the cold breath of winter in southern Alberta, so do small towns — even to a writer who fled one — have their saving graces. Sharon Butala's fierce condemnation of small towns is followed immediately by a huge "but." It seems that small towns are warm and caring places, even as they are parochial and mean-spirited.

"What I have observed in the town," says Butala, speaking of Eastend, Saskatchewan, close by the ranch where she lives, "is this great contradiction. Both sides of the story are true. There's a tremendous amount of gossip and mistreatment and everyone knows everyone else's secrets. On the other hand, they *do* look after the old people, keep an eye out for them, they support the widows. There's no isolation. For example, in our town a woman had a nervous breakdown — she was a single parent — and her child was seven years old. Another family just took him over, and everyone else made sure the woman got the treatment she needed. If she had been alone in the city, I think they would have just locked her up and taken her child away, he would have gone to strangers."

Literature for centuries has portrayed small towns with a

broad and heavy brush: they are either as close to heaven as we are likely to get on earth or hellishly insufferable. As warm as Thornton Wilder's *Our Town*, as suffocating as Sinclair Lewis's *Main Street*.

In his book *Welcome Home: Travels in Smalltown Canada,* Stuart McLean marvels at the spirit and character of smalltown Canada. If you want to know what it's like to live in small places — such as Nakusp, B.C., Dresden, Ontario, Foxwarren, Manitoba, St. Jean-de-Matha, Quebec, Sackville, New Brunswick, Ferryland, Newfoundland, or Maple Creek, Saskatchewan, read *Welcome Home*. The author spent weeks at a time living in these places.

At one point, he spoke with an eighteen-year-old girl in Nakusp, a handsome mountain town about sixty miles outside Nelson. I know the place. Good hot springs there. The girl was talking about how hard it is to find privacy. No doubt her lament is shared by sensitive teenagers all over smalltown Canada. "You walk down one side of the street," the girl told Stuart, "and there are your friends. You walk down the other side and there are your mother's friends. It'll be nice to get out from the suffocating pillow."

A school guidance counsellor I know tells me that city-born teenagers transplanted to smaller places are quite "antsy" and miss the action and adrenalin of the city. And with little or no public transit in small places, they are constantly relying on their parents to drive them to and from friends, until, one day, they get a licence of their own. Almost all teenagers battle their parents over the car, but in the country teens want the car that much more and parents worry that much more.

But rural adults and teenagers sometimes find common ground. In August 1994, Camden East put on a barn dance for a teenage girl. Jacintha Shenton is very blond (her mother was born in Holland), very smart, very pretty, and Kurt as a five-year-old seemed to swoon a little when she came to babysit. But that spring she was told she had acute leukemia, and her brilliant career (she had won a scholarship to the University of Toronto and intends to be a forensic scientist), her life even, were put on hold.

It occurred to someone that Jacintha would be unable to earn tuition money while undergoing chemotherapy and, later, a bone marrow transplant. What about a fund-raising barn dance? The idea was broached with Jacintha and her parents, who pondered it, then welcomed it. Planners planned, organizers organized, word got out. *The Whig, The Beaver, The Guide* — every newspaper in the region lunged at the story and offered a variation of this headline: Village Rallies Round One of Its Own, Camden East Does It Again.

All my life I have valued the small over the large. Big organizations, in my experience, are unwieldy, slow, inclined to bring out the worst in people: institutions create a hierarchy, a pecking order, and someone always wants to be rooster. Small organizations, on the other hand, are goal-oriented, mobilize quickly, offer less space and time for ego, less habitat for roosters.

The fund-raiser for Jacintha reminded me of what small places can achieve. An old Quonset-hut auction barn west of the village, Tom Harrison's, became a charming dance hall for one warm August night. David Slack, a neighbour who lives with his family next to Lyle (or Lyle's, as country people are wont to say when describing not just someone's house but those who live there), is the drummer for a gifted and versatile band called SecondSet. He and the band, all friends since they were twelve, played for free. Pals of Jacintha's decorated, no, transformed the auction barn.

Auction barns can be sad places: here is where once-prized possessions are picked over by people who wear masks of disinterest to keep the bidding low. "What-am-I-bid, what-am-I-bid, what-am-I-bid," the auctioneer calls out in that inimitable cadence to coax and shame and jolly the crowd into bidding higher. I am a sentimental bird who values old things for the stories they tell. An auction barn temporarily displays an estate, maybe that of a widow on her way to rest home or grave.

Sometimes these old people come to see who buys and what they bid, but their eyes always seem a little wet. Many others cannot bear to look on as their life's accumulation of furniture and tools and books is carted off by strangers.

But on Friday evening, August 26, 1994, Tom Harrison's auction barn was, as I say, transformed. The most imaginative touch of all were two avenues the length of the barn created by potted miniature trees with soft and tiny white lights, lending a café aura. Some wooden lattice at the entrance had been similarly graced with lights; there were candles on the tables set up along both sides of the barn, and at each table helium balloons straining for the roof. The spot where Tom typically stood during auctions to sell off job lots was now a stage. Behind the stage — where cattle and horses are stabled before auction — were a bar and more tables.

Dozens of businesses had donated items for auction, and I was astonished by the generosity of both donors and bidders. Tom's "What-am-I-bid, what-am-I-bid, what-am-I-bid" got a playful, even comic response. The village mechanic, for example, had donated a case of motor oil and the final bid was about triple what you would pay for the same at Canadian Tire. At this auction, the smart bid was the high bid. The mood in the hall was euphoric.

Near midnight, according to country custom, food and coffee — the lunch, as it is called — appeared. There came white sandwiches on plates the size of pontoons, all tarted up with orange cheddar-cheese trays and green sweet pickles. The Camden East Community Association happily ran the bar and business was brisk.

Some cried when Jacintha's mother and father, Margaret and Brian Shenton, went to the microphone — I'm not sure who was holding up whom — to express their gratitude, their astonishment, that the community would go to such lengths. They had only lived in the village for five years or so.

Then the dancing picked up again and I found myself out there with David Slack's nine-year-old daughter, Claire, and her friend who both twirled their fingers in the air to a Beatles tune. As if we did this all the time.

We raised $7,400 for Jacintha's education and had a fine party to boot. The last thing organizers did when the party shut down some time around two was to ask for volunteers to help clean up in the morning. Damned if they didn't come. This being the country, work was divided along traditional (read, sexist) lines. Boys and men to lift the tables and chairs onto someone's flatbed truck and haul them to the community hall in Newburgh. Women and girls to sweep the hall and dismantle everything so that Tom's auction barn could revert to what it was — a low-bidder's paradise.

Right neighbourly it all was.

To be sure, the barn dance was as much about the terror that a young girl with cancer can inflict on a community as it was about community-mindedness. Jacintha was there that night, just briefly, wearing a baseball cap to cover her naked scalp. What we felt under that barn's arcing roof was a crazy mix — of fear (it could have been *my* daughter), of generosity (it's a crazy world but here is something I can do), of group dynamics (the village versus a disease we all loathe) and of pure exhilaration (the chance to dance).

It is one of the defining things about the village that we find, or invent, so many occasions — fairs, fund-raisers, concerts — where young and old can mix. And they do mix.

In the country, the places where people meet are far fewer and smaller than in the city. Local store, post office and ball diamond rank as critical junctures. The result: you *do* meet your neighbours, you *do* brush shoulders with them. So while village and country life seem best suited to the young and the old, and perhaps least suited to teenagers, it is also true that the generation barrier is often and easily crossed.

Young people who grow up in small places often flee them, but it goes the other way too. Terry Black and his wife, Kathy Pringle, are two smalltowners in their thirties, he from the outskirts of Sault Ste. Marie, she from Napanee. They tried the big city, found it not to their liking, and moved into a newer house on the edge of Camden East in early 1995. Their two-acre property is tucked well back from the road behind a rock face.

Kathy, an occupational therapist, says, "I enjoyed the lifestyle, the shopping the first few years in Toronto. But then I missed not knowing people and feeling a part of it. I had a beautiful apartment. I knew my landlord and a colleague down the street, no one else. Now that I'm here, I'm frustrated that at the moment my long hours mean I can't hook into the community network. That will change. Coming here was also a gift to my parents. They'd say, 'When are you coming home?'"

In the meantime, Kathy finds consolation in the space, in the stars, the birds at the feeder and the deer that amble through the woods behind the house. "It's like living at the cottage," she says.

Kathy and Terry had only been in the house a few weeks when a welcome wagon of villagers dropped around with muffins and a village directory, a who's who of local tradespersons. One villager gave them a word of advice: it would be three generations before they would be seen as "local." On the other hand, Kathy has discovered that her last name has made a huge difference in being accepted. The Pringle and Hinch families, to which she is related, are both prominent in the area. It's a kind of trump card to say that your blood lines are local, and she's learning to play it often.

For his part, Terry, a computer systems analyst, found Toronto intimidating, his suburban condominium claustrophobic. "I felt out of place. I was dying to get to a place and *fix* things." An attitude persists in both cities and small towns that only those who can't cut it in the city live in wee places, but Terry believes that is changing. "I know a lot of guys my age who are in the city just to get enough work experience, then they're getting out."

Edo and Linda Knopper, both fifty-five, had barely moved into their house in the country — a lone A-frame on twenty-three acres with a commanding view of the Napanee River valley — in the summer of 1995 when they saw a porcupine one evening from their back door. Under their car, in fact. Thought Linda, "We love the country. Nature is so close."

Next day, Sunday, the car would not start. Bev and Sue Smallman live next door and heartily recommended a mechanic named Joe down County Road 4. The Knoppers called him, and he came out to investigate. That he did so amazed Linda, a blond, ebullient woman who would take animal and child company over adult company any day. In Toronto she had worked in a vet clinic and also volunteered at another centre rehabilitating injured and orphaned animals.

Joe's diagnosis: an animal — the porcupine, almost surely — had eaten the ignition wires.

But nothing, it seems, can take the sheen off country life for Linda and Edo. Edo was born in Amsterdam and retains an unmistakable Dutch accent. His hair has largely come and gone but what's left has been gathered into a neat little pony tail, the red of the ribbon a jaunty counter to the grey of the hair. For ten years Edo worked in the restaurant business and constantly travelled the freeways of Toronto. "It drove me crazy," he says. Likewise Linda.

When I meet with them, it is early evening and though the moon is a brilliant globe cresting a lip of cloud, the stars are visible over the A-frame. "Some nights," says Edo as we stand on the back deck, "the Milky Way is so thick you could walk on it." His voice strikes a note of wonder, as if he has never seen such stars in his life.

So private is the property and so heavily treed that during the heat of high summer Edo sometimes arrives home after work and begins to shed clothes after closing the car door. He leaves a trail of shoes and shirt and underwear. By the time he gets to the pool, he is naked.

He laughs. "How many places can you do *that?*"

"It's a park," says Linda of their spread, "and we have to keep reminding ourselves that it's ours." Nature park is more like it. Besides the porcupine, raccoons dine at their compost bin. They have seen bear tracks in the forest; indeed, they saw them before buying and the tracks sealed the deal. There have also been mice, squirrels and bats — *inside* the house.

Asked to describe what she values about the place, Linda rapidly, gleefully, lists them. "It's the peace and before that the wildlife. It's life. I can't explain it. Even watching the bugs destroy the trees seems terribly interesting to me. Making coffee in the morning and looking out the window is a joy."

Edo and Linda have had to make some adjustments. There are no restaurants nearby, so they have to cook at home more. Edo wishes he was a better handyman; their house in the country is also their first house. One day the power went off for a few hours and Edo remembered, too late, that the water pump is an electric device. Soon there wasn't a drop of water in the house. Linda — "like Mrs. Robinson Crusoe" — used water from a watering can outside the back door to wash her face and brush her teeth.

In time, a frozen water line or backed-up septic system or well gone dry will almost surely take a bit of the air out of the Knoppers' balloon. For now, it's all bliss. "We're never leaving," says Linda. "I just wish I hadn't wasted all those years in the city."

The irony — one that career-minded country dwellers face — is what little time they have to enjoy the splendour. Edo and Linda run a nature store in downtown Kingston that specializes in bird-houses, -feeders, -seed and anything to do with birding. At the moment, they work seven days a week. The planned potluck to meet the neighbours has been put off until after the new year. Nonetheless, the neighbours have been around.

Bev Smallman has brought over fresh honey from his hives, Sue Smallman bread from her oven. Wes and Pat Garrod, whose distant riverside place you can see from the A-frame, have brought fresh eggs, and Wes has used his tractor to clear the old paths in the forest up on the ridge. Jennifer Daneshmend, who lives down the road, has brought strawberry jam. Other neighbours have heard of them through the grapevine and sought them out at their store. How unlike their condo in Toronto where they knew one person in the whole building.

Still, the Knoppers' somewhat frantic existence may serve as a reminder that living in the country may put the Milky Way over your house and the freeway far behind, but the pace may yet be relentless.

Perhaps retirement would offer some relief? I look around Camden East and I see lots of retired folk, some well into their eighties. Lula Yorke, the widow who lives across the river in a tiny house, stays on in part because the neighbours to the east, the Bakers, are so generous about cutting her lawn and shovelling her driveway.

Other old villagers in larger houses seem to move to nearby towns when their health begins to fail or death takes a partner. The typical old country house is a two-storey affair and old legs balk at all those stairs, all that vacuuming, all that yard work. The Carrolls moved to a small brick house in Napanee for just those reasons.

June Lakins, whose house I can see from our porch, did the same when her husband, Ron, died a few years back. Ulrike remembers being invited, along with several dozen other village women of all ages, to an afternoon tea and send-off put on for June at the church hall. Close friends told June stories, and it seems they all had one, for June, it turned out, was much livelier and funnier among her female friends than in mixed company. Marion Lawlor, usually shy about speaking in crowds, animatedly told the gathering about sharing a room with June on a Florida bus trip, how pressed they were one morning to make the bus and how, finally settling into her seat, she looked over at June, who had applied a bright smear of lipstick — to both eyebrows.

Ulrike came away from the event a little astonished at this informal community of village women. She realized there was more here than meets the eye. Or eyebrow.

August 12. Last summer, after Kurt and his pal Jonas had been playing by the falls one afternoon — Kurt on his newer bike, Jonas on Kurt's older model — the latter was left behind. When we went back next day, the bike was gone. In all the years of living in the village, we had never had a thing stolen from us. The bike incident seemed like a blemish and I regretted the loss, for the plan was to pass the bike on to one of Kurt's younger cousins.

But a year later, the Coyle kids, John and Chris, were riding down the river on inner tubes when they spotted something in the water. They remembered the sign we had posted at the store — something about a missing bike. (I could not bring myself to write the word *stolen*.) Could this foul-smelling, rusted thing with the dead tires be it? Indeed it was. For a lark, someone had thrown Kurt's bike in the river.

I let the bicycle dry out in the sun for a day or two, then took a wire brush and steel wool and lubricating oil to it. Miraculously, it has come back to life. Even the mottled tires have taken, and held, new air.

I wonder what the beavers and the fish made of it, a little black bike, its spokes gaily beaded with plastic, its tires slowly turning in the current, then fixed in the winter ice, then free again with spring.

August 19. Tournament time. From here to Kaladar and beyond, every kids' and mixed slow-pitch and village baseball team is gearing up. The Newburgh mites fastball team has been competing and practising weekly since late May, and this weekend-long tournament caps the season. I coach, Kurt often pitches, team colours are white and red.

We take inspiration from Napanee, which routinely hosts the provincial championships. I like to watch a few such games as a preamble to our own tournament, and to admire the artistry. These pitchers must spend countless hours with buckets of balls perfecting their delivery. *Underhanded* seems a coy word for what they do: the ball comes in so fast and dips so hard that for a batter even to make contact and foul one off strikes me as a great accomplishment.

Our own thirteen-team tournament — on diamonds south of Napanee with fields of barley waving beyond — offers only a little artistry but every year a little more tension. The bleachers teem with players' siblings and parents and grandparents, some armed with full coolers and deep lungs. Every pitch is cheered; strikeouts and home runs bring them to their feet. One loss and you're in the "B" division; winners keep playing in the "A" division until knocked out. A large handwritten scoreboard on the side of the canteen plots the results until only four teams are left on Sunday.

At our team bench, it takes two coaches and two assistants to usher fifteen boys and girls through a game. To help the catcher in and out of equipment, to keep score and rotate players, to coach at first and third, to keep skulls clear of bats, to pass out bubblegum before the game and Freezies after, to keep spirits up and order on the bench and the shortstop from making sand castles.

Kurt et al. seem not to mind the heat, but they are rattled by the wasps. The mild winter spared their kind, and they multiplied, and eating and drinking outside has been an adventure all summer long. Wasps love Freezies, and so we eat them on the move.

My fellow coach is Pete Madden, father of Andrew. The latter has late in the year perfected a windmill delivery, and we ride his arm Friday evening, all through Saturday, and right to the final. This morning we play for the big trophy. My kinetic son is playing first base, bobbing on his toes like a human pogo stick. I lean on the fence, trying to look casual, and failing — though the game has yet to begin, the shortstop yet to make his first sand castle. Pete looks over. "You're not gonna get all serious on me, are ya?" We both laugh and the laughter feels like a cool shower.

In other years, our team often made it to the final and lost out. This year, the Newburghers — like Camden East's Useless Nine of old — confound the opposition. The score in the final game: 19 to 2. We take the big trophy home.

August 31. The last day of this month always feels like the last day of summer. It has been a good summer, for baseball, for seeing birds — hummingbirds and woodcocks and black-billed cuckoos, all spotted while I sit barefoot below the shade of that maple between our house and the garage. This tree seems uniquely capable of generating a breeze beneath its leaves. The shade of it and all the other trees on our property has kept the grass soft and green, despite the months and months of sun.

Unlike my neighbours just north of the village, I do not usually hear coyotes at night. But this summer on the deck I hear them often, making those wild haunting yips that village dogs feebly answer. It has been a summer of respite from the quarry, and I banish all thoughts of it.

September

KURT WITH A K
MEETS THE THREE RS

Save our school.

The battle-cry goes up whenever school boards try to close little schools, which are the lifeblood of little places. When I think of all the small schools across Canada, some bad, many good, that have been shut down in past decades, I think of that book by Friedrich Schumacher, *Small Is Beautiful: Economics As If People Mattered*. Is it? and Do they? are the questions I find myself asking. Bitter experience has taught me that yes is the usual answer to the first question, no to the second.

Perhaps, I muse darkly, each province will one day pare down to just one mega–school board and one mega-school to which buses from every far-flung corner will roll in daily. Thus would centralization be taken to its logical conclusion.

In November 1983, a memorable meeting took place in the public school, a one-storey red-brick rectangular box built in the village in the early 1960s. A most undistinguished building, as country schools often are. But looks deceive, for the meeting — an emotional one on a wind-tossed evening — was about all the reasons for keeping its doors open.

I wrote an extended piece in *The Whig-Standard Magazine* about that night and events leading up to it. "Save the School, Save the Village," the headline read. "It is difficult," I wrote, "perhaps impossible, to make urban man understand what a school means to a village. Villagers say that when you kill the school you cut out the heart. At the open meeting and during subsequent interviews, the point was made repeatedly, until it became a chorus. School. Heart. Village."

The aim of the meeting was to let school trustees, then making noises about budgets and cutbacks and closure, hear what defence the village could muster.

The teaching principal, Rowena Reynolds, a tiny woman with sharp features and a bundled energy, was clearly born to teach. Two years beforehand she had been named Ontario's teacher of the year by the provincial school trustees association. A former county superintendent once said of Reynolds: "Administrators admire her, teachers hold her in awe, children worship her and parents believe in her." A male principal once criticized Reynolds for loving the children too much.

The astonishing thing about the school was its connection to the village, and how Reynolds fostered it. The whole village, in effect, served as a school resource. A child's trip to Florida, a village elder's open-heart surgery, phone company workers laying cable at the four corners: all were springboards to learning by experience, a distinguishing aspect of the school's methodology. Many people in the community, not just parents, were drawn into the school as helpers, readers, instructors. June Lakins, the school custodian, was also the seamstress for the annual Christmas pageant, a gala affair to which the entire village was invited. Few declined.

Reynolds deployed a British model of teaching called family grouping, in which classes are integrated at certain times of the day and older pupils help younger ones. The system took the best aspects of the old one-room schoolhouse; Reynolds herself was taught in one not far from Camden East. Reynolds's three Rs were not just reading and 'riting and 'rithmetic but recognition, respect and responsibility. Pupils were taught to recognize and respect each other's strengths, to respect themselves and to be responsible for their actions.

When students left the school (kindergarten to Grade 3 was offered), they typically scored higher than the county average academically, and in language and social skills, graduates ranked far ahead of their peers. You would call the school and hear: "Good morning. Welcome to Camden East Public School. This is a student speaking. May I help you?"

Here was that rare thing — excellence in education. Reynolds had become something of a legend in the area. Students in the faculty of education at Queen's University often came to watch her work and to learn from her; one day a film crew from the university came to record her teaching. The school's pupils — some with fresh experience of shoddy teaching elsewhere — loved it here. One after the other, parents stood up at that meeting in November to testify, often tearfully, on the school's behalf.

A few days later, a group of outraged people gathered around our kitchen harvest table — for I numbered myself among the outraged. We were plotting kitchen strategy to save the school, and I remember that everyone took a turn suggesting a course of action.

At the end of the table sat James Lawrence, then publisher of *Harrowsmith* and *Equinox* magazines and the father of two daughters, one of them a recent graduate of the school, the other still a student there. He doodled away as people spoke, saying nothing, barely looking up. It was dark at that end of the table, and I had placed a little lamp there. The light shone on his doodling. Then it came his turn, and he proceeded to outline a hugely ambitious plan to sway public opinion in favour of the school. Using the resources of his publishing company, he said, we would send to every taxpayer in the county an elaborate information kit on the school and a referendum question on whether the school should be closed.

This was a wonderful idea, and it should have done the

trick. The referendum was mailed out and got an unusually hearty response for such things; some 29 per cent mailed back ballots, with 86 per cent of respondents in favour of keeping the school open. On the eve of the school board's decision, editorials ran in local newspapers, including *The Whig-Standard,* all in support of the school. Regional radio and TV reported the issue. *Morningside* called. The move to close this tiny school of twenty-eight students had become a national issue.

The trustees, most of them, were unmoved. "If Camden East School were to burn down tomorow," the school board's director of education later said, "the world isn't going to grind to a halt." About that, at least, he was right. The sun still rose late in June 1984 when Camden East Public School ceased to exist and Rowena Reynolds retired. Flowers at the front of the school wilted and died; weeds consumed the lawn. The school building languished on the real estate market for many years before someone finally bought it for a fraction of its worth and converted it into apartments.

But the measure of both the village and the school is that the school in Camden East did not die.

From Camden East Public School, like a phoenix from the ashes, arose Camden East Community School. James Lawrence proposed — again in a meeting around our harvest table — an alternative. As angry as any of us, he said his publishing firm would fund a new school, but the community would have to pitch in. Rowena Reynolds, he told us, had confided to him that she would come out of retirement if a new community school was launched. Happy day.

We at the harvest table — Jane Good, Larry McCormick, Virginia Thompson, George Gauld also among that number — were now the de facto board of directors of the new school. It would be housed at the four corners, in the old Farmers Bank building, where *Harrowsmith* had taken its first breath in 1976. Mountains of work lay ahead that summer, and it would all have to be done by volunteers.

Jim Pauls, Reta McCormick's brother and a drywaller by trade, worked for nothing, as did local painters, carpenters, electricians. Villagers signed up Jane Good's duty roster to paint walls, to scrounge for supplies. We got desks from Harold's Demolition in Kingston and painted them over with a cheery blue rust paint. Somebody gave the school a fridge. Then came a stove, a couch, and from *Harrowsmith* a computer along with scads of books and office supplies. People from the region who had read about the closure of the old school and the opening of the new one came around with donations of goods and cash. The small defiance of our action, the picking-ourselves-up-by-the-bootstraps sentiment, all struck a chord out there. We were the village that could. The school's list of needed items was long, but every day it seemed one or two more got scratched off by someone's often anonymous generosity.

The water supply was not reliable, so Lyle Lawlor built a cistern in the would-be school's basement. Maureen Gauld, George's daughter, lent her piano, which got wheeled into the adjunct portable building that served as the school gym and music room. Billy Skinner, then a gas jockey at McCormick's (and later the school's Santa Claus) bought a new clock and proudly presented it. I donated an old but still serviceable piston pump, which plumber Ron Lalande hooked up. Every item in the school had a history.

From the old school we plucked the integrated teaching program that was its heart and the old school's principal, who was its soul. We had our school back. Two elegant signs proclaimed in black and gold lettering that the old bank building now housed the Village Commons. A James Lawrence touch of class. The school, the library and post office inside, I suppose, did constitute a commons of sorts.

"Good Thing, Small Package" was the title of an elegant brochure on the school we produced to inform prospective pupils and parents. James Lawrence had intended all along that the umbilical cord connecting the magazines and the school eventually be cut, and so every year our fund-raising grew more ambitious. Sundae Sunday, the annual end-of-summer ice-cream sale on the hill opposite our house, grew to become an annual fair under a sprawling circus tent that drew a thousand people or more.

A local dairy, Beatrice, donated ice cream at wholesale prices. A local wholesale supplier, Loeb's, similarly slashed the price of everything we needed to make sundaes and banana splits. The first year we put on Sundae Sunday the thermometer plummeted, and the last thing anyone wanted that day was ice cream. Larry passed around trays of McCormick's coffee, and even I drank some, hoping to coax some warmth from it. But after that first event, the sun seemed to shine on our endeavours.

Sundae Sunday remained the pivotal fund-raiser, but there were book sales, bake sales, baseball tournaments, plays and musicals, dinner theatre and sales of T-shirts and sweatpants. The most lucrative and most detested fund-raiser was the staffing of bingos at an emporium in Kingston: we all hated breathing cigarette smoke. As a bingo caller, I was too quick for some, too slow for others, and patrons were not shy about venting their displeasure.

My memories of Camden East Community School are of countless meetings, many hours of hard work and a lot of fun. On Sundae Sunday, the hill was a carnival of kids wearing face paint and ice cream. George Gauld got to blow up helium balloons and hand them out; nothing made him happier. I can see him yet: in straw hat, the helium tank strapped to a telephone pole, a line of kids forming, and overhead the odd stray balloon drifting skyward, followed by a child's cry, and back the child went to George for another. It was, as Mr. Rogers might say, a wonderful day in the neighbourhood: the flea market, students offering guided tours of the school, pony rides, clowns, Larry McCormick criss-crossing the hill and beaming out a heartfelt joy and the certainty that Camden East truly was, as he had long proclaimed, the centre of the universe. School. Heart. Village.

Kurt was born September 9, 1986, two years after Camden East Community School was formed. The pupils played on the hill opposite our house each recess, and when Kurt was a toddler he would hear their squeals of delight and he too wanted to be out there. I remember how the older ones gently let him in to their circle. When the photographer came around for school photos, he posed like the big kids did.

We in the village had fought the good fight to save the old school, then to launch and maintain a new one. But by the time Kurt was old enough for junior kindergarten, both schools had vanished.

The community school had a short but glorious life of six years. Burnout eventually took its toll. At one point twenty sets of parents and thirty other villagers were active in the school. James listed as "guest faculty" a host of luminaries, all of them connected to the magazines: Terence Dickinson, later named to the Order of Canada, would lecture the kids on astronomy; Wayne Grady, a gifted editor and author, would teach creative writing; the brilliant and peripatetic photographer Patrick Morrow would describe his ascent of Mount Everest.

The school closed for all kinds of reasons. The same people were doing all the work. Fund-raising goals kept escalating, and then precipitously after a corporation bought the magazines from James. Though willing enough for a while, the corp soon lost its zeal for community charity work. Had we been wiser we might have sustained the school. Flying at first by the seat of our pants, and smoothly for a time, we eventually came down to earth, and the landing was hard. In the summer of 1990, the village bade farewell — seemingly for good this time — to its school, to Rowena Reynolds and its other fine teachers. James drove up from Vermont for the occasion, and I remember how choked with emotion he was when it came time for him to speak.

These days Kurt takes the bus — as almost all rural pupils must — to another village school five miles away. Camden

East is diminished by not having a school of its own. There is still great heart here, but it's a little smaller these days, less visible.

In June 1995, Kurt marked his last day in Grade 3 at Newburgh Public School. His teacher that year was Fiona McAlister, a young woman on exchange from Carrickfergus, Northern Ireland. She had an insatiable desire to explore Canada and that year saw more of it than most Canadians do in a lifetime. I liked her spark. Kurt once observed that she revealed her true personality to the kids. There was no classroom veneer. Kurt valued that honesty. When she left Newburgh she cried, the kids all cried, even parents and staff got out hankies. As it should be.

I onced asked Fiona to compare Irish kids and Canadian kids. She observed that Irish children are more inclined to respect authority, Canadian children more inclined to challenge it. But something happens to those children, she added, because she found Canadian adults a timid bunch compared to their Irish counterparts. Maybe that's why little schools in Canada rarely last for long.

The truth about rural education is complicated, but when *Harrowsmith* did a report on the subject in 1992, journalist Susan Rogers concluded after much research that where a strong link exists between community and school, the quality of education is very good. And the odds of that bond forming, she wrote, are higher in smalltown Canada than in downtown Canada. In my experience, parents of children in rural schools tend to be more involved in their children's education. Ulrike is part of an ongoing design workshop at Kurt's school, a publishing centre in which pupils create their own books; I conduct two-day tutorials for would-be writers in the county.

Of course, sometimes involvement is forced upon us by cutbacks. When the music program was cut at Newburgh Public School, two parents organized a private one in the evening using Queen's University grad students.

The urban conceit holds that there are lots of bad rural schools in Canada, which is probably true. As much as I defend things small, I must concede that little schools do have inherent disadvantages: smaller budgets, less clout with bureaucrats, often less ambition. Sometimes grades must be blended when class enrolment dips, and a student, for better or for worse, may face the same teacher two years in a row. In small schools, pupils' reputations, families' reputations, precede them. As in a small town, there are few secrets. Common knowledge can be just that: common. The notion of making a fresh start gets tricky when every teacher in the school has you pegged as the original rotten apple.

Sometimes fresh starts are expedited by fresh teachers. Experts will tell you that a school is the sum of its parts, and if the parts are old and unchanging, students will suffer. Well-read and well-travelled teachers are valuable, and in small places there are too few of them.

The other blemish on rural education is bussing. Rural children can spend up to three hours a day on buses, meandering along country roads. And while studies suggest no *significant* difference in either academic achievement or dropout rate between those who bus and those who don't, a more worrisome aspect of the studies is that academic performance declined as the distance increased. School buses are tight, cramped spaces where discipline is often problematic and the little ones are a captive audience for the older ones' antics. These are all reasons that fights to save rural schools are so bitter, because bussing is always the alternative.

Bussing can be hell for the driver, hell for parents, hell for children. I know a soft-hearted woman who drove a school bus in the Camden East area for several years. She would rather sell encyclopedias door to door in the desert than do it again. Another woman was so angry at the bus driver for allowing her child to be repeatedly bullied on the bus that one day she waited for him at the bus stop and when the door opened she tossed a water bomb at him.

There is a pecking order on buses, with no escape for those at the bottom. Choice seats are gobbled up by the bigger, more aggressive kids. Waiting for buses, children get rained on in the fall, they freeze in winter and in spring the blackflies feast on them. Ulrike passes the school en route to her office each morning, and Kurt leaps at the chance to go in with her and thus cut his bussing — and bussing's attendant woes — in half.

But good schools can also come in little packages. Like the one in Youngstown (pop. 300), nearly two hundred miles northeast of Calgary. The Alberta dropout rate is 20 per cent; Youngstown's is under 1 per cent and the students routinely clobber their Calgary counterparts in academic quiz shows on television. Seventy per cent of students go on either to university or technical school.

The school's ten teachers oversee 120 students in Grades 1 to 12. The ethic at the school is conservative: the school's motto is All Hard Work Yields a Profit. Senior students routinely take home two to three hours of homework every night. And because the school enjoys such a high academic standing, principal Stuart Ian Wachowicz enjoys great freedom to blend the new and the old, the computer course with phonics. As was the case in Camden East, community and school are on the same wavelength.

"There is a general agreement between teachers and parents," says Wachowicz, "that we want to operate like a big family. There is great strength in that unity." He cannot say with certainty that rural education is any better, or any worse, than urban education. What he does say is that rural education often benefits from both low teacher/pupil ratios (smaller classes also means more individual access to computers) and a homogeneous student population. In most country schools, unfortunately, *homogeneous* means white. The farther from the city you go, with the exception of reserves, the whiter it gets. In Kurt's school of 170 children, there is one child of colour.

Ethnic minorities in Canada seem rooted in cities, where cultural diversity flourishes. In the big city you can find a world of difference — a Sikh temple, a Thai restaurant, an Ethiopian grocery. Small towns more likely offer a United church, a Chinese/Canadian restaurant and the A&P.

Viren Oogarah was raised a Hindu on the island of Mauritius, where his ancestors had come from India to work in the cane fields. He remembers how rich in world cultures the island was, a far cry from Centreville, where his wife, Dorothy, was born and raised and where they have lived since 1976. Baptized decades ago, Viren has been active in St. Luke's Church. I see him often at McCormick's, gassing up his red van and chatting long with his cronies. If you ask him about racism, he seems almost surprised, as if the issue might have occurred to him once or twice but a long time ago.

Still, I cannot say whether small places or their schools are any more, or any less, inclined towards racism. But then, race rarely is an issue where all the people are the same colour.

If the school in Camden East serves as a reminder of how good some country schools *were,* then the school in Yarker tells me how good some still are.

I was much heartened to learn about Yarker Family School from a friend of ours, a mother of five who once had children in the school in Camden East. She spoke glowingly of the school and of its head teacher, Janet Hartel. "A young Rowena Reynolds" the woman called her, and there is no higher praise. Word of the school had spread, she said, and several families had moved to the village just so their children could take advantage of it.

I was curious to meet Hartel. And so, one day in June 1995, I introduced myself on the telephone, and I could hear in her voice the qualities that would serve her well in the classroom: bright, chipper, open, confident. Of course she would talk to me. Would tommorow suit?

The woman I met next morning was smartly but casually dressed in shorts. Janet Hartel looks younger than her forty years; the thick hair sandy, swept back, the features sharp, the build athletic. She radiates energy. No matter the game at hand, here is someone you want on your side.

"I grew up in Killaloe, Ontario," she began. "And so in teaching here I've sort of come home. In my fifteen years of teaching, I've taught in Toronto, I've taught English as a second language, I've taught in Jewish schools. The school in Yarker is the most comfortable and natural situation of them all."

As it was in Camden East, school and village fit like hand in glove. Births, deaths and house fires become central events in the school. Twice in the four years that Hartel has taught at Yarker Family School, she has helped to orchestrate rebuilding when one of her pupils was left homeless after a fire.

Hartel lives in Kingston, where her husband is a financial adviser, and they have two children enrolled in that city's schools. She remembers her first week at the Yarker school after living for years in Toronto. She had stayed late and gotten a flat tire just outside the village by the cemetery. Panic set in: only days beforehand a young woman in the London area had been murdered on Highway 401 when the Good Samaritan who stopped turned out to be nothing of the kind. A local man driving past offered to change Hartel's tire. At first she was reluctant, but the panic subsided as they conversed. From that moment, she began to feel safe again.

Especially intriguing were Hartel's thoughts on the differences between urban and rural children. Essentially, she says, city kids are indoor kids; country kids are outdoor kids. "The whole connection among country kids is to the environment," she says. "I taught Grade 5 in Toronto. Their idea of outdoor education is a groomed park in a green space. These kids in Yarker are totally in touch with their environment. Here we teach outdoor education right from the school's backyard. The students hike, they know all the trails between Colebrook and Yarker, they know where the poison ivy is, they know about tadpoles and luna moths — their vocabulary is much different from that of a city child. I saw a lot of latch-key children in the city, spending too much time in front of computers and TV and video."

Sue Smallman is a neighbour and retired research psychologist. I mention her credentials lest the point that follows be seen as simple bias. Sue volunteers and dresses in period costume at Macpherson House, a restored nineteenth-century house-cum-museum in Napanee, and she observes after years of guided tours that city school kids are decidedly more hyperactive and less prepared to listen than their country school counterparts.

At Yarker school, a local farmer has built a pen alongside the building so that pupils can bring in animals for show-and-tell. The pen has housed calves, goats, piglets, fox kits, turkeys, sheep, rabbits and ponies. Many of the students live on farms and know where food comes from, how animals are bred and butchered. Many of their parents hunt. Small wonder that the emphasis at Yarker school is on science and the environment. In the weeks preceding my visit, field trips had taken children to a local wetland and to Larry Traynor's Garage to watch the spectacle of cars being crushed and recycled. The village as resource.

"I always bring it back to the environment," says Hartel. "Country life is a good life for children." She observes that country people tend to be less materialistic than city people, their lives simpler. Many have moved to the country, she says, because the cost of living in the city is beyond them. There is less peer pressure, and no doubt less money, to buy those $80 Nike running shoes or other fashion statements (though that all changes once the kids hit the higher grades). Finally, there is the atmosphere in the village school, making Yarker the family school it claims to be.

Parents all come to a potluck dinner at the school each fall, to a pre-Christmas evening of music and to a picnic at the end of the year. The school also holds a grandparents' day, a four-year-old tradition in which children introduce their nannas and grampas and give them the grand tour. Many end up spending the day in the classroom. Hartel knows all sixty pupils in the school and all parents by their first names.

Of course, the threat of closure is constant. Parents in Yarker believe (naively, I would say) that an excellent school stands a better chance of surviving than a poor one. On the contrary, a fine school can become a target because it accentuates the mediocrity of schools nearby. A parent once told Hartel, "We're going to make this school so good they *can't* close it." In her first year at the school, Hartel marshalled the parents into a fund-raising brigade that raised $5,000 for new playground equipment. Academically, the school ranks at or near the top in the county.

It all sounds wonderful, but was not always so. Villagers will tell you that before Hartel's arrival, the school was, in the words of one, "the pits." Hartel pulled off the library's bookshelves such gems as *Dick and Jane* and *Little Black Sambo.* I have the sense that Hartel is persuasive in her dealings with those who hold the purse strings. She managed to extricate $1,000 to buy literature. She procured five computers and four CD-ROMS, arguing before the bureaucrats that she needed the technology to compensate for the lack of a gym. (Hartel believes that outdoor play — the school backs onto fields and woods — is far better for the kids' health anyway.) As a result, Yarker Family School has a fine school library and one of the better on-line computer setups in the county.

Hartel's one caution about country schools is that when you enter one in kindergarten, your classmates will essentially be the same classmates years later. In the case of Yarker school, which goes from junior kindergarten to Grade 3, the pupils know each other well. Maybe too well. "They're with each other for five years," says Hartel. "That does not favour those on the bottom. You *have* to get along, so we teach a lot about peace-keeping and conflict-resolution."

The flip side of all that continuity of friendship? A colleague who grew up outside a small town points out that many of his high-school classmates had been in the same maternity ward together! "Going on to university," he said, "was a huge shock for them because it was the first time they'd ever had to consciously make friends."

Andrew Nikiforuk has much to say on the subject of rural schools. He worked at *Equinox* when I worked at *Harrowsmith;* what I remember about my second-floor neighbour at the mansion was his booming laugh, the little plastic skeleton that hung from his desk lamp, his wild office overrun with newspaper clippings, and his unerring journalistic sense. That, and his strong opinions on just about everything.

A much-travelled former teacher and award-winning journalist, longtime *Globe and Mail* columnist on education and the author of two books on education (*If Learning Is So Easy* and *School's Out*), Nikiforuk believes that North America's spiritual and cultural renewal will begin in back-country towns. Just as convinced is the American poet-farmer-philosopher Wendell Berry, the author of *The Gift of Good Land* and countless other smart and eloquent ruminations.

Nikiforuk has written widely, and disparagingly, about what he calls "the continent's battered school system." He was the *Globe* columnist whom teachers loved to hate. "If there is any hope," Nikiforuk once wrote, "of reviving the school system, it rests in the country, not because of any virtue that rural educators might possess but because of the nurturing environment a rural community can provide for its school. Good schools, whether urban or rural, thrive on high common standards, parental involvement, accountable leadership and shared work ethic. In small towns and villages, these values are not only easier to marshal but more likely to be a community priority."

You cannot generalize about rural education; anyone pondering a move to the country should investigate the local school, which might be as good as the one in Youngstown or like those in remote areas I know of where some teachers, never mind students, wrestle with the subtleties of grammar. Country kids often face long bus rides, enjoy fewer facilities than in city schools and have fewer choices in teachers. So how does one explain this finding? Since 1983, Alberta has regularly tested rural versus city kids in Grades 3, 6 and 9 and has consistently given the nod to rural pupils. Must be the air.

"In general," says Roger Palmer, Alberta's assistant deputy minister of student programs, "rural schools tend to do very well and in some ways better than their urban counterparts on provincial tests." He can't explain the discrepancy and refrains from concluding that rural schools are better than urban ones. Palmer does point out that city schools are presented with different challenges, such as more children with physical and mental disabilities and more pupils for whom English is a second language.

An American study published in 1994 found that school size, not classroom size, is the key influence on student performance. Small rural schools in the west and midwest consistently achieved the highest scores on scholastic assessment tests.

Imagine that you have left the city and found a country place you love — until that cosy two-room schoolhouse at the edge of the village suddenly closes its doors. And all of a sudden your children face two hours on the bus each day to and from a school that is your, and their, worst nightmare. What are your options?

Start your own school. The usual cautions apply here. As the Camden East model illustrates, burnout from fund-raising poses a genuine threat. Our board of directors never did charge tuition: we feared the school would become less a community school and more an elitist facility, available only to those who could afford it.

On the other hand, independent schools are spared the burdens imposed by school board bureaucracies, and I like to think that the mere existence of alternative schools helps keep the mainstream honest. Consider the example of the fifteen or so Waldorf schools in Canada, part of a loose network of more than four hundred in twenty-three countries.

Waldorf schools owe their existence to Rudolph Steiner (1861–1925), an Austrian scientist and philosopher who believed that to change the world you start with children. Makes sense to me. The goal in the Waldorf school is to create a sense of family in the classroom. Each pupil has the same "class teacher" until high school. Art and ecology, writing and illustration are focal points. Every school has a garden where pupils plant, weed, compost and harvest. German research suggests that graduates tend to excel academically later on and typically land jobs in the humanities.

But these community-controlled schools come at private school prices, albeit at the low end of the scale. The tuition at the Waldorf school is $3,000 to $4,000 a year in British Columbia (where the province offers help with funding) and in Toronto can range as high as $6,000 or $7,000 a year, with those of greater income subsidizing those of lesser means.

Keep them home. About 35,000 families across the country do just that. Wendy Priesnitz, coordinator of the Canadian Alliance of Home Schoolers, lives in the country near the town of St. George, in southwestern Ontario. She observes that home-based educators tend to be university-trained, religious and self-employed; they are equally split between city and country.

"Most home-schooled families," says Priesnitz, a former teacher who home-schooled her own daughters until they reached high school, "have no particular beef about the education system. They just think they can do better. They use the education system as a consumer would." Such parents thus move their children in and out of the school system to avoid poor teachers and to take advantage of good ones. This flexibility becomes more important in the country, where choices of schools and teachers within a school can be limited.

Home-based educators typically follow a home schooling program or their provincial school curriculum. The good news about home schooling is also the bad news about home schooling: the teaching is constant. Studies suggest that about 90 per cent of home-educated students who are subjected to standardized testing score above average.

Make the local school better. No easy task. But research suggests that parental involvement in the school can make a huge difference. No one knows that better than Henry Hedges, a retired professor of education at the Ontario Institute for Studies in Education. "We can make dramatic improvements in learning," he says. "It's so simple, so obvious. When volunteers work in the classroom, the teacher tends to double up on what we call the vital tasks, such as initiating new learning. It gives what all teachers want — more time to teach."

Ironically, says Hedges, good teachers welcome help from the community; bad or insecure teachers fight it. The advice, from Hedges and a great many others, is to offer your services in the classroom as a helper, reader or storyteller. Share your experiences and your expertise. Get involved.

September 13. September is not just about school. In September, the leaves start to turn, our thoughts turn to winter and how the weather will soon turn on us.

A man came today to give the furnace its winter tuneup and cleaning. Tuning our six-year-old "high-efficiency" furnace has confounded more than a few furnace men in the past, so I decide to give this Napanee fellow a try. Like every other furnace man before him, he is appalled at what the previous man has done, shows me how this or that jet has never been set or is badly set. I believe him absolutely, just as I believed all the others. This man's efficiency gizmo shows that our furnace — because badly tuned by all those other guys — was only 64 per cent efficient and is now 87 per cent efficient. I expect our fuel bills to drop through the floor. I expect forced-air miracles. I am in awe of men with gizmos.

I am in awe of winter. City people — in apartments and condos especially — simply turn up the thermostat when winter approaches. I do that too, but I also gear up. I have learned to approach winter as a chipmunk does — with much fore-thought. All this goes with the territory of an old country house built in pre-Confederation days, not R2000 days: every fall I check the weatherstripping around every door and ground-floor storm window, I clean all the windows to let in more sun-light and the heat that comes with it, I split kindling and pile more wood than I need. Every winter I am more prepared than the last, every winter I love winter a little less. I clean the chimney. I watch furnace men come and go.

September 27. At 7:50 a.m., a school bus heading north stopped several hundred metres from the village to pick up a passenger. A county sand truck coming south had seen the bus's flashing lights and stopped as well. Just at that spot, at the bottom of the hill, had settled thick fog. And so neither the driver of the grey van that sped down the hill and into the fog, or the three drivers hard on his heels, had any inkling of the bus or the truck.

I have been in Toronto all day, hear the story in the evening from someone on the phone, and am numbed by it. The road, I am told, was quickly closed, fire engines came with the jaws of life, a helicopter took from the scene a pregnant woman. The driver of the van and his two children were severely injured and lie in the intensive care unit of Kingston General Hospital, where the mother in the family maintains her vigil. I know her; she and her family live not far from Tamworth. I try to imagine what is in her mind. Maybe she second-guesses where they live. Maybe she is thinking, how perilous these country roads, how distant the sirens.

There is a postscript to all this. The woman's son would spend months in hospital. The communities of Enterprise and Tamworth overwhelmed the family with cards and food and other tokens of kindness. "They kept it up for weeks," the woman said. "That outpouring of love and support was quite extraordinary. I have seen it but I have never been on the receiving end of it." She hopes never to be on the receiving end again.

The woman is a doctor, and I thought she might have wished — given the accident — that home and hospital were less far apart.

Not for a minute, she told me much later, for she finds city freeways far more perilous than country roads and a city hospital can seem a long way off during rush hours. "I tell you what I *have* been thinking about since the accident," she said. "I've thought about gravel trucks from a quarry on that road, where there is so much fog. That would be a nightmare." And she would know better than most what a nightmare looks like. She was the doctor called to the scene that day when the fog descended and clung to the base of the hill.

October

HARVEST MOONS AND HEALTHY BODIES

From spring to fall, less often in winter, my habit before bed is to walk out the back door, along the limestone path, up the single step to the cedar deck that overlooks the river. I lean on the railing to take in the air, listen to the river, and on clear nights take in the stars — watch for shooting, thank my lucky. When, for almost two years, I worked the first part of each week in Toronto, I would return on the train each Wednesday evening and be out on that deck in the dark, listening to the sounds of wind and water. I could feel my shoulders drop, my spirits lift.

You can find something like it in the city too, but you must know where to look. I remember pondering a job offer in 1988 from *Morningside*. A colleague who had worked at *Morningside* counselled me to take it but warned that my days in Toronto would be equally rewarding and stressful. "Whenever you're feeling overwhelmed," he said, "just walk down Jarvis Street to the arboretum at Allan Gardens. It's peaceful there." The Victorian glass greenhouse is cathedral quiet, dense with tropical foliage and tall blossoms; you can sit at a bench, close your eyes and take in the smell of damp earth, the sound of trickling water, the feel of hothouse heat.

Small wonder that I plant trees on our village property. Obsessively do I plant trees. Ten years ago I planted about 225 white cedars to make first a south-facing hedge, then a west-facing one; both now stand eight feet high. I trim their height in June lest I become known as the village hermit, cloistered behind cedar. The hedge reminds me of one at my grandfather's farm. But more than nostalgia led to hedges; village dogs were more numerous then and they had made our yard a crap joint. One spring day I was collecting in a pail the usual winter's worth of turds, and I snapped. A fence. Had to have a fence.

A white picket model was dismissed — too much money, too much maintenance. I opted for a natural fence. An Ottawa Valley farmer was selling two-foot cedars for $2 each in a Kingston parking lot and I would stuff them, a dozen at a time, in the trunk of my '84 Corolla. Cedars are tough, as tough as the Corolla, which, after 301,000 kilometres, still rattles on more than a decade later. Not one tree has died.

After that, I was hooked on tree-planting. I planted islands of birch and white pine on the lawn, mountain ash at the front, honey locust here, a spruce there, red and white pines on the riverbank.

On our acreage in Prince Edward County we have planted thousands of trees, and across the road, on the land owned by friends David and Claudine Carpenter, hundreds of grape vines for a winery we dream of. Every fall, we and half a dozen others mound up the vines with soil and wish them safe passage through the winter; every spring we replace plants lost to frost; in summer we rototill along the rows, evicting the grass and dandelion and Queen Anne's lace.

Hand-crafted wooden signs at the end of each row proclaim that here are the Chardonnays, here the Pinot Noirs, here the Cabernet Sauvignons, Rieslings and Merlots; twelve varieties in all. Every year it looks more like a vineyard. We will call it Wicked Point Winery, after a local place-name, and no one seems much to mind that the winery dream is so elusive. Weather, soil, birds and deer, finance and circumstance could any or all of them turn on us.

It's play-farming, but it's also hard work and every year more costly as the list of supplies grows. What sustains the co-op (we never call it that) is the appeal of working on the Land (we always call it that), the prospect of good wine, and the joy of each other's company. Parties on work weekends always feature live music, good food and, naturally, fine wine chosen by our master vintner David Hutchison, known as Hutch.

The kids who come — Kurt, Hutch's daughters, Amy and Sarah — have the run of the fields and the paths through the woods; the farmer close by is happy to have them visit her horses, chickens, ducks, goats, barn cats and, invariably, barn kittens. This is freedom of the open-prairie kind, and we all take something from it — the young ones setting off with walking sticks, and vicariously, the adults who watch them go. Because the playground is nearly eighty acres in size, the children are gone from sight for hours. It's like stepping back to another, more innocent time. The three children traditionally sing as they walk a silly song that circles back on itself, and I have come to associate that song with working on the Land: it begins "This is a song that never ends, It goes on and on, my friends ..."

An unexpected bonus of living in the country has been this connection with soil — with vegetables, trees, flowers. When the leaves fall in October I am always a little sad, for I miss the continual susurration of the trees, the whisper of the wind through the green.

My affinity for trees, in fact, explains my loathing of beavers. I remember a short story called "Leiningen Versus the Ants," written in the 1950s by Carl Stephenson. It concerns a man's attempts to outwit army ants bent on overrunning his house in the jungle. He makes the house a fortress, with all manner of ingenious moats. Moats watery, moats oily, moats fiery. But the ants' instinct is never to go around, always to go through.

Is it instinct? Or something else? Like piranha, and as voracious, the ants attack en masse, stripping the flesh off a deer, say, in minutes, strategically taking the eyes first. As the enemy counters Leiningen's every move, he is astonished by the force of its will. I am a Leiningen of sorts, and the beavers are my ant(agonist)s.

Every morning from spring through fall, I come down into the kitchen and before grinding coffee cast a wide-angle glance. I am looking for cream-coloured chips at the base of a stump where once was a tree. I can forget names, birthdays, the punch lines of jokes, but our inventory of trees is etched on my brain. Only in winter, when beavers cease their marauding, do I cease the morning roll call.

The beavers must scale a precipitous bank to get at our trees, but like Wolfe against Montcalm, they work in the night to attain the plain. There, on the heights and on the bank itself, the beavers have taken at least a dozen trees. After each loss, I wrap more trees with chicken wire to a height of two feet. And plant a replacement.

Now it happened one night several years ago that I was moving across the lawn to put Kurt's tricycle in the garage. And in the dimness — beside an island of birch and white pine I had painstakingly planted that day — was an inexplicably large shape where only lawn should have been.

I moved closer. The thing turned its head a fraction and eyed me lazily. Its look said, "Well?" I moved closer still. It did not budge. When I was three feet away, it turned oh-so-slowly and began to lumber back towards the river, no doubt miffed at the lost meal of birch. Was this the fellow that ate the cedars last week? And the pines before that? I had presumed (1) beavers eat only deciduous trees, and (2) beavers stick close to the safety of water and would never venture this far up on the lawn. Wrong.

I have seen a beaver on the riverbank opposite completely ignore the Bakers' dog on whose lawn he sat. Even when the beagle circled him, barking a territorial warning, the beaver

left his flank exposed and went on grazing the grass, until finally, the thoroughly humiliated dog slinked away, feigning disinterest. Another time, I spotted a beaver under a truck near
the four corners in Camden East, at least a hundred yards from
the river. That was the year Larry McCormick lost a slew of
trees in his open-air nursery, the saplings all lined up like steaming hors d'oeuvres on a tray.

Like Leiningen, I admire the enemy but I hate him. As I
herded my beaver to the river that night, the anger rose in
me, especially when he insisted on moving so slowly. In my
hand was a poor prod — a length of quarter-round trim, left
from some porch repair and on its way to the garage along with
the tricycle. I whacked him with the flimsy wood, which, of
course, broke on his broad back like balsa, but this — along
with my yelling "Gedouddahere!" — nudged him into a kind
of fat canter and he was picking up steam as he rocked and
rolled across the lawn, then through the garden. He slid on
his belly down the bank before leaping into the water, making
a sound like a boulder heaved from a bridge. Even then, he
seemed without fear. He quickly circled on the surface, staring
back at me, his chin resting on the water. The look said, "My
ancestors ate trees where you now stand. Who do you think
you are?"

This past May we lost two more trees to beaver teeth: a tall
pyramid cedar at the back, a foot from the house, and a hemlock on the eastern perimeter. Neither was wrapped with chick-
en wire. I had presumed (1) beavers would not venture so
close to the house, and (2) beavers don't eat hemlock. Wrong.
Beavers, I now know, will take any tree to keep their teeth
short and sharp. Though my posture in these battles remains
defensive, I did once try painting the freshly gnawed bark of
a still-standing tree with Scanlan's Hellfire, a vengeful concoction of pepper, chili sauce and Tabasco. I am sure the beaver
scoffed at it.

After years in the country on the river, I have learned that
chicken wire and duct tape are the two indispensables: the tape

for in-a-pinch plumbing and car or other repairs; the wire to preserve chickens and trees.

The first thing I ever built on what my neighbour George Gauld once called the Mill Street Ranch (he routered out a sign to that effect and it hangs yet by the chicken-house) was a chicken run of two-by-fours and chicken wire. But the great bulk of such wire on our ranch has gone into confounding the powerful incisors of *Castor canadensis*.

My battles with beavers aside, I am convinced that my stress levels are far below what they were in the city. To the question, What does it mean to our health to live in the country? I answer, A great deal. I have been struck by the work of psychologists who make a connection between green space and good health. The power of nature to heal, of wilderness to restore, of gardening to induce peace and tranquillity: all this is well documented. Nature, says Pierre Bourque, former director of the Montreal Botanical Garden and currently mayor of Montreal, is replacing religion. He's only half-joking.

Some studies, hotly debated (because measuring health is tricky business), suggest that people who live in the country tend to enjoy better health, are more contented and less stressed than their urban counterparts. At least part of that well-being, I believe, stems from all that green.

In her memoir *Revolution from Within,* Gloria Steinem observed that women, especially, typically lose contact with nature during adolescence. She argues, as many do, that human well-being lies in closer connection with nature and that women can often reconnect by revisiting a place where they once felt free — a particular garden or tree house, a mountain path or lake.

Steinem talks about "the saving grace of nature," and I wonder how many women, and men, have rediscovered that truth. Often at sunset, Ulrike and Kurt and I will walk north of the village along the old railway track. We still call it that though the actual tracks were torn up years ago. In high summer, wild grape and raspberries and milkweed grow thick as a hedge on each side. Walk east to a frog pond where the limestone is shaped like benches, a good spot to sit and cogitate. Walk west, and a path in a field of clover takes you to a place where the Napanee River cuts through a gorge, with cliffs dropping thirty feet to the water. Always our walks take us past fields, rarely into the village, as if the fields themselves were pulling us to them.

"I do love these fields," Ulrike told me one evening on a walk. When she was eighteen, she made her first return visit to northern Germany, to Linderte, the village of her birth, where she felt for the first time a true sense of the country. Her grandparents lived in a house with a backyard vegetable garden that ended where the fields began. "Somehow," said Ulrike, "those fields behind my grandmother's house and the ones around Camden East seem all of a piece." She looked west as she said it — past goldfinches on a fencewire, to yellow grain bowing to the breeze, to the sun dipping behind banks of stormclouds coloured purple and grey. Emperor's colours.

Rightly or wrongly, urban North Americans believe that the country is a healthier place to live. Rural Americans, who were *perceived* to be happier than their dour urban counterparts in a national survey undertaken in 1992, came up smelling like roses — "more likely to be warm and friendly, honest in their business dealings, to be concerned about the problems and needs of others, to get real fun out of life, to be in good health and to have a close-knit family."

The imagined village may pale beside the actual one. But why are urbanites so convinced the grass is greener on the rural side? In 1976, the University of Michigan's Institute for Social Research set out, ambitiously, to measure quality of life in the United States. They found, in their voluminous study, that the grass does not just *appear* to be greener in the country. It is.

Darryl Hobbs teaches in the department of rural sociology at the University of Missouri and he's done a little math. He points out that of two million farms in that country, one-quarter account for the lion's share of production; three-quarters — operated by part-time and hobby farmers — generate but a fraction of production. "They not only are not earning income from farming," says Hobbs, "they're subsidizing their farm income from off-farm income." All these people are playing farmer. Why?

Hobbs challenges the assumption that quality of life is related to standard of living. And he cites the University of Michigan study: "Among persons in all parts of the country, from all walks of life, those people with a 'lower standard of living' express the greatest satisfaction with their lives. Furthermore, those most satisfied of all are living in rural areas." An intriguing graph in that study shows that overall satisfaction with community rose progressively as you moved from big cities to suburbs and small cities and towns, but was highest by far in rural areas — in villages and on concession roads.

Now just stop it right there, as Howie Meeker would say. Am I to take it that less is more, that small is beautiful, that farm life is blissful? Not exactly. Real farm life is hard. Farmers joke that they work eight hours like everyone else — eight in the morning and eight in the afternoon. Many farmers are poor, debt-ridden and weary. Why, then, do farmers cling to farming? And why do people hobby-farm?

Sharon Butala thinks she has the answer. In an essay called "Time, Space and Light: Discovering the Saskatchewan Soul," she observed that for all the dark truths about farming, "something about farm life ... remains beautiful and good, and that is the true source of the myth of the family farm as the ideal way of life." Searching for what that something is, she wonders if it is the freedom of the farmer — though chained by debt and banks and duty — to sculpt a daily or weekly schedule of work.

Butala wonders whether the tug of community is another integral part of farming's allure: how you can feel secure in a far-flung network of family, friends and lifelong acquaintances.

"Even what appears to the city dweller," she writes, "as a sea of emptiness, the spaces between farms, does not seem that way to the farmer." A farmer will know intimately this sprawling territory of farms and hamlets, back roads and rights of way, know it better than city dwellers know the few blocks of their neighbourhood.

In her essay, Butala fixes on time, space and light. By *time*, she means the agrarian round — seeding in spring and harvesting in autumn, rising, more or less, when the sun does and sleeping, more or less, when it sets, as opposed to urban obeisance to clocks. Butala finds central to the connection with land the sense of uninterrupted *space* on a farm. Finally, there is the natural *light*, for farmers work outside most days of their lives.

Butala contends that lifelong, generations-long attachments to land work mysteriously on human memory and imagination and dreams. What starts as something physical and literal — dirt under the fingernails — becomes in time more spiritual; the land gets under your skin in another way. "It is this sense out of which *place* comes," Butala concludes, "and it is also the one out of which the myth grows." The myth, that is, of the family farm as the ideal way of life.

A friend of mine, Wes Garrod, a high-school principal who lives with his family upriver, showed me something his father had given him. Elegantly scripted and framed, it's called "The Country Boy's Creed" and was penned early in the 1900s by an American crackerbarrel philosopher named Edwin Osgood Grover. It reads, in part: "I believe that the Country which God made is more beautiful than the City which man made; that life out of doors and in touch with the earth is the natural life of man. I believe … that life is larger and freer and happier on the farm than in the town."

It is thanks to such romantic writing that the myth of country bliss has endured. Some of us want to believe there's a heaven, though we doubt it very much; we want to believe in a happier life on the farm, even when the facts speak against it. It has been estimated that the number of rural poor now exceeds 10 million in the United States, where family farms are constantly being swallowed by mega-farms. Five per cent of American land-owners, many of them banks and insurance companies, now own 75 per cent of the land. By the year 2000, the fifty thousand largest farms in the U.S. — and remember, that nation is home to two million farms — will account for three-quarters of all agricultural production.

The family farm and smalltown life are intricately connected. The village of Camden East, were it not surrounded by small farms and farmers, by cattle and horses on its very periphery, would lose its defining character. Kill the family farms and you kill the towns, at least as we know them — or think we know them. That myth again.

Various writers on nature, Butala among them, talk about allegiance to place, how the land has a life of its own beyond anything we do with it, and how fitting yourself into the rhythms of something bigger than you are can be psychologically soothing. I try to fathom why that might be so, and it occurs to me that working on the land offers freedom — as Butala suggests — but it also to some extent robs one of choice, and maybe there is relief in that. The particularities of the land, the seasons, the weather, all tell you when to till, what and when to plant, when to harvest. Partaking in those rituals and rhythms can be a comfort because it challenges the tyranny of the self: that way we have of living with our own thoughts and inner voices, so self-possessed and -obsessed and -conscious that the world around us is barely noticed.

Here's an example close to home. A garden is a farm in miniature, offering a little of the farmer's heartache and wonder. From spring through fall, Ulrike makes her rounds, as we have come to call them, of her flower gardens. Every year more ground is given over to flowers: they run circles round the linear contours of the house, grow in burgeoning shapes by the winding limestone paths, inhabit curving islands of their own.

I will see her, walking slowly, then stopping to bend over in her scrutinizing pose. One morning in June, when her rounds were done, I asked her to tell me in detail what she had seen. I had never asked her that before, though I had long been struck by the time she took.

"Well," she began, "I noticed that the petals were opening on the zinnias. The seed packets described them as purple, but they're more magenta than purple. And on the deck I noticed a lot of baby spiders in a seed flat of dwarf cosmos. In another section I had looked at many times before, near the back door, I realized that the lobelia plants from last year had self-seeded. When plants are tiny, you can't recognize them until the 'true leaves' come. That was the clue. And the lupins — they were cream last year, pink this year. Don't know why. There have never been pink ones.

"I do rounds every day, often twice a day. Sometimes they're practical — I check the asparagus, for example, to make sure the spears haven't bolted. The herb garden also needs attention: the cilantro, for instance, will develop fernlike leaves that make the plant bitter. At the same time, I'm thinning.

"Morning and evening are best for rounds. The best light. If I sit on the sandbox by Kurt's playhouse in May I can see the light shining *through* the tulips. It's absolutely gorgeous. You get a sense of distance and overlapping textures, like a landscape in miniature. All because you're sitting low to the ground. The mornings are misty and dewy, the colours stronger.

"Of course, gardening is a curse too. I'm obsessive about it. Sometimes I long not to think about it; the flowerbeds have to be perfect in my anal-retentive way. Yet they're a source of great pleasure. I look on the garden as a sculpture. I'm always shaping.

"And because I know where things are planted, I can savour their progress. The life of a plant is so amazing. One minute there's a clump, after the snow goes, and then when it's in bud you can hardly wait for it to come out. You've seen it in flower a hundred times but the unfolding is still really exciting — partly because you've been watching it every day. Paying attention is the key. And there is always something unexpected to go with the something planned. You put it there but it's still a surprise. There might be something you've never planted before and you say, '*That's* what the flower looks like' or '*That's* this plant's habit.'"

You hear those words and you catch a glimpse of the satisfaction that regular contact with growing things and open spaces can offer. Nothing permanent, mind you, and nothing easily won, but something intricately linked to good health and a positive outlook.

A book that stayed with me long after I read it is *The Age of Missing Information,* by *New Yorker* staff writer Bill McKibben. He's a charming Luddite whose target — television — is an easy one. But I like what he says and I like his quirkiness.

Here is what he did. On May 3, 1990, he and friends videotaped the two thousand hours of television programming that issued from a Fairfax, Virginia, cable station over that twenty-four-hour period. During that same summer, he spent another twenty-four hours on a mountaintop by a small pond, where he hiked and swam, made supper and watched the stars before falling asleep. The book, as McKibben puts it, "is about the information each day imparted."

His thesis is that information from TV and the time we spend absorbing it come at the expense of something. What is now missing is the deeper understanding, a physical grip — on the natural world. Are we so free, he asks, when we are freed from the soil? Are we so much smarter than a nineteenth-century farmer who knew the ways of a horse or used the moon and the clouds to plot weather to know, in turn, when to plant or harvest?

"The idea," writes McKibben, "of standing under the stars and feeling how small you are — that's not a television idea. Everything on television tells you the opposite — that you're the most important person, and that people are all that matter." You can just as easily get couch- and TV-bound in the country as you can in the city: cable, satellite dishes and rotating or rusting antennae keep us ruralites more or less tuned in. But I can be in the woods or upriver and into silence in minutes. Nature is so accessible. And partly because of that, so inviting.

I once asked Kurt to think about how he, as a country boy, might be different from, say, his city cousins Darren and Laura. "If we're all walking along and we see a snake or a beetle, I want to stop and look. They're not as interested," he says. One might think that the opposite might be true: that being so close to creatures and semi-wild space, Kurt would lose interest in nature. Not so. Our little ecosystem in Camden East — our lawn in particular when I let it get too long in summer — is the hunting ground of garter snakes and frogs and bizarre beetles.

In the summer of 1995, the three of us witnessed, twice in a twelve-hour period, something we had never witnessed before: a garter snake devouring a frog. The first spectacle we observed in late evening under the glare of a flashlight, the second under the morning sun. Both lasted at least half an hour. We were drawn in both cases by the birdlike, plaintive cries of the victim, and were tempted to interfere, but did not.

What was extraordinary was the snake's technique, how it managed to keep a grip on the frog's one foot while reaching for the wildly flailing other. The mouth stretched horribly, steadily. It was a magnificent trick. The frog, for its part, made ever more pitiable and weaker noises. The final moments saw the snake's eyes and the frog's eyes almost come together, the two heads piggybacked like some grotesque hood ornament.

This regular contact with the natural world, though not always pretty and usually far less dramatic, nevertheless counts for something. Human society matters, all right, but it's *not* all there is.

Gardening is also contact with the natural world. You get earth on your hands, you get low to the ground, get tired and sore, sometimes you get mad when the potato bugs breed faster than you can pick them off. But it's absorbing work, as ancient an activity as there is. And when you garden you plug into that continuum, and you forget — for a time, anyway — all the things that TV says we have to buy.

I know, I know. City people garden too, and I am glad of it. When I was a boy in Scarborough, only Italian immigrants ploughed up their backyards to grow tomatoes and grapes. We thought them odd; that's all changed now and gardening has most of us in its grip. But inner-city people are either deprived of that privilege or till minuscule plots, sometimes desperately. Lacking any backyard to speak of, Ulrike's mother grows a few tomato plants in pots on a second-floor walkway — only there does the sun penetrate the inner-city canopy of trees. But even so, she must place the plants in a wire cage to protect them from marauding squirrels.

People who live in condominiums or apartments may turn to community gardening, in which a family is allotted a certain space to grow vegetables. It is a fine idea, but prize tomatoes — prized the more because ersatz winter tomatoes are so awful — tend to get pinched, say my friends who garden this way.

The frustration of these gardeners is amplified, in part, by their fanaticism. I saw a survey in the *New York Times* in which the number of American gardeners growing vegetables between 1993 and 1994 increased by 10 million. Sales of lawn and garden materials are increasing steadily in the United States by 10 per cent each year. Americans — here is a yardstick — annually spend more on gardens than on pizza!

Canadian data suggest the same trend, which is especially noticeable among the baby-boom generation. Revenues from the garden and landscaping industry in Canada, estimated at $5.4 billion a year in 1992, doubled in the past decade. Eighty per cent of Canadians now garden in one way or another. What is driving all this?

Michele Landsberg, the author and *Toronto Star* columnist, wrote a piece in May 1995 describing what sustained her after she was diagnosed with breast cancer a year earlier. Family and friends certainly, but what she really wanted to talk about was her garden. She found that studying the hues and filaments of a clematis blossom would quell the cancer-induced terror — "and happiness would fill me like cool water rising in a glass."

Landsberg filled her head with knowledge from gardening books and magazines, nosed around nurseries by the hour, saw flowers as if for the first time. A line of poetry from Canadian poet Lorna Crozier stuck with her: "The garden going on without us."

"I've no idea why such a reminder of my own mortality should have soothed me," Landsberg wrote. "Maybe, on my knees in the grass, I could feel comforted by being part of nature's great wheel. This year, with spring and regained health, I was doubly and richly rewarded: I'm astonished at how much I tilled and worked and planted, and how much beauty has come rushing back to delight me. I am grateful, grateful to the garden."

The village puts me close to what Landsberg calls "nature's great wheel." In the fields and forests near our house, the cycles of dearth and abundance work themselves out from year to year.

One winter we were overrun by rabbits. The evidence of rabbitry was everywhere: on cross-country ski trails around the village I could see by the fur and blood in the snow where a coyote or hawk had dined on one here, another one there. Rabbits darted among village hedgerows at dawn and four or five gathered at night under our bird-feeder to nibble at fallen seed, to gnaw at our apple boughs and raspberry canes. I applied urine, which is said to repel rabbits, to the canes. I applied it, in direct fashion, at night, our garden being dark enough for such bold preventive measures.

Rabbits, mice, tent caterpillars, June bugs, wasps, flying ants, cluster flies, ladybugs — the waves come to let you know how small you really are, how someone else is in charge. I do not mind the feeling, nor do I mind peeing in the cold in the garden below stars.

We are doomed to be self-obsessed creatures, but nature spells occasional relief, for its says, "Stop. Look outward. Look at this!" In 1989, two University of Michigan psychologists, Rachel and Stephen Kaplan, examined the benefits of wilderness trips and discovered that participants found them profoundly restful, even healing and restorative. "They found nature more powerful, and at the same time more comforting," the authors wrote, "than they had ever imagined; they left the wilderness at the end of the trip worrying about how they could maintain their contact with this unexpectedly significant environment." A hundred other studies of wilderness experience all found the same thing.

What I have observed, on whitewater canoeing trips into northern Ontario, is that when you move through wild places, time stretches. A day on a river is a long time; a week is like a month; two or three weeks feel like a season. In the city we are always looking ahead, ever mindful of the clock. In the wilderness, there is only food, shelter, this journey, this paddle stroke and the next and the next and the next, the body hardening with each one. Demands made, demands met.

A wilderness trip, a walk in a park, a stroll through your own garden: all are aspects of the same thing, and their power to restore has been known a long time. Frederick Law Olmstead, the landscape architect who created, for example, Central Park in New York City, argued in the 1860s that visual contact with nature improved psychological and emotional well-being. "The attention is aroused," he wrote, "and the mind occupied without purpose."

Many scientists now believe he was right. One study found that students stressed by exams relaxed when shown colour slides of rural settings. Slides of urban scenes had no beneficial effect; better, though, were slides of urban scenes with at least *some* vegetation.

Following surgery, patients given a room overlooking a grove of trees recover more quickly and require fewer painkillers. Views of greenery reduce, almost immediately, blood pressure and muscle tension. Breast cancer patients get on with their lives more quickly when they tend plants, or even enjoy them from a distance. Two groups of prisoners were once studied. The jail cells of one group looked onto farmland and forests; the other overlooked the prison yard. Guess which group reported fewer calls for health care?

You need not be in nature to enjoy its benefits, just be able to see it or be close to it. Ease of access to nature was shown in one national American study to be the strongest predictor of satisfaction with where you live. In another study, only marital circumstance ranked higher. "Nature," concluded Rachel Kaplan, "is not merely an amenity, luxury, frill, or decoration. The availability of nearby nature meets an essential human need."

CBC Radio broadcaster Shelagh Rogers works in Toronto, lives in Eden Mills. Her job is stressful, the village restful: she knows this in her heart. Her house backs onto the Eramosa River, and its greenery and wildlife calm and delight her as the Napanee River calms and delights me. Shelagh once had her blood pressure tested in each location, city and village. There was an astonishing ten-point difference.

But wouldn't any home — whether in the city or in the country — be more relaxing than any office? Doesn't *that* explain the difference? "No," said Shelagh, and she was adamant. "My place in the city was extremely stressful. Neighbours played heavy metal music and there were stabbings in the area. Now, when I walk along the river after a day at work, I find it so restorative. I feel grimy, almost soiled in the city, and going home to the country washes it all away."

You can live in the country and not be touched by nature at all, but you'd have to be wearing oversized blinkers. One day this past summer I wheelbarrowed our ailing piston pump — an old one we use for watering the garden directly from the river — up to Lyle's garage for his diagnosis. "Motor's shot." Pretty soon a beer was thrust in my hand, and neighbours there got telling bird stories. Virginia Thompson had seen a loon on the river. Don Simpson had observed three red-tailed hawks circling north of the village.

My offering was to describe a great horned owl that, one night the week before, had cosied up to its plastic counterpart on our TV aerial. I had been out on the deck for my nightly constitutional and had seen a massive dark shape above the roof. Puzzled, I had moved towards the house and the bird had exploded into motion. I was dumbfounded both by the size of its wings and the sound they made as the owl lifted off and took up new lodgings in the maple out front, crashing through the branches with the delicacy of a fullback.

A few days later, in midafternoon, I looked up into that same maple because robins there were making a terrible racket. A large crow was poised over their nest, about to take nestlings, while both robins dive-bombed it. I was as angry as the robins were, but helpless to intervene, for the nest was forty feet up. "Hey!" I boomed, and the crow took off, robins in hot pursuit.

Nature has the power to make us pause and reflect, and we are starting to make conscious use of it. Those who work with prisoners, with the mentally ill, with Alzheimer's patients, with the alcohol- and drug-addicted, all know that growing things or being in their midst has a healing effect. Horticultural therapy is a new name for an age-old treatment.

In ancient Egypt, physicians urged their "disturbed" patients to take walks in the garden. In the sixteenth century, it was thought that the discipline and regimen of farm life would restore order to the psyche of deranged patients. In the 1800s a Scottish psychiatrist had patients working on his farm. "The physical activity of working the soil," he said, "appeared to alleviate many emotional problems." And in 1896, three American authors published a book called *Darkness and Daylight or Lights and Shadows of New York Life,* in which they described the effect of plants on street urchins:

"In the schoolyard a small greenhouse was built on top of the bathhouse. The best children in the school were allowed to take a plant home with them, and if they brought it back in a few months, improved and well cared for, they received others as premiums. Soon in the windows of the poorest, most tumble down houses and tenement rookeries one saw flowers growing, or met the little savages of the district carrying a plant more carefully than they did the baby entrusted to their care."

The plant/people relationship, say those who have thought deeply about it, is ancient and for that reason a comfort. For primitive humans — and we show few signs of having outgrown our primitivity — green space meant refuge and food. We still feel that in our bones.

Gardening writer Jennifer Bennett, another *Harrowsmith* alumna, is both passionate and dispassionate about gardening. What she says brings us a little closer to understanding why this generation has rediscovered plants.

"Having plants around is important to us because they're alive and still *at the same time*," she says. "Every other living thing moves, which can create some anxiety that's maybe a throwback to the time when we had to catch our supper. But plants aren't going to run away, nor do they just sit there like stones. They're always flowering and producing fruit."

And more, the plant neither knows nor cares whether you are loved or shunned, a "good" person or a "bad" one; it needs you all the same. Even a small garden offers lessons in self-esteem and self-reliance. Plants, it turns out, can bring otherwise forlorn communities together. The literature on plants and people is full of stories describing how rough inner-city neighbourhoods and moribund towns found new hope when volunteers created community flower gardens.

Among our friends in the community, seeds and bulbs, cuttings and produce circulate like tokens. Sundrops from Jane. Yukon Golds to Lyle. Irises from Maria. Bleeding hearts to Marta. Four-o'clocks from Virginia. A little bit you, the tokens say. A little bit me.

All this time in the country, and, like Ulrike, I still admire the fields. How the geometric pattern of bales — some shaped like wheels, others like bricks — alters as you drive past, up a hill or down. I love the summer smells, when you're driving at night with the windows down past fresh-cut hay; how the smell is stronger in valleys and near water. I love the colours: that new green in spring, how the setting summer sun can splash a field of hay with melted copper, how dusk can turn a field to mauve, how the blackbirds swarm in those same fields in the fall, spinning like tornadoes in the cold clear light.

I like to watch a farmer out in a field on a tractor, making perfect furrows in the spring, taking off that last crop in the fall. I like the way cows will often face the same direction, according to the sun and the wind, the way they sit on manure piles in the winter for warmth, how cows when I jog by them look at me with blank bovine curiosity, as if they were seeing a two-legged creature for the very first time.

The daily commute from Camden East to Kingston — a seventy-minute round trip on an old two-lane highway — was no trouble and even a small pleasure for us when we did it in the 1980s. Traffic was a breeze. The sight of those fields, those farmers, those cows, as the seasons wheeled endlessly on, struck us as little moving pictures of contentment.

Farmland is tame land, and to tame it we first made war on it. "Nature, red in tooth and claw," Tennyson wrote. Imagine how pioneers must have cursed the land that some of us now want to get back to. Read Annie Dillard's *The Living*, her fictional account of harrowing life in the American northwest of the nineteenth century. Or Susanna Moodie's *Roughing It in the Bush*, about her life in the woods not all that far from Camden East around the middle part of that century. All those trees to be cleared. How they must have loathed trees! Moodie came to appreciate her new country, but not before first feeling "a hatred so intense that I longed to die, that death might effectually separate us forever."

This was the pioneer legacy, an abhorrence of nature — and it goes back further. Edward O. Wilson, the renowned entomologist and twice winner of the Pulitzer Prize (he alone holds that distinction), observed in his book *Biophilia* that "for millions of years human beings simply went at nature with

everything they had, scrounging food and fighting off predators across a known world of a few square miles ... Nature was
something out there — nameless and limitless, a force to beat
against, cajole, and exploit."

But now, Wilson believes, an inner voice is saying *You went
too far.* The voice whispers how foolish to try controlling nature,
and what joy in simply watching it. Wilson is mesmerized by
the insects, bacteria and fungi by the millions in a handful of
earth. Every species, he says, is like a magic well: the more you
draw, the more there is to draw. *Biophilia* argues that we humans
have an innate tendency to focus on life and its processes. To
dip and dip again into that magic well.

Wilson contends that as we come to understand other organ-
isms, we value them, and ourselves, more. He believes that "to
explore and affiliate with life is a deep and complicated process
in mental development. To an extent still undervalued in phi-
losophy and religion, our existence depends on this propensity,
our spirit is woven from it, hope rises on its currents."

October 24. Water from last night's rain beads in the morning
light on the cedars outside my office like tiny glistening balls
of silver nitrate; ground spiders, I see, have set dewy webs in
the still long grass; I can look out every window and spot paper-
thin leaves circling lazily in the breeze like errant ships.

The harvest is in: herbs hang from rafters in the garage,
the last of the green tomatoes line the kitchen sills and ripen
in the sun, the potatoes and squash are bagged in the mud
room. Ulrike has packed the freezer with peas, tomato sauce
and strawberries.

Out in the garden the pea fences (made of old posts and
chicken wire — what else?) are rolled up and put away for
another year.

The harvest moon showed itself last night and I thought
of our friends up on Bethel Street, Jane and Peter Good, and
the moon walks they take on their farmland. "One night,"
Jane remembers, "when Patrick was little we woke up him and

Allison and all of us — in our pyjamas and nightgowns — put on rubber boots and walked out into the fields. I thought: has it ever been this bright at night before? The land looks so different in moonlight. I see my kids differently in that light. Another night we took out a tape recorder and played the call of a screech owl, and by golly, one answered. It was *so* eerie. I didn't know whether to cheer or scream. Some nights we go out to watch the northern lights dance. The moon walk is such a small thing, but so memorable. There's a kind of freedom in it."

October 31. The morning brings "frost on the pumpkin," and I need only look in our own garden to find the literal frost, the literal pumpkin. Rogue pumpkins at that.

We had, lazily, last year left a jack-o'-lantern to compost in the garden after Hallowe'en, and this summer, camouflaged among the squash leaves, came the thick and fuzzy, wild and insistent tendrils of pumpkins, five of them. A serendipitous orange harvest.

If seasons in the country mark the passing of time, so does tradition. You can get a country person to pause for tradition's sake; I am not sure the city ever pauses in quite the same way.

Hallowe'en remains a much-anticipated event around the village, and I am struck by how elaborately country people decorate their houses and properties beforehand. Every year in Newburgh, the same villager concocts a spook house — with fake graves on the lawn, a "body" in the driveway, a chain-saw massacre theme in the garage and ghoulish music playing from speakers. For weeks before tricks or treats, sheeted white ghosts are strung from the branches of old maples, straw people with orange pumpkin heads are arranged on porches, black-hatted witches set out along driveways.

Tonight, as soon as darkness drops, they will come to our door in waves of two and three, gleeful village creatures so keenly costumed and masked we know them only by their chaperoning parents waving from the sidewalk, watching their children haul in pillowcases of candy, wishing for a dental plan.

November

PLANNING THE GREAT ESCAPE

I believe in fate, or something like it. Circumstance brought me to this village, to this old house in rural Ontario not ten miles from the rock-rich, dirt-poor farm near Tamworth where I spent many summers as a child. My grandparents doted on me then, as later I would dote on them. Coming to Camden East was like coming home, but only later did I see that.

After my grandfather Leonard Flynn died one night in his sleep during his ninetieth year, in November 1982, we buried him in the church cemetery at Erinsville near the farm. The sky that day seemed a shifting battleground of grey and black clouds, the wind from some roiling northern sea, as we stood around the coffin and watched its descent. Wise to the end, Leonard was a storytelling genius, delighted in human company, now and then cheated at euchre and made mischief whenever he could. For me, he *was* the country. And if I came back to the country I knew as a child, I was also re-embracing him and his good wife, whom he called the Mother.

Witold Rybczynski talks of *feng-shui* in his book *The Most Beautiful House in the World*. The Chinese word means wind and water and it describes a complex method of divining whether a prospective site is auspicious, or not. My house, my village seemed right both to live in and, when the time came, to wake my Irish grandfather. I obeyed an instinct that said "This is the place. Here." Ulrike was of the same mind: we knew this house would be home the minute we entered it.

I once wrote some doggerel verse — I called it "Ode to a Celtic King and Queen" — to mark the fifty-seventh wedding anniversary of Leonard and Gertrude Flynn three years before my grandfather died. Ulrike, a fair calligrapher, set it out on parchment in black ink and drew a green harp at the bottom before framing it. It's home-made poetry, all right, but some lines seem prescient, and I wonder as I read it now (for it's come back to me and hangs on my office wall) how many like me have gone from the city to the country in search — without realizing it — of childhood memories.

Michael Pollan, editor-at-large of *Harper's* magazine, penned a smart rumination on the garden called *Second Nature: A Gardener's Education*. "Much of gardening," he wrote, "is a return, an effort at recovering remembered landscapes." Later in the book he writes that "some private Eden shadows every garden."

I take Pollan at his word. My garden, my country life, connect me in a way to a treasured past. In his youth, my grandfather rode the rails west, built roads north of Napanee, drove logs on the Napanee River. But for most of his life he farmed. Grew things. Had cows, horses (giant gentle Clydesdales named Bessie and Queenie), pigs (I remember the day one was butchered by the driveshed, can hear its screams, can recall Nanna frantically pulling down blinds and striving to keep us from the windows), geese (which chased and terrorized us), chickens (which we chased and terrorized), and there were always a dog or two, always collies, and cats to catch the mice.

The farm seemed such a bountiful place. We took back to the city maple syrup by the gallon tin, apples by the bushel, heavy jars of preserved raspberries and pears and sweet pickles, trunkloads of potatoes. Grandpa must have missed those spuds when they left the farm. Sold it for a song in 1962.

The tiny house on a working-class street they retired to in Kingston had a backyard, but Leonard Flynn had no use for it, other than as ground for potatoes, with a few feet stingily allotted to other vegetables. The high porch at the front afforded a semi-panoramic view of Markland Street, and on good days he occupied there a swinging metal couch; inside, an oak rocking chair with flat armrests gave him a similar vantage.

He was a man always looking out, taking it all in, but in another sense, giving it all away. Children on the street soon realized he was a soft touch for candy money; little kids chased by bigger ones sought sanctuary there. The Flynns drew people of all ages, like a pot-bellied stove draws toes of all sizes in winter.

Neither prosperous nor poor, Leonard Flynn was a good horse trader with a reputation for coaxing fair harvests even from reluctant land. He had many hats, huge hands and a philosopher's knack for seeing silver linings. This latter gift convinced him he was rich in ways that count, and when the government sent him a pension cheque every month he could not believe his good fortune. All this, for being old. Home was where he held court, and the stream of visitors was constant: his son and two daughters or his twenty-one grandchildren. When he was happy he whistled and told yarns and went on road trips to visit family; he whistled and palavered and travelled constantly.

In the spring the snow had barely gone before he started planting his Pontiacs and Irish Cobblers. I get the same fever each spring, remembering how my grandmother adored new potatoes. I remember the pink hollyhocks in her flower garden along the high picket fence (a portion of it stands yet), and I cannot see hollyhocks without seeing her. She gave us — my many brothers and sisters and cousins — the run of the farm, overruled our parents when we ran wild, fed us pie till we finally declined.

Gertrude Flynn was a great star in our galaxy and we, her grandchildren, moved in her orbit like so many tiny satellites. "Well hello my little man," she would say to me when I was a boy, expressing amazement at how I had grown since last seen, how handsome I had become, how perfect in every way.

I was not perfect, but she was. When she died, at ninety-four, her funeral was of a kind reserved for bishops, the mass concelebrated by three priests, with one actually using the word *saint* in his eulogy. She had been a school teacher, almost as beautiful in her youth as her twin sister, Loretta, and though content by the rules of her generation to listen to others, to cook for others, she was an educated woman for her time and an engaging conversationalist, especially on politics.

She went to mass daily, three times on Sunday. But her piety was personal, not something she inflicted on anyone. Gertrude Flynn, née Dalton, loved what she called foolishness — a room full of people all talking at once, competing for laughter and doing whatever it took. When she laughed, and she laughed easily, her eyes closed shut, and her ample body shook like the jelly she insisted on serving with potatoes. Markland Street and the farm before it were like drop-in centres: everyone was always welcomed, always fed. "Sit in, sit in," she would say, pointing to the dining-room table, then whipping up the meal as if you were a field hand anxious to get back to haying.

My private Eden, to come back to Michael Pollan's phrase, was that farm at Tamworth, and all manner of smells and sounds and tastes can call it up again. The feel of hot milk on my skin recalls my grandfather nailing us as we passed him at his milking stool. The taste of warm milk conjures my grandmother's breakfasts, the milk still warm in the puffed wheat — too warm, I complained. The way light slants through barnboard calls to mind days in the hayloft, a rope hanging from the rafters, us swinging like pirates and dropping into seas of straw. The hollow feel of a hand pump as it draws air from below, then the full gushing sound as it grips water — this takes me back to the small kitchen-sink pump, and from there to the cookstove and the pies. The sight of children playing in the rain serves up a remembered scene of naked siblings and cousins, shivering gleefully below a gushing rainspout, my grandfather laughing at the doorway. Maybe we asked his permission, knowing he'd say yes. Maybe the idea was his.

Why does the countryside exert such a pull on some people? My gut feeling is that to go to the country is to embrace something old and faintly familiar. Janet Rosenberg, an award-winning Toronto landscape architect who helps clients design the gardens of their dreams, says, "People are interested in what they had as children. They remember the smell of lilacs, they remember watching the ants on the peonies. They have these images of what they want to create."

For Michael Pollan, a fragrant strawberry can conjure up an ill-conceived market garden that he and his friend Jimmy Brancato once grew. "As everyone knows," he says, "it is not so much the eye that summons the gardens of childhood, but the nose." Inhaling the perfume of fresh strawberry can call up that garden for Pollan, complete with the image of Brancato bent over a hoe. "For me the acrid chemical smell of Ortho Rose Dust," Pollan adds, "still has the power to summon an August afternoon in my grandfather's garden. Not terribly romantic, but there it is."

The graveyard in Erinsville affords a view of a small emerald lake, which I am sure my grandfather appreciates, along with the company of the Irish dead. With him are great numbers of Cassidys, Donahues, Doyles, Flanagans, Kearnses, Murphys (a great many Murphys), Finns, Gaffneys, Hooleys and, of course, Flynns. The stones, all facing the setting sun, declare that some of those below came from Counties Wicklow, Meath and Wexford in the eighteenth and nineteenth centuries.

I like the feel of the Church of the Assumption cemetery. From the farm right next door come the sounds of cows in conversation, calls that would have been familiar to those buried here. But for the stirrings of the farm and of birdsong in the hedgerows, it is quiet. A solitary beech grows in the centre of the graveyard, which is presided over on its high eastern flank by a life-sized brown crucifix.

One tiny white stone on the hilltop, set flat into the earth, finds words to describe a better future than perhaps the hard farm life. It goes:

Beneath this stone I'm doomed to lie
Till the last trump comes sounding by
And the Angel beck'ng o'er my tomb
Saying rise John Murphy rise and come.

The Celtic monuments, the sheer Irishness of the place, help explain why so many people in Erinsville (*Erin* is the poetic name for Ireland), though born in Canada, as Leonard and Gertrude Flynn were, spoke with an Irish accent. My grandfather used *me* as an adjective (as in "Where's me slippers?"), said *gar*-antee for guarantee, began stories with "I mind the time" and not "I remember," and was often asked by strangers how long he had been in Canada.

When our patriarch died, all the grandchildren and uncles and aunts returned to our house in Camden East to drink to his memory. Old memories, fresher ones. I remembered how he slapped his knee and laughed at my complaint that the rooster I bought at a farm auction crowed all night and kept me up. In anger I once put the rooster in a feed bag and he still crowed. Maybe, it occurred to me, light was entering the feed bag? I put the bagged rooster in the dark basement and *still* he crowed. In the end, my grandfather made potpie out of him.

I'll bet he had fun telling that story to his cronies, many of them retired farmers like himself. Easier, he might have said, to take the boy out of the city than to take the cock-a-doodle-doo out of the country.

My own coming to the country, and to familiar country at that, seemed preordained. Circumstance took me to Kingston, noise sent me packing, a village took me in. Your own journey from the city to that place in the country you are keen to call home may be as serendipitous. Some people plan their departure like a military campaign, wisely leaving nothing to the imagination.

They do the smart things. They talk, and they listen.

They talk to friends with homes or cottages in the region under scrutiny to get a sense of the place through the seasons, not just when the grass is high and winter impossible to imagine.

They spend weekends there in bed-and-breakfast places. Proprietors of B&Bs tend to put a rosy hue on the locality, for they hope guests will remember it fondly and return; on the other hand, they are deeply interested in both the history of their community and its future. At least they can offer names and numbers of key people in the community.

Talk to people in stores, on the streets, in cafés. Eavesdrop on conversations. Drop into the hardware store and ask the kinds of questions I would have put to Ferd Hartman when I moved to the village. Do "cidiots," as I have heard them called, get the rolled eyes and a brushoff? Or genuine help?

The operative word in a move as big as the one from city to country is *careful.* Before you move into that lovely century farmhouse on the hill, take a pad of paper and make a long list of questions. Then seek answers. When you think you have the perfect house, but have doubts, hire the services of a private building inspector, someone coolly rational who will act as a counter to your romantic longings. Someone, say, like Don Tubb.

If you drive directly south from Camden East you will eventually hit Lake Ontario. A ferry there will take you to Amherst Island, where about four hundred people live on farms and cottages. There you will find the sheep farm that Tubb operates with some others. He has lived on the island since 1973, and he helps put out a small monthly newspaper called the *Amherst Island Beacon.* My sense is that Tubb feels committed to his community and to country life, but not blindly so. He sees clearly, and if you get close to signing a mortgage on a place in the country, you would be wise to have someone like him look before you leap.

"It must be quiet where you live," I say. Quiet, Tubb replies, is a relative term. When the wind is right, or rather wrong, he can hear the intercom at the Ontario Hydro plant three miles away on the mainland. All during the summer he keeps a fan going as white noise in his bedroom. "The owls," he says, "drive me nuts."

What Tubb does have, unreservedly on the farm where he also operates his building inspector business, is space. And it is the desire for space, he believes, that is in large part driving people from city to country. "They want space to swing their arms around in," he tells me. "People get claustrophobic in the city." But in their desire to escape, they sometimes let the heart rule when the brain might have saved them.

"It's a romantic notion, moving to the country," says Tubb. "Maybe it's an irrational notion. People buy five, ten acres, more than they can ever handle. They don't realize the time it takes to cut an acre of lawn" — five to six hours — "or the cost of a riding lawn mower" — $2,000 at least. Or the time and skill it takes to build and maintain fence lines sometimes required on a big farm property.

Where you might see a century farmhouse with ginger-breading on the porch as a dream home, Tubb might on closer inspection sketch a drafty, uninsulated old house built by a tippling carpenter in hard times using second-rate materials, a house that will require rigorous upkeep and a skilled upkeeper. Flatly he says: "A hundred-year-old farmhouse can mean a big drop in the quality of life." Such a house might be heavenly for a handy tinkerer, hellish for the uninitiated.

For $225, Tubb will play what he calls the big detective game: he will assess the house's strengths and weaknesses. Find the fatal flaw, if there is one. Paint a picture of what needs to be done to the house, what maintenance is required, and what might happen if it's not done. Ensure that house and buyer are well matched. If they are not, moving to the country can be like stepping into a cow pie.

To repeat: in the country (here I mean villages and concession roads), water and sewage — and all that go with them — are the homeowner's responsibility. Tubb's job, your job if you are up to it, is to avoid post-purchase surprises, and he strongly advises that you get answers to questions such as the following.

Is the well up to the demands you will put on it? It may have been fine for the older couple who occupied the place for forty years, but will it deliver on demand to your dishwasher, to your teenagers' epic showers, to the Jacuzzi you have planned, or to the enlarged vegetable garden you want to water even through droughts? Mortgage lenders, says Tubb, now want wells to deliver no less than four gallons a minute, which is not much. Find out who drilled the well, and get that report.

Has the water been tested for contaminants? Private companies and local health units will test for fecal bacteria and residue from fertilizers and herbicides. These tests can be cheap or expensive, depending on what they're looking for.

How old is the septic system? If it's been regularly pumped and maintained, it could last many decades. If not, you might have to replace it. The tank may be old and small, too small for a large family. Ask if the system has ever malfunctioned, and if so, talk to the firm that fixed it. You would be amazed at the encyclopedic memories of backhoe operators and honey-wagon drivers.

Get a quote from a local contractor to see the going rate for a new one. Look in the yellow pages under Septic Tanks — Installation. Health inspectors are rigorous these days, and a good thing too, but they are especially stiff and unyielding — because of pollution concerns — whenever a septic system is installed on waterfront property. In some cases, there is insufficient land to accommodate a conventional system, and the only alternative is a costly one, a large holding tank that must be pumped out every month.

How far away are emergency services — fire, police, ambulance? Your house insurance will be higher depending on your distance from firefighters, who could all be volunteers lacking the equipment and technical knowledge of their counterparts in the city. The response time from a volunteer fire department is remarkably quick, but not as quick as in the city. If the volunteers arrive on the scene of a fire at an older clapboard house and ten minutes have elapsed since the fire started, they will not enter the building. They presume that its collapse is imminent. This is the speed of fire in an old house.

Increasingly, estate houses built in the country have a pond constructed nearby. What appears to be an esthetic complement to the house is also a source of water for firefighters. Insurance companies take note and cut their fire insurance fees accordingly. Without hydrants or a water source nearby, rural firefighters often have to fight a fire cautiously. A city pumper may throw 6,000 litres of water per minute at a fire; an older rural pumper may call on 4,000 litres per minute — but only if the water supply is continuous. A house near a river or lake thus has a better chance in a fire.

If you do buy a house in the country, you can have the house inspected at no cost by a member of the local fire department. The firefighter will examine the fuse box, furnace, dryer and water heater and suggest ideal locations for smoke detectors.

Finally, my own insurance company recently sent us a note that describes a $75 annual surcharge to be levied in 1996 on all policyholders who use woodstoves. Having our stoves examined by a qualified inspector will reduce the surcharge to $25. But it seems clear that fire losses to insurance companies from woodburning stoves are high. The fire department will, for a small fee, examine the chimney and woodstove and check for proper clearances from walls. The certification may save you grief later on.

If the first question is, How high are the taxes, the second question should be, What do I get for them? The answer, warns Don Tubb, may be apparently very little. You look after your own water and septic requirements, you typically take your own garbage to the dump, and the police, medical and fire protection may pale beside what you had in the city. And yet you may be shocked by how relatively high your property taxes are. The rates vary wildly from township to township: those with meagre populations and little industry (i.e., no tax base) hit up property-owners to keep schools open and roads paved.

We paid about $1,000 in property taxes in Camden East in 1995. One of my brothers lives in a house the same size as ours but in a fairly upscale neighbourhood in Toronto (which city he loves, by the way): he paid $3,000. Neighbours not far from him pay $4,000. I do not envy him his tax bill, but there are times when I wish for more services too.

On the other hand, says Tubb (an "on the other hand" sort of guy), many costs of country living are hidden. Rural municipalities, for example, must often dig costly test wells at landfill sites and monitor them over the course of years.

Get to know the township clerk, advises Tubb. "The township clerk is the most important person in the whole township," he says. No one works harder. No one knows the area better. In my experience, township clerks are knowledgeable and discreet. They can tell you about the township debt load, about new projects that may burden taxpayers, about the location of any polluting industries. They can tell you where the nearest quarry is, whether plans are afoot for more and what the likely truck route is. They can tell you where the nearest landfill site is, whether your area is being targeted for city garbage, and all about the road in front of the place you might buy.

A word or two on roads is probably in order here. A quiet concession road sounds nice in principle, but such roads tend to be unpaved and dusty. I know someone who lives on such a road, and his house has been set well back from the road for privacy. A good thing too: his family's laundry would otherwise easily coat with dust from even the odd passing car. The vents of his own car plug up badly and regularly from driving through dust clouds. Wags are forever writing on the rear of his car, Wash Me.

A house removed from the road may well offer privacy. But a long driveway will require a snowblower or tractor — or a kind neighbour — to keep it clear in winter. If the driveway is dirt, not asphalt or gravel, it may become icy in winter, muddy in spring, dusty in summer and fall. And if security is a concern, then houses unseen from the road can become primary targets.

For years, it seemed, house break-ins were rare around Camden East. We felt almost immune in our house, with the river behind us and vigilant neighbours all round. Then one day a few years ago, Larry McCormick had his car stolen from outside the store in midday; he had left the keys inside, as country people often do. He is now cured of the habit. Theft is still rare, but people on the outskirts of the village now and again lose tools and VCRs to thieves during brazen daylight raids. Houses out of sight on back roads seem particularly vulnerable. A friend outside the village has posted a handmade sign on his doors that reads: "No money, no booze, computer and VCR 20 years old. Nothing worth your risk."

On the other hand, a paved road — especially a flat stretch — may be an inviting track for speeders. I like winding and hilly roads because they force me and everyone else to slow down; road engineers apparently despise them and are forever ironing them out. Township make-work projects.

A road you might choose to live on is one used by school buses: such roads are by necessity maintained and snowploughed early and often in winter.

What are the house's windows like? Our house had old-style storm windows, about three feet wide by six feet high and held in place by sash-fasteners. Removing second-storey windows in spring and reinstalling them in fall was a high-wire act requiring an extra set of arms and a head for heights. I lacked both. Modern, efficient windows with screens are in several ways a smart investment but extremely expensive, so if the windows are old, get an estimate on at least replacing the upstairs windows — which is what we did — and then brace yourself for a shock.

Ask, too, how well the house is insulated and how old the furnace is; the old ones are appallingly inefficient. Examine heating bills and hydro records. Get a fix on what it will cost to keep the house warm in winter. If there are no large shade trees on the south and west sides, expect the house to be hot in summer.

Are the telephone lines adequate for your needs? When we moved into Camden East, it was a long-distance call to Kingston, and those charges added up alarmingly. If you intend to set up an office in your new country place, find out whether fax and modem lines are available and how much they cost.

Zoning in the country often makes for strange bedfellows. If the zoning allows your would-be neighbour to operate a framing shop, then you will have the daily whine of a radial saw to contend with. If the house sits on a side road, are there plans to build more houses nearby? And what might that do to your well? I know a farmer who lived in the same house for decades and never lacked for water — until bungalows began popping up on his road like mushrooms overnight. Is your well safe from contamination by cow or horse manure? Proximity of tilled fields to the house is an important consideration if the farmer uses chemicals that can drift during spraying and foul the well. And before you buy a house in the country, talk to your prospective neighbours and get a sense of how neighbourly, or not, they appear to be.

Subscribe to the local newspaper for six months or more. Most smalltown newspapers want to avoid bad news, preferring to accentuate the positive and to make their editorial pages safe havens for advertisers. Nevertheless, the *Weekly Gleaner* and its ilk do paint over time a composite picture of an area — the burning issues as they appear in letters to the editor, the price of day care and real estate, employment opportunities (or lack thereof), community events, the latest crises, such as house fires, and how people respond to them, when and where the auctions are.

Talk to the newspaper's editor. What is that person's take on the community? Is there an active community organization? Corruption on town council? Might planned developments affect the local water supply or taint the air? Is the school being eyed for closure, and is it any good?

Realtors, like tame weeklies and B&B operators, err on the bright side. But they too can be a source of valuable information. Sometimes their data tell a story. If housing prices in a community, for example, have doubled in recent years, then you can expect high turnover in the neighbourhood as locals bail out of a market they can no longer afford and newcomers hop on the real-estate meteor.

If you are prepared to stuff your belongings in a U-haul and hit the road, you might consider one of ten towns identified by *Chatelaine* magazine in its April 1992 issue. The magazine regularly consults relocation experts to identify what it calls ideal places to live, though its notion of ideal has undergone a radical transformation.

In 1988, experts told *Chatelaine* that Canadians preferred "urban centres with strut and swagger." By 1991, city house prices and "unsettled" big-city life, the experts said, saw Canadians seeking towns or cities where community spirit and family-oriented activities might thrive. By 1992, the long recession, the Gulf War and apparent surges in urban crime, race-related problems and homelessness had taken their toll: Canadians now listed affordable housing and safety as top priorities. Things you can find, relocation experts were saying, in small places.

The experts selected ten towns: Penticton, B.C.; Okotoks, Alberta; Sarnia and Waterloo in Ontario; Kirkland, Quebec; Sussex, New Brunswick; Truro, Nova Scotia; Charlottetown, P.E.I., and Grand Falls–Windsor, Newfoundland.

None of the towns cited were mentioned in another resource worth looking at, *The Townsearch Guide: Your Handbook for*

Finding the Best Place to Live. This is a self-published book that considers sixty-four towns across Canada, listing information on average real estate costs, education, recreation and health services, and a brief profile of each community.

The authors, Mark Gauley and his wife, Dale Chambers, both in their late thirties, ex of Winnipeg, Edmonton and, most recently, Vancouver, had tired of what they called the urban treadmill. They chanced upon the story of Rossburn, Manitoba, running an ad in a Toronto newspaper promoting itself as safe, clean and affordable. The dramatic response to the ad, along with demographic data they had seen, told Gauley and Chambers that people all across Canada no longer speculated about moving to the country, they were doing it.

The authors set out to accomplish twin tasks: find their own small town to live in, and write a guidebook to help others find theirs. They sold their house and cars, quit their jobs (he sold eyeglasses, she sold computer systems) and spent four months travelling across the country in a recreational vehicle, checking out small towns along the way. They finally settled in St. Andrews, New Brunswick, and there in the summer of 1995 published their handbook.

The Townsearch Guide is a useful enough survey, and what I found astonishing is the low price of real estate in some western towns — $35,000 will get you a decent house in Snow Lake, Manitoba. The weakness of the book is the smallish number of towns surveyed, and the profiles are written by the communities themselves, who paid a listing fee. Those expecting critical analysis, not boosterism, must look elsewhere.

Mark Gauley, for his part, has no regrets about their move. He told me that in the year they have lived in St. Andrews they have come to know more people than in five years in Vancouver. "The climate is great, the people are great. There's a good sense of community." His advice to anyone pondering a new life beyond cities is just "get in the car and go." Talk to as many people in the town as you can, he said, and take your time: "I'd avoid being too quick to pick my spot."

I could find no independent guide to smalltown Canada, but perhaps that is as it should be. The ideal town or village does not exist. Weather, architecture, landscape, proximity to urban centres and cultural amenities, makeup of the population, cost of real estate, the work available locally or nearby — these are all matters of personal preference. Guidebooks and magazine articles may cause you to investigate a certain community, but you must trust your own judgement.

One way of at least gaining a sense of rural life is to swap houses for a weekend with a country friend or relative, or house-sit when someone you know goes away on vacation or sabbatical. It won't be the same as actually living in the country, but if you find being there comforting, your hunch will have been confirmed.

If you already own a city house, you might want to hedge your bets. Rent the city place and do the same in the country until certainty sets in that you have found the right spot, that, as in my own case, heart and mind agree: "This is the place. Here."

November 8. Overnight frosts have dispatched all the flowers in Ulrike's various gardens save for the chrysanthemums and, by Kurt's old playhouse, some rugged mauve hollyhocks. I can see them from the kitchen door and will officially log in winter when I wake up one morning and find them black and limp.

The river is a river again thanks to heavy fall rains. All the rocks exposed in summer are once more hidden, the current once again has both heft and speed. This morning I see from the kitchen a great blue heron at the base of the U-shaped hollow in the bank where the stairs lead down to the river. I freeze when his stern golden eye meets mine, hoping he will think me a piece of furniture, which he evidently does, for he goes on fishing as before.

Hunters in bright hats with ear flaps and long loud jackets — from a distance the men look like oversized orange popsicles — are huddled these mornings outside McCormick's. I see pickup trucks parked at random on the side of roads, pass several gun-toting popsicles out in fields staring intently into the trees, hear the odd shot in the woods to the north. Deer season. Not a time for nature walks.

November 14. Goodbye hollyhocks, hello early winter. Over at McCormick's, Chuck Clark has issued a storm warning. By way of preparation, I move the red canoe from its summer spot on the riverbank to its winter lodgings in the rafters of the garage, set out four bird-feeders along the bank and put heavy stump-sized blocks of wood in the back of the pickup to aid with traction in the snow. A few inches of the wet stuff drape the ground and the trees. The dozens of sparrows and finches in the cedar hedge no longer seek insects there, but refuge.

November 15. I don't have to raise the bedroom curtain to know what's out there. My ears tell me. The usual morning stirrings of the village are lost in the falling snow. Eight inches of the heavy stuff have already fallen. The cedar hedge is splayed and bowed in the middle under the snow's great weight, as if an ogre has been sitting on it, and my very first task in the morning — even pre-coffee — is to take a broom and give the bent conifers and birches a break from the heavy load of snow. No branches snap, but my broom does. School is cancelled. Kurt and his pals build snowforts all day.

This evening he and Ulrike walk along the river road by the now swollen river, the still falling snow muffling all sounds but those from the rapids and the falls. My wife and son walk in a black-and-white silent film, but only the river is black, the village is all in white.

November 19. Spend the afternoon hauling away and chain-sawing about half a cord's worth of dogwood and poplar that has mysteriously collected five feet off the riverbank near the foot of the stairs. The tangle seems haphazard, the kind commandos use in war movies to float down the river past thick guards on bridges. Closer inspection reveals nothing accidental at all about the arrangement, which is brilliantly anchored by heavy deadhead logs in the fast current. It's either a food cache or the start of a lodge.

Beavers. Back, and for the first time in all the time we have lived here, eyeing our backyard as home base.

December

ON THE SIDE OF COUNTRYSIDE

In the early 1980s, the custom of decorating houses with Christmas lights faded around the village. The economy was shuddering and the old notion of plugging in lights suddenly seemed ostentatious, not right for the times. Then, as if to say "recession be damned," the tradition returned and with new vigour. Larry McCormick, for one, never let anything — certainly not hard times or hydro bills — defuse his Christmas spirit. People drive a long way to see his over-the-top many-thousands-of-lights display on the conifers along the river road. One year I counted fifty-six trees with lights on them. The lights lend a twinkling, elfish look to the woods by his house, where life-sized cutouts of reindeer, sleigh and manger folk pose in the floodlights for slow walkers and drivers, sometimes for tour buses.

Years ago Larry built near the bridge a small barnboard manger the size of a shed with cedar-shingle roof. I can see it from a kitchen window. And each Christmas he would lay in straw, a crèche and a wee corral for (his) donkeys and (borrowed) sheep. Crowning the barn is a wire star wound with a string of white lights, flashing each night during the weeks before Christmas.

The manger draws the village — and those on far-flung concession roads for whom Camden East is centreville — out into the cold in mid-December. Drawn to the star as well are three bearded kings, a shepherd or two and a chorus of tiny ski-jacketed cherubs, their ribbed wings edged with tinsel.

Behind us someone tends a crackling bonfire as warmth against the damp cold that comes swirling up from the river, which is these days throwing off steam and turning to ice along its banks. We sing carols, the forty or so of us gathered round the manger, we listen to a nativity reading, and afterwards the wide-eyed kids jump onto a vast tractor-driven, high-framed wagon and sit on bales of hay while riding through the village.

Oh what fun / it is to ride / on a one-horse open sleigh.

The tractor is not one-horse at all, but Fred Galbraith's 125-horse Case International. Immune to the cold, the kids sit singing in the hay wagon in the glare of the tractor's rear highbeams. A single float in a night-time Santa Claus parade, we stare into village windows and wave as we pass; those on the other side of the glass wave back.

We have several Christmas traditions around here. Until it closed, the school in Camden East staged memorable and elaborate concerts. These days there is the concert-cum-talent-night at the United church in Newburgh. Another custom is having neighbours drop in to our house for drinks, mulled wine and German cookies; I pass on the hot wine but I savour the fragrance from the cinnamon sticks that wafts through the whole house. Some of Ulrike's bigger cookies, gingerbread rings inlaid with almonds and glazed green and red half-cherries, are hung with ribbon on the Christmas tree and then put away with the other ornaments for next year. We used to hang them high when Kurt was a toddler because he quite liked four-year-old cookies.

But the one tradition I value most is the tree-trimming at the Smallmans. If my community of friends has a patriarch and a matriarch, it is these two. Bev Smallman is the former head of the biology department at Queen's University, now a hobby farmer and beekeeper. Sue is seventy-odd, Bev is eighty-one.

We buy our honey from them every fall in thirty-gallon pails and are learning to appreciate the subtleties of flavour and texture in fresh honey. Like a grape harvest, every honey crop is different. In 1994, the basswood trees near Bev's hives were heavy with both blossoms and bees, and the yellow and white clover on the roadsides thrived — as did blueweed in the fields, lending a creamy texture to the ensuing bumper crop. Here was honey you wanted to eat by the spoonful. Putting it in tea or on a peanut-butter sandwich was like putting ice in single-malt scotch.

In 1995, the summer-long drought meant that though flowers bloomed they offered little nectar to foraging bees. The honey that Bev took off his hives, though still fine, was sharply reduced in flavour but especially in quantity. Fresh honey, I now know, reflects the weather. It's like looking at a tree stump and measuring the distance between rings. The difference here is that your eyes not your palate reveal meteorological vagaries.

Bev is still the professor, and when he explains all this he does it with his usual enthusiasm. Countless times I have asked him questions, about raising, dispatching and eviscerating chickens, about dealing with wasp nests, powder-post beetles in firewood, tent caterpillars and gypsy moths, and his answers are unfailingly learned and detailed. Invariably he will ring back with some fresh or forgotten insight.

Bev is a humanist. A scientist who puts his faith in science. An atheist who counts among his closest friends deeply religious people. An erudite man who stands in awe of the knowledge of particular locals who possess little formal education.

Drives a heavy brown-and-white GMC truck, an ancient thing, or an ageing blue Tercel with white sheepskin seatcovers. Wears a white Tilley hat cocked up one side Aussie-style and leans forward slightly as he drives. Sports a fringe of grey hair round a naked pate, an artist's white goatee. Has the habit of running the palm of his hand over his dome as he speaks. Squints a little as he launches into an argument, which he manages by good manners never to make personal. Possesses what Ulrike, who is quite taken by them, calls laughing eyes. Like all truly engaging people, he is a storyteller and in his best stories he is the butt of the joke.

Sue is a weaver, an accomplished gardener, someone who combines strong opinion with discretion and diplomacy. She has great love for Bev, and I have seen her gently chide him, to balance his stories when they err on the side of excess. "Mad-keen" is one of his favourite adjectives; mad-keen describes Bev and Sue Smallman.

Conversation with them could range over the mixed blessing of ironwood as firewood (easy to cut because of its slim trunk, devilishly hard to split because, well, they don't call it ironwood for nothing); how to keep raccoons out of your corn patch (black nylon mesh all around, for the coons fear getting their feet caught up in it); the wisdom of an underground sprinkler system in the garden (it dramatically reduces the volume of well water required); the latest news in *The Economist* or *Discovery*, or the social issues of the day. They travel often and widely: in their hallway is a world map thickly dotted with red pegs to mark where they have lived and wandered. One of the highlights of the year is Bev's slide show from the most recent trip — he is a gifted photographer and his travelogue goes down as well as Sue's home-made soup and breads.

The Smallmans are, as Ulrike and I are, converts to country life. But they were here long before we were, and they have taught us much. More than anything, they teach by example the meaning of community. This is why Bev sat on the Camden East Community School's board of directors — when he was older than most pupils' grandparents — and why Sue was such a lynchpin in the ongoing restoration of Macpherson House when no one much wanted the job.

If you move from city to country, may your new community be rich in people like them. It is in their stucco farmhouse midway between Camden East and Yarker that Ulrike, Kurt and I and a dozen or so others in the Smallman circle gather for the tree-trimming just days before Christmas.

It goes like this. Come in the side door, through the always open garage where the ironwood is neatly stacked. Into the kitchen where the Findlay Oval cookstove beckons like a hearth. Potluck dinner set out on white linen and built around the best of the basics: Sue's home-made breads. Turkey and ham and a slew of salads. Aged cheddar and curds from the cheese factory in nearby Wilton. Camembert and its companion, good wine.

Kids toss paper airplanes from the top of the stairs yet restrain themselves. The house has a certain refinement and they feel it. The tree gets trimmed eventually, a trinket at a time as you pass, but that task seems incidental to the real business of the evening — catching up with neighbours after a busy fall. Talk in the kitchen one year turned variously to the teachers' strike/lockout, the intelligence of dogs and whether anyone can imitate the sound that bats make in your attic. A child, puckered in imitation of adults kissing, came closest.

In the living room by the fireplace a neighbour, emboldened by wine, baits Bev on a religious question and he politely declines at first, then lightly spars. In the dining room, the kids are circling the mounds of fresh cookies and Christmas cake like turkey vultures. When, finally, we head out into the cold night, we leave warmer and fuller than when we came. If our friends and neighbours are spread out for miles, we still manage to meet in what feels like the centre — the village, of course, but also that stucco house and tiny farm, the one that Bev mockingly calls SmallManor.

When I ponder the future of small towns and villages, it is always with an eye to the people who live there, for they can make, or break, them. Little places seem so fragile in one way, so durable in another. After spending a year thinking about little places in general, and mine in particular, I am left with the sense that these miniature settlements have much to teach their sprawling counterparts, but the reverse is also true.

And as living in the country becomes less and less distinctive from living in the city, I begin to wonder, What does the small town still have to offer? Is there a distinct rural society any more with so many ex-urbanites coming to the country? Or does living in the country change the way you see the world? This confluence of people and place is fraught with difficulty, but rich in possibility. And I feel compelled, in closing, to look at both.

One Saturday morning — it was April Fool's Day, 1995 — I demonstrated my intelligence by doing two things at once, reading the newspaper and listening to CBC Radio. (These are perhaps the *only* two things I can do at once.) The program was *Fresh Air,* and the subject that day was Maritimers coping with the city, Toronto in particular. Gradually, I became engrossed and put the newspaper down.

The panel of three agreed that among the many things they missed about home — by the ocean will always be home — was what they perceived to be the warmth of their birthplace; the city seemed to them cold by comparison. They missed saying hello to people on the street, even strangers, and getting a response. When decades ago I hitchhiked with my friend David Carpenter all over Newfoundland, we had a name for such a greeting. We called it the Newfie nod, and it consisted of the head moving gently and slightly down towards the chest, then quickly to the left. It said all at once "G'day," "How are ya?" and "Isn't life just the grandest thing?" Almost everyone, even children, gave us — two come-from-away guys with packs on our backs — the nod or some verbal greeting. Two nods, we figured, would be the mark of lunacy, but we never saw two. Just the one and the smile that went with it.

The three Maritimers on the radio were saying that such a nod on city streets would likely be met with a scowl, or worse. They had formed a club where they could meet, eat cod tongues and, I presume, nod to their heart's content. The closest thing to home, they said, was rural Ontario.

In my village it is unusual to walk to the post office or McCormick's without being greeted. Sometimes a trip to the store — forty-five seconds away — takes forty-five minutes because I have stopped to talk with someone, then another villager stops and we either form a threesome or change dance partners. The effect of being helloed to this extent is somehow reassuring. Using Descartes' logic, it is not so much "I think, therefore I am" as "I am greeted, therefore I am."

My friend Wayne Grady once wrote a *Harrowsmith* piece he called "Wave Mechanics": the etiquette involved when country folk pass each other while driving. Grady identified four levels of wave, set out in gradients of familiarity. Here, then, is his code, and you who contemplate moving to the country should pay heed.

1. *The one-finger wave.* The index finger rises casually from the top of the steering wheel. This, says Grady, is "for two people who do not know each other from Adam who generally approve of each other's existence."

2. *The two-finger wave.* A form of "G'day" used between people of casual acquaintance, such as, says Grady, "between you and the electrician whose estimate for rewiring your workshop last July was 30 percent higher than that of the general handyman who eventually got the job."

3. *The full-hand wave.* Meant for two drivers who know each other but do not generally socialize. The hand is still kept on the wheel but all five fingers come up and stay there until the other driver is well past. Grady's translation (and he won a Governor General's Award for French-English translation, so we have to trust him on this): "Hello again. Nice day. Keeping busy, I see. Yeah, I had to go all the way into town for a box of number 8 wood screws. Well, gotta be off. See you later."

4. *The arm wave.* This one, says Grady, has the hand coming off the steering wheel, is accompanied by a smile and is strictly reserved for "some" family members, immediate neighbours and the drivers of school buses and tractors. This wave says it all: "whether the new fertilizer you tried out in the north

hayfield seems to be working, if the silo auger that snapped last week has been welded yet, whether you are still selling brown eggs, and didn't I hear the other day that you applied to the Township Council to sever an acre and a half of waterfront down on Clear Lake?"

5. *The after-wave.* This is my own addition to Grady's list. Not everyone looks into the eyes of oncoming drivers to check for familiar faces. Sometimes the car is past and you have just, out of the corner of your eye, caught a wave motion (#4 — see above). Quickly, you look in your rearview mirror, and if they do the same they will see you throw your left arm out the window and up, like a pupil's in a classroom. This wave says, "Jeepers, Jane, I must be half asleep. How are ya, anyway, and isn't this your *second* trip into Napanee today?"

Soon after Stuart McLean published *Welcome Home: Travels in Smalltown Canada,* I asked him to reflect on all that he had seen and heard on his journeys. This was in the fall of 1992. We talked at length in his home in an older Toronto neighbourhood called Seaton Village, walked his young sons to a nearby rink for a hockey practice and continued talking in the cold stands. Stuart is an affable sort, with sandy curly hair and a storyteller's love of audience. He seemed to know most of the other rink dads.

After living in small towns for weeks at a time, Stuart realized that his own little neighbourhood offers some of the same features. "Everyone in big cities," he told me, "has this romantic notion of small towns. But there are too many pastels in that vision. Likewise, the smalltown vision of cities is too dark, too ominous." True enough. Self-serving stereotypes about big burghs and little ones remain deeply entrenched: the villager thinks of the city as crime-infested, and her home seems sweeter by contrast; the uptowner imagines how dull and incestuous a village, and the bright lights below his fourteenth-floor condo seem to shine that much brighter.

Stuart occupies a more middle ground. In the seven small

towns in which he lingered, he talked to many hundreds of people, and only one person failed to welcome him and answer his queries. That says something about Stuart, something too about smalltown trust. Try stopping people on a busy city street and see how quickly the human traffic flows around you like a river round a rock.

He learned that in smalltown Canada children found their own sanctuaries. A young girl he met would go skinnydipping in a creek and catch catfish; one boy would go to a lighthouse and just watch the sea. "Children in the country," he told me, "get the wind in their hair more than we do. I felt kind of sad that my kids, growing up in the city, don't have that kind of freedom."

Some of these towns are on the ropes, yet Stuart admired in the people he met "their quiet sense of belonging, their sense of place." He kept encountering in these towns quintessentially Canadian touchstones, such as working the family farm, harvesting maple syrup, taking the train, playing hockey on the pond and facing unmitigated winter — all of them, in his eyes, succumbing. To the greenhouse effect. To the global economy. To circumstance.

"When I was in these small towns," said Stuart, "I was mad as hell. I thought, How can we lose this way of life? Small towns are a cradle of values. At our peril we let them die. Would it make any difference to the country if Foxwarren, Manitoba, disappeared? No, but it would make a difference to our sense of ourselves. These are our roots. We grew from this. We would be diminished."

A friend of mine who now lives in Kingston after decades in the country lost his job a while back, and what a great pity, because he was awfully good at what he did. He worked with words and wordsmiths. "What will you do?" I asked him. "We'll live with less," he replied. "And that's not such a bad thing." Those words of his are much in my mind when I look at the case to be made for living in smaller places.

You can make more money in the city but you can live on less in the country. You can cut wood to heat your house, grow much of your own food. You can barter and trade, put solar panels on your roof and kiss the hydro grid goodbye, achieve a level of self-sufficiency only dreamed of in the city. What I describe is an old notion that *Harrowsmith* simply celebrated — the independent, alternative way of living in which neighbours count for a lot — and it still has merit. Maybe now more than ever.

But you cannot say that small places are all warm and larger places all cool. Each neighbourhood is only as generous or as mean-spirited as those who live there. Safer to say this: that the country still feels like something apart from the city. My own life is markedly unlike that of, say, my siblings in Toronto and Vancouver and Ottawa. Heating with wood, gardening on the scale that we do, living in a village on a river and all that that entails: my life *is* different, far more retro than metro.

In a place the size of Napanee, for example, the church and the hockey rink (each a cathedral in its own right) are far more likely to be community crossroads than they would be in the city. The Legion hall, the bingo hall, the Women's Institute and the 4-H club all help define the place and reflect its rural roots and sensibility. The manner of dress (conservative and casual, never chic), the patterns of speech (drawl is not too strong a word in many cases), the preponderance of pickup trucks, the pace: these and countless other aspects set country and city apart.

But the gulf between country and city is closing. Some 70 per cent of Canada's farm households now have at least one member working off the farm, often in towns and cities. Owing to more and better roads, cable television and the Internet, the culture of the city easily reaches what some of my downtown friends call the hinterland. My son, nine years old as I write this, shares with city kids an interest in Pogs, skateboards and Lego. And while his musical tastes may run more towards Garth Brooks than to Tom Cochrane, he is no country cousin in the city, staring up at skyscrapers and mumbling his geewillickers.

I am glad of that, but another part of me wants differences between city and country maintained. If rural starts to feel like urban, then the rural option is lost to us.

The essence of towns and villages, at the moment defined by the farms around them, can disappear. In Ontario, some locals who live in St. Jacobs, Niagara-on-the-Lake and Stratford will tell you that the throngs of urban strollers — drawn to Mennonite artisanship, the theatre or the fudge, tea and gift shops — have revitalized the towns; others complain that living there has become a nuisance. Congestion, parking problems, crowded sidewalks: city woes on smalltown streets.

If the migration from cities to country continues or increases, then some villages and towns will be overwhelmed. Land once useful for agriculture, flood control and forestry has already been lost, especially land close to cities.

R. Alex Sim, in his book *Land and Community: Crisis in Canada's Countryside,* laments what he calls the tragedy of our time — the rural way bowing to the urban one. When Sim thinks of rural Canada, he sees both light and dark. He sees, on the one hand, respect for nature, sensitivity to others and their needs and a sense of plugging into an organic whole. But along with those positives, he lists "the negative rural attributes of narrowness, insularity, and conservatism," which ill equip rural people to counter the powerful forces of urbanization.

The city, Sim argues, possesses the same sort of duality: high culture and rich resources on the one side, "destructive and colonizing violence" on the other. The ideal buttress is a strong and distinct rural culture. "Correcting and restorative impulses," Sim writes, "could come from ruralization. That is my faith and my vision." Mine too.

But if there is to be any smalltown buttressing against the juggernaut of the city, then sense of place, allegiance to place, has to be more strongly felt. In *The Great Good Place,* published in 1989, author Ray Oldenburg quotes from another book, *America as a Civilization,* written by Max Lerner more than three decades beforehand. Lerner argued that nostalgia for the small town, felt even in the 1950s, is really a "quest for community."

"The critical question," Lerner wrote, "is not whether the small town can be rehabilitated in the image of its earlier strength and growth — for clearly it cannot — but whether American life will be able to evolve any other integral community to replace it. This is what I call the problem of place in America, and unless it is somehow resolved, American life will become more jangled and fragmented than it is."

The city, for all its merits, rarely inspires in those who live there allegiance to the place. Particular neighbourhoods may coalesce *against* unwanted development or plans to chop down trees. And I know of one neighbourhood in Toronto that is pushing for positive change: in village fashion they are fundraising and using volunteer labour to build an eco-centre at the local school. But in many other neighbourhoods the word *neighbourhood* hardly applies.

I have lived in three Toronto neighbourhoods, and my actual neighbours remained in most cases strangers to me. Many of the country people I interviewed for this book remembered, and not fondly, that sense of anonymity in their former city neighbourhoods. Where Europeans still gather in piazzas and squares, in cafés and local pubs, most North Americans retreat to their epic urban homes to watch on average four hours of television a day.

For most North Americans, home is almost literally a castle. I see that in 1940 the typical American single-family house measured 1,300 square feet; by 1992 it had leapt to 1,920 square feet, a 50 per cent jump. In parts of Toronto, builders typically raze two old houses side by side and throw up one customized monolith in its stead. Such dwellings demand of their owners a huge income to pay for mortgage, heating and landscaping, so the occupants' gaze is pulled ever inward, rarely outward into the community.

Some psychologists put two and two together: the absence of meaningful social contact in most North American communities (putting pressure on home or work to meet social needs), and some of the highest divorce rates in the world. Here is a measure of our retreat behind closed doors: in the late 1940s, North Americans drank in bars and restaurants 90 per cent of all the alcoholic beverages they consumed; today, the figure has dropped to 30 per cent. Public life is declining on this continent.

Rural life at least offers more opportunity for connectedness. Sheer necessity dictates it. You are more likely to be drawn out into the community — to take a shift scooping ice cream at the village fund-raiser, to fill in as umpire at the ball game, to bake for the church social. There are rewards for all that scooping and umping and baking, but this may not be what the city-bred are used to.

What happens, I wonder, when people who feel no affection for their city or suburb move out to the country where commitment to place is an important part of rural life? What happens when people more used to impermanence (16 per cent of Canadians and 20 per cent of Americans, most of them urban, change addresses every year) go to places where locals feel an ingrained sense of obligation to their neighbours?

Maybe the urban sensibility overwhelms the rural, just as Wal-Mart wipes out Main Street. You end up not with a cohesive and still distinctive town or village but with a transmogrified rural retreat. A bedroom community. And a place that has always defined itself as small, in opposition to the big and impersonal, feels suddenly, calamitously, big and impersonal itself.

My erstwhile colleague Alexander Scala, who wrote exquisite essays in *The Whig-Standard Magazine* — they are collected in a book called *Under the Sun* — described in one how he left Toronto in dramatic fashion. He and his family lived in a house with bizarre neighbours on both sides; Alex served up details of around-the-clock revellers, ceremonial drumming, throbbing music and a black Lab baying at the moon. He lived, as he put it, "in the middle of the worst country song ever written." When, one evening, he found his wife, Gail, lying face down on the sofa, in the dark, with a cushion over her head, he knew it was time to go. The Scalas and their two daughters lived from 1981 to 1987 on a ninety-acre farm in Lanark County, east of Kingston.

But there are few sentimental bones in Alex's body. He never *fell* for the country, never swallowed the belief that a distinct rural society — as opposed to the urban one — still exists. In an essay called "Death of the Country," he wrote: "The current outpouring of city folk into the countryside may restore the rural landscape to something like its old level of population, but it will not restore the lost distinction between rural society and urban society. Quite the reverse. The movement out of the cities is, in fact, the last stage in the long process of urban imperialism. First the city coerced or seduced vast numbers of country people into entering the gates of the city itself. Next it stealthily imposed its manners and usages on those who remained in the country. Finally the city has sent forth an army of occupation. It scarcely matters if some members of this army believe that by shifting themselves to the country they have renounced the city and its works. The first Europeans to settle in North America learned to imitate the Indians, but this did not make them Indians. They carried Europe in their minds."

The last line in the essay reads: "I am content that the city should prevail."

I disagree, but not entirely. If you breathe country air long enough, you may well take on a sensibility that changes the way you think. But, of course, it is not as simple as that.

R. Alex Sim has likened rural Canada to a raft heading down a fast, frothy river of change. The raft hits a rock, and part of it breaks off, carrying away some occupants. Others, new people, try to scramble aboard, but the ones left, even as they struggle to rebuild the raft, "are undecided whether to welcome them or cast them adrift."

Paul Delaney has clambered aboard that raft. He teaches physics and astronomy at York University, but home — and he means *home* — is in the nearby village of Beeton. He and his wife, Lynne Frankonseca, previously lived with their son in Etobicoke, a city just west of Toronto. "I felt like we couldn't let our child play outside without posting an armed guard," he said. As a parent, he hated the paranoia; as an astronomer, he missed the stars.

The village of Beeton erased Delaney's anxiety and gave him back his stars. The village offers streets lined with magnificent maples, and good houses on half-acre lots are $80,000 cheaper than they are in Toronto. Delaney's children (they now have two) walk four minutes to school and feel the freedom to roam. "The university is forty-five minutes away," Delaney says, "but I drive through countryside. It's gorgeous. When I drive back at the end of a day I always feel a great sense of relaxation when I reach the village limits."

But surely there is the odd wrinkle? Are you, I asked Delaney, connected to the community? He concedes without hesitation, "We'd like it to be more. Beetonians live in their own world and it's hard to beat that down. Still, there is a sense of support, and there's no question of it being offered if we asked for it." Meanwhile, Beeton is growing at an unprecedented rate — two hundred new families in the past three years. Delaney can choose from five car pools to get home, suggesting that many teaching colleagues are doing as he has done. The sudden growth of Beeton, insists the new guy in town, has not changed the character of the place. You wonder if locals are saying the same.

My hope for small places such as Beeton and Camden East is that born-and-bred locals and from-the-city newcomers form an alliance, uneasy though it might seem at first. The city folk, most of them, could learn something from locals about what it means to be "right neighbourly." The newcomers, some of them, could teach the locals a thing or two about standing up to authority — to things like school closings and quarries and mega-dumps.

What I have discovered from my own time in the village of Camden East is that though I still carry the city in my head, I have acquired some country blood too. If I ever belonged to what Alexander Scala called an army of occupation, then my allegiance has shifted. Assimilation has not been total, but assimilation there has been. When I sit among country friends, the conversation often reflects not just who we are but where and how we live — "Got your firewood all in? How's the honey crop this year? Did you lose any chickens in the heat wave?" It's a bit like singing a song in another language. The language of the country is not my mother tongue, but a language I have come to speak.

December 8. An early winter, with more snow and cold than anyone can remember, has also put the kids skating on the pond in Newburgh well before the usual time. Alas, the pond in Camden East that forms at the base of the hill will only be breathed into being by warm winds and a serious thaw. No sign of that yet.

The river is still high and fast, but every day the banks inch out a little farther into the current, and the dark channel narrows. This morning watched an otter lift his black rubbery body up onto the shelf of ice for a looksee, and am glad of the sight. The beavers, I presume, have hunkered in somewhere for the winter. There has been, thankfully, no attempt at reinstating the food cache so close to home.

December 31. After this year-in-the-life — mine and that of my village — I feel compelled, like a columnist for a weekly newspaper, to bring the reader up to date.

It's been a hard year for two Mill Street men. Lyle Lawlor gamely soldiers on, but he misses Marion, and at times seems lost without her. George Gauld endured two major operations for a pinched nerve, and still walks with a cane. Doug and Virginia Thompson have gone south to Florida for two months, Bev and Sue Smallman are eyeing New Orleans and Arizona as their next destination. Township trucks, for the first time in memory, failed to fill in Mill Street potholes at tax time. Another tradition sacrificed to the deficit god at Queen's Park.

Last I heard, Bernie Duhamel was operating a tourist lodge near Kaladar. Ottawa has virtually swallowed Larry McCormick, MP, and I miss his "G'dayneighbour," though I still see Reta out walking their dog early each morning. We could use them, even Puddles, in the quarry fight. HOWL mailed out a snappy four-page newsletter before Christmas, and its sarcastic headline — "Welcome to Camden East, Welcome to Quarryville!" — woke a few people up. By summer we should know whether that battle is won or lost.

Jacintha Shenton, leukemia behind her (we hope), is studying hard at university and thoroughly enjoying Toronto. The Daneshmend house is batless finally, but a sudden thaw put two feet of water in their basement. Still, they love where they live. Ditto their neighbours Edo and Linda Knopper, who frantically borrowed heating oil and bought firewood and sand when several thaws were followed by deep freeze and the fuel truck could get no traction on their steep and icy driveway. Welcome to the country.

Oh, yes. The Newburgh pizza parlour has expanded, even got a liquor licence and a billiard table! And the grand old limestone building at the four corners in Camden East finally sold — to a couple from Toronto.

In the house that Squire Clark built for his sons before Canada was conceived, the water line has not frozen, the water pump goes -*ha!* and shuts off when it should, and though the cold has seemed unrelenting, the winter light has been generous. I am still waiting now for the thaw and the skating pond to form at the base of the hill; only then will I feel that the great wheel of days and months and seasons has turned a full circle.

FURTHER READING

The Age of Missing Information, by Bill McKibben, Random House, 1992

An American Homeplace, by Donald McCaig, Crown, 1992

A Better Place to Live: Reshaping the American Suburb, by Philip Langdon, University of Massachusetts, 1994

The Big Picture: What Canadians Think About Almost Everything, by Allan Gregg and Michael Posner, Macfarlane Walter & Ross, 1990

Biophilia, by Edward O. Wilson, Harvard University Press, 1984

The Bird Artist, by Howard Norman, Farrar, Straus & Giroux, 1994

The Blue Jays' Dance, by Louise Erdrich, HarperCollins, 1995

Broken Heartland: The Rise of America's Rural Ghetto, by Osha Gray Davidson, The Free Press, 1990

Camden Township History, 1800 to 1968, compiled by the Camden Township History Committee of 1967–70, 1970

Conflict and Change in the Countryside: Rural Society, Economy and Planning in the Developed World, by Guy M. Robinson, Bellhaven Press, 1990

Cottage Water Systems: An Out-of-the-City Guide to Pumps, Plumbing, Water Purification, and Privies, by Max Burns, Cottage Life Books, 1993

Dakota: A Spiritual Geography, by Kathleen Norris, Ticknor & Fields, 1993

Endangered Spaces, Enduring Places: Change, Identity and Survival in Rural America, by Janet M. Fitchen, Westview Press, 1991

The End of Work: The Decline of the Global Labor Force and the Dawn of the Post-Market Era, by Jeremy Rifkin, P. Tarcher/ Putnam, 1995

Far from Home: Life and Loss in Two American Towns, Ron Powers, Random House, 1991

Fields of Vision: A Journey to Canada's Family Farms, by Phil Jenkins with photographs by Ken Ginn, McClelland & Stewart, 1991

The Gift of Good Land: Further Essays Cultural and Agricultural, by Wendell Berry, Gnomon Press, 1981

The Great Good Place: Cafés, Coffee Shops, Community Centers, Beauty Parlors, General Stores, Bars, Hangouts and How They Get You Through the Day, by Ray Oldenburg, Paragon House, 1989

A Guide to Residential Wood Heating, Natural Resources Canada, 1993

The Heart of the Country: From the Great Lakes to the Atlantic Coast — Rediscovering the Towns and Countryside of Canada, by Fredric A. Dahms, Deneau, 1988

If Learning Is So Natural, Why Am I Going to School? by Andrew Nikiforuk, Penguin, 1994

In the Skin of a Lion, by Michael Ondaatje, McClelland & Stewart, 1987

Land and Community: Crisis in Canada's Countryside, by R. Alex Sim, University of Guelph, 1988

Life After the City: A Harrowsmith Guide to Rural Living, by Charles Long, Camden House, 1989

Little Town Blues: Voices from the Changing West, by Raye C. Ringholz with photographs by K.C. Muscolino, Gibbs-Smith, 1992

The Living, by Annie Dillard, HarperCollins, 1992

Living the Good Life: How to Live Sanely and Simply in a Troubled World, by Helen and Scott Nearing, Schocken Books, 1987

The Most Beautiful House in the World, by Witold Rybczynski, Penguin, 1989

One American Town, by Donald S. Connery, Simon & Schuster, 1972

Out Our Way: Gay and Lesbian Life in the Country, by Michael Riordon, Between the Lines, 1996

Paradise: Class, Commuters, and Ethnicity in Rural Ontario, by Stanley R. Barrett, University of Toronto Press, 1994

Penturbia: Where Real Estate Will Boom After the Crash of Suburbia, by Jack Lessinger, SocioEconomics, 1991

The Perfection of the Morning: An Apprenticeship in Nature, by Sharon Butala, HarperCollins, 1994

Pilgrim at Tinker Creek, by Annie Dillard, Harper & Row, 1974

The Popcorn Report, by Faith Popcorn, Doubleday, 1991

The Role of Horticulture in Human Well-Being and Social Development, edited by Diane Relf, Timber Press, 1992

Roughing It in the Bush, by Susanna Moodie, Virago Press, 1986

Rural Canada: A Profile, Government of Canada, 1995

Rural and Small Town Canada, edited by Ray D. Bollman, Thompson Educational Publishing, 1992

Rural Communities: Legacy and Change, by Cornelia Butler Flora et al., Westview Press, 1992

Rural Sociology in Canada, edited by David A. Hay and Gurcharn S. Basran, Oxford University Press, 1992

Second Nature: A Gardener's Education, by Michael Pollan, Atlantic Monthly Press, 1991

A Sense of Place, A Sense of Time, by John Brinckerhoff Jackson, Yale University Press, 1994

Sex, Economy, Freedom and Community: Eight Essays, by Wendell Berry, Pantheon Books, 1993

Silent Spring, by Rachel Carson, Houghton Mifflin, 1962

Smalltown America, photos and text by David Blowden, introduction by David McCullough, Abrams, 1994

The Smiling Wilderness: An Illustrated History of Lennox and Addington County, by Frank B. Edwards, Camden House, 1984

The Townsearch Guide: Your Handbook for Finding the Best Place to Live, by Dale Chambers and Mark Gauley, Townsearch Information Services, 1995

Under the Sun: Occasional Essays, by Alexander Scala, Quarry Press, 1988

Villagers: Changed Values, Altered Lives: The Closing of the Urban-Rural Gap, by Richard Critchfield, Anchor Books, 1994

Welcome Home: Travels in Smalltown Canada, by Stuart McLean, Penguin, 1992